Transnational Corporations and International Production

For Penelope and Daniel

Transnational Corporations and International Production

Concepts, Theories and Effects, Second Edition

Grazia Ietto-Gillies

Emeritus Professor of Applied Economics
London South Bank University
Visiting Professor, Birkbeck University of London, UK

Edward Elgar
Cheltenham, UK • Northampton, MA, USA

Published by
Edward Elgar Publishing Limited
The Lypiatts
15 Lansdown Road
Cheltenham
Glos GL50 2JA
UK

Edward Elgar Publishing, Inc.
William Pratt House
9 Dewey Court
Northampton
Massachusetts 01060
USA

A catalogue record for this book
is available from the British Library

Library of Congress Control Number: 2011932901

ISBN 978 0 85793 225 9 (cased)
ISBN 978 0 85793 227 3 (paperback)

Typeset by Cambrian Typesetters, Frimley, Surrey
Printed and bound by MPG Books Group, UK

Contents

Boxes

Summary boxes at the end of chapters

Abbreviations

CEE	Central and Eastern Europe
EC/EU	European Community (up to 1992)/European Union
E-NIDL	electronic-age new international division of labour
EPZ	Export Processing Zone
FDI	foreign direct investment
FPI	foreign portfolio investment
GATT	General Agreement on Tariffs and Trade
GDFCF/NDFCF	gross domestic fixed capital formation/net domestic fixed capital formation
GDP	gross domestic product
IC	international company/corporation
ICTs	information and communication technologies
IE	international enterprise
IFT	intra-firm trade
IIT	intra-industry trade
IMF	International Monetary Fund
IPLC	international product life cycle
JVs	joint ventures
M&As	mergers and acquisitions
MNC	multinational company/corporation
MNE	multinational enterprise
NIDL	new international division of labour
NAFTA	North American Free Trade Agreement
OECD	Organisation for Economic Cooperation and Development
OLI	ownership, location and internalization
R&D	research and development
TNC	transnational company/corporation
UNC	uninational company
UNCTAD	United Nations Conference on Trade and Development
WID	World Investment Directory
WIR	World Investment Report
WTO	World Trade Organization
WWI	First World War
WWII	Second World War

Preface and acknowledgements to the second edition

In the seven years since the first edition, the book has had a fairly happy life. It has been used by many researchers and as a text – mainly for postgraduate students – in several countries. The first edition was published alongside an Italian edition by Carocci in 2005. This second edition will be published in Japanese by Dobunkan Shuppan Co. Ltd.

In the last six years several reviews have appeared and colleagues and friends have given me their feedback on the book. I have also devoted further thoughts to some of the topics in the book while working on other projects in the field of international business. Moreover, the literature on TNCs and their activities has moved on.

This second edition is the result of all these elements taken together and of my desire to attempt to address them. It is also a reflection of the growing relevance of transnational corporations in the world economies in both the developed and developing countries. The recent financial crisis may further enhance their role in the global economy. In fact, many smaller, location-bound enterprises may find it more difficult to survive. Moreover, the full economic, social and political repercussions from the financial crisis are not over yet and they will be felt for many years to come. It is possible that disillusion with the unbridled financialization and liberalization of the last three decades may lead economists and politicians to reassess the fundamental roots of the globalization process (Ietto-Gillies, 2002a: ch. 9). This can be done by an analysis in terms of what contributes to the development of the productive forces in the new globalizing phase of capitalism. This may shift the discourse on globalization away from the emphasis on liberalization and financialization on to the TNCs: to their organizational and technological power specifically in terms of their ability to organize production across border and via the utilization of the ICTs.

The current edition differs from the first one in the general updating of content, empirics and references in most chapters as well as the correction of minor mistakes. There are also some major revisions and specifically the following:

- Part I has been restructured into one chapter only (instead of two as in the first edition) and the Appendix. The tables have been eliminated though key updated empirics have been left as part of the text.
- An extra chapter (Chapter 15) has been added to Part III (Modern Theories) dealing with Penrose's approach to the firm and its possible implications for TNCs; it also deals with the network theories of the TNC.
- Chapter 11 (corresponding to Chapter 12 in the first edition) has been enhanced by the discussion on the theory of Kogut and Zander alongside the one by Cantwell.

- Chapter 14 (corresponding to Chapter 15 in the first edition) has been rewritten and restructured to reflect developments in my thoughts and work as well as developments in the real economies.
- In Part IV the first chapter (Chapter 16) has been rewritten and restructured. Chapter 17 has been shortened and restructured and now concentrates only on innovation.

Acknowledgements

First I want to thank John Cantwell, Mark Casson, Jonathan Michie and John Dunning for their generous endorsement of the first edition of the book. My special thoughts to the late John Dunning who showed towards me and my book his usual warmth and generosity which he gave to all researchers in international business throughout the world.

My debt of gratitude to all the colleagues and friends who have helped me with the first edition continues. The current edition has benefitted from comments to the published book by: Francesco Abbate, Giovanni Balcet, Jeongho Choi, John Ottomanelli, Pallavi Shukla and Mohammed Yamin.

John Cantwell has read the new Chapter 11 and given very useful comments. So have Mats Forsgren and Christos Pitelis in relation to Chapter 15 (respectively for the section on network theories and the one on Penrose). To all three my warmest thanks; their comments have helped me to finalize the relevant chapters.

I have read with great care all the reviews of the first edition of the book and taken on board most of the comments. The perceptive review – a mixture of generous remarks and constructive criticisms – by Ana Teresa Tavares has led to the addition of Chapter 15 (on Penrose and on the network theory) and to the rewriting of the first two chapters of Part IV (Chapters 16 and 17). The major changes made to Chapter 11 owe much to the comments I received personally from Mohammed Yamin and – via her review – from Ana Teresa Tavares.

Once again the team at Edward Elgar has been a pleasure to work with. I am particularly grateful to Jo Betteridge for her high competence, efficiency and kindness. Many thanks also to Dee Compson Wragg and Caroline Phillips for their excellent editing work.

I extend my thanks to Oxford University Press and the President and Fellows of Harvard College for permission to reproduce Figure 5.1.

Grazia Ietto-Gillies
London
May 2011

Preface and acknowledgements to the first edition

The last three decades of the twentieth century and the beginning of the twenty-first century have seen a considerable growth in academic interest in the economics of international business, in parallel with the growth of cross-border activities in all their modalities.

The interest manifests in the increase of units – or indeed of entire courses – teaching the subject often from a multi- and inter-disciplinary perspective. It has also manifested in a growing number of research works in the field including the development of a variety of theories to explain why firms become transnational companies (TNCs) and why they engage in specific activities. Most of these theories have been developed in business schools or economics departments in the last 55 years following Stephen Hymer's seminal doctoral dissertation (submitted in 1960 and published in 1976).

These developments indicate both a large and growing demand for the subject and a large and growing supply of material emerging from research work. It is a classical situation in which there emerges a demand for textbooks that summarize and present in relatively simple form the main elements contained in various pieces of research.

There are indeed many textbooks on international business and some are, in fact, excellent works. Many of these books are targeted at specific units in business strategy or international marketing. A few take an economics perspective instead of – or in addition to – the business and marketing perspective.

Whichever the perspective, there are, however, currently no textbooks – as far as I know – that present in detail summaries of all the main theories of TNCs and international production or that present a full analytical framework for dealing with the assessment of effects of TNCs' activities. My 1992 book did indeed deal with theories and – to a less satisfactory extent – with effects.

The present book – though a development from the 1992 work as well as of other work done in between – differs from the 1992 work in the following respects. It deals specifically with conceptual issues (in Part I); the modern theories are dealt with in a more inclusive and exhaustive way; the effects of TNCs' activities are presented within a stronger and explicit analytical framework; the whole book is presented in a more reader-friendly mode.

The latter objective is achieved in a variety of ways including the following: development of boxes which highlight specific elements in each chapter; presentation of summary boxes at the end of each chapter and of suggestions for further reading at the end of chapters. Attention is paid to clarity of concepts and to explaining terminology which may not be fully familiar to students. Not much prior knowledge is assumed; however, knowledge of basic economics is of great help. Further details of the book content as well as a discussion of why we need theories of TNCs' activities are in the Introduction to the book.

This book is designed to be of use to three sets of audiences. The main one is students of: a variety of courses/units in business and international studies; economics and international economics; international relations; and development studies. The level of courses is likely to be that of final year undergraduate or postgraduate. The second audience is likely to be the lecturers who want to familiarize themselves with the theoretical development of the subject in order to decide which approach to present to their students. The chapters on the theories are self-contained and therefore lecturers may select the ones they want to present to their students without fear of didactic difficulties. The third audience is relatively new researchers in the field who want to gain an overall view of the development of the subject before concentrating on specific elements of it. The critical appraisal of various theories and the problems and issues raised by them, at the end of each chapter in Parts II and III, may help new researchers to find out about some of the unresolved problems in the field. The wide citation of works in the text is specifically designed to whet the appetite for the subject and to encourage new research by pointing to further issues, problems or possible solutions. The comprehensive list of references should also be of help to this audience.

If this book stimulates undergraduate, postgraduate and research students to take a further interest in the subject and possibly develop it, I will have achieved my aim.

Acknowledgements

I am indebted to several friends, colleagues and indeed family members for reading draft chapters of this book and offering comments or giving me help with presentation issues. Any remaining errors are mine alone.

I owe a specific debt of gratitude to the following: Francesco Abbate; Paul Auerback; John Cantwell; Sabrina Corbellini; Howard Cox; Lucio Esposito; Marion Frenz; Marco Gillies; Donald Gillies; Antonio Majocchi; Marcela Miozzo; Joanne Roberts; Helen Sakho; Grazia Santangelo; Roger Sugden and Antonello Zanfei.

Working with the editorial team at Edward Elgar has been a great pleasure. My special thanks go to Jo Betteridge, Julie Leppard and Karen McCarthy for their kindness towards myself and their competence in dealing with the book.

I would also like to thank the President and Fellows of Harvard College and John Wiley and Sons, Inc. for permission to reproduce Figure 6.1.

Grazia Ietto-Gillies
London
December 2004

Introduction*

I Overview of the book

The subject matter of this book is the transnational corporation (TNC) and its activities, particularly its direct production activities abroad. The book deals with the following three major areas:

*   Evolution and Concepts in Part I;
*   Theories in Parts II and III;
*   Effects in Part IV.

The first part is designed to introduce the reader to basic concepts such as foreign direct investment and international production. It will also give a glimpse into trends and patterns in the population of TNCs and the modalities of their activities, particularly foreign direct investment (FDI). A brief excursion into the historical evolution of the TNC leads to a discussion of the favourable conditions that made possible the growth of TNCs and their activities on the scale we have seen in the last 60 years.

The existence of favourable conditions tells us why it was possible for such developments to take place. However, we still have to explain why the companies wanted and want to develop internationally. On this issue we have a variety of theories which will be presented historically in Parts II and III of the book.

The reason for the historical approach is twofold: first, because it allows the reader to see the links between a specific theory and the social and economic circumstances and environment in which it was developed; and second, because it facilitates the historical analysis of ideas in our field. It therefore allows us to analyse the antecedents to a theory as well as its effects on later theoretical developments.

Comparisons between each theory and the ones preceding it will, in fact, be made, in the critical analysis of each theory. This will be presented at the end of each chapter on the theory – or in a few cases group of theories – after the presentation of the theory itself. The presentation and the critical analysis will be kept separate deliberately, to avoid confusion in the mind of the reader and, indeed, to encourage the students or the lecturers to develop and present their own criticisms. This approach is rooted in the belief: (a) that critical analysis is an integral part of the learning process, particularly in higher education; and that, moreover, (b) it is the essential ingredient in the development of any subject and, therefore, in doing worthwhile research.

The two parts on theories deal with two different historical periods demarcated by the Second World War (WWII). The chosen demarcation is important for two reasons: first, because the decades after WWII have seen unprecedented growth in the activities of transnational firms; and second, because the theories of the TNC and its activities – as we know them today – only began after WWII. Nonetheless there are some historical antecedents which are worth exploring and this is what Part II does. In this part the theories are grouped into two major sets: Marxist (Chapter 2) and neoclassical (Chapter 3) approaches.

Part III presents all the major modern theories of the TNC and its activities. It is structured in 12 chapters, starting with the theory of Steven Hymer developed as a doctoral dissertation in 1960 (Chapter 4). In this part, I have tried to be very inclusive, though I have no doubt that colleagues will find some missing authors or theories or some misrepresentation. In fact, the current edition responds to some criticisms by colleagues that some works were indeed missing from the first edition (see Preface to the second edition). If more are missing, I plead ignorance, not deliberate neglect.

Part IV presents a framework for the analysis of the main effects of TNCs' activities. It is structured in five chapters dealing with: boundaries issues (Chapter 16); effects on innovation (Chapter 17); effects on labour (Chapter 18); effects on international trade (Chapter 19) and on the balance of payments (Chapter 20). The thematic structure here mirrors a similar structure in Part I. In both parts this allows us to deal with the various relevant elements. In some cases historical perspectives will be touched on within the themes.

Suggestions for further reading are given at the end of each chapter. These are presented as *indicative further readings*, thus leaving to the individual lecturers the choice of alternative or additional suggestions. The end of each chapter has a *summary box* which highlights the key elements dealt with in the chapter. It also gives references to other relevant chapters in the book.

Most chapters and parts are self-contained and can be read and understood on their own. Therefore, teachers and students who are only interested in selected chapters of the book can still have the full benefits from them. However, the first two chapters contain concepts that are relevant throughout. For this reason, reference to these chapters is omitted from the suggested references to other chapters. The chapter on the issues of boundaries in the assessment of effects (Chapter 16) is essential reading for the following chapters on specific effects (Chapters 17 to 20).

The reader may notice some repetitions of concepts presented in slightly different contexts. This is a deliberate strategy – particularly in Part I – designed to facilitate the absorption of some key concepts. The book has a relatively low level of empirical content though facts and cases are cited here and there. Detailed empirical results of theory testing or of effects are deliberately avoided for the following reasons. First, because there are just too many empirical studies out there and mentioning only a few would not have done justice to the existing large literature. Second, because empirical studies become obsolete very quickly as new ones are published. Third, because I wanted to have enough page space to concentrate on the fundamental concepts with regard to both theories and effects.

2   Do we need specific studies of the transnational firm and its activities?[1]

As mentioned in the previous section, the main body of the book deals with theories and effects of the transnational corporation and its activities. There is now a very large body of literature on theories of the TNC and the subject has reached a suitably mature stage in which it becomes appropriate to present the material and controversies related to various theoretical approaches in textbook format.

Before dipping into the concepts and the details of the subject matter of the book, I should explain why I consider a study of international production important and indeed necessary in the current phase of capitalist development. To the layperson it would seem obvious that we need to study the activities of the most important economic agents operating today: transnational companies. Moreover, it would seem obvious that we must try to explain their most relevant activity: international production/foreign direct investment.

Yet the subject has made few inroads into the main theoretical body of economics. Why is this so? We could dismiss this issue as just some evidence of the divorce between theory and reality on the part of many mainstream economists. There may be some truth in this but it is certainly not the whole story. There are deeper reasons – linked to both methodology and subject matter – why economic researchers have been unable or unwilling to fit the TNC and its activities into the main body of their theories. There are also very good reasons why the topic should now be given a stronger role in the economics curricula and research. To both of these I now turn.

Let us begin with trying to see the reasons why the TNC and its activities have no place in economic theory, particularly in macroeconomic theory. Let us assume for a moment a wholly theoretical world in which all national barriers and frontiers have come down; one single currency circulates; a single tax regime is in operation. In other words, the world becomes one single country/nation-state and is governed as such. In such a world we would have no theory of international production: there would be no need for it. We would work within the confines of spatial location theory to explain where production is located and with theories of the firm, business governance and market structure to explain the growth of firms, their boundaries, their organization and their behaviour vis-à-vis other firms. Thus we would not need a theory of transnational companies to understand *who* invests, *where* and *why*. Theories of transnational companies and of foreign direct investment are needed because we have nation-states and frontiers.

In fact we do not attach much relevance to the identity of the investors when they originate from other regions within the same nation-state, for example when a Texan firm invests in Michigan or a Tuscan firm invests in Calabria. Why should we consider the origin of the firm as relevant when it is from a foreign country?

In general, when analysing economic activities, economists tend to ignore the actual nationality of the investor. Instead, the main focus has been on issues such as: the firm in general or in relation to its size; the market structure of an industry; the production, investment or trade of the macroeconomy independently of the nationality of the firm producing, investing or trading. This is exactly what we do when we study, for example, international trade theory: we analyse the comparative conditions and advantages of the trading countries and/or the impact of trade on them independently of the national identity of the exporter firm. Why should we bother with such identity when the operator is someone investing in many countries?

Does this mean that theories of TNCs and foreign direct investment are redundant and trivial? Could it all be subsumed under theories of investment independently of the nationality of ownership or the investor? Or under the theory of the firm in general? Is there much point in developing theories of 'international' production and investment or the 'international' firm? Would not theories of production, investment and the firm take care of everything there is to know about the location of investment and production, and of the behaviour of firms and their entry modes into foreign markets?

This is indeed the – tacit – approach taken in most traditional economics departments in which the international economy is dealt with at the macro level by teaching and research into issues of international trade, the balance of payments and exchange rates. Moreover, at the micro level, theories of the firm and investment are not usually analysed in the context of the 'nationality' of the investor or the country in which the investment has taken place. Characteristics of companies other than multinationality (such as size) are considered in the context of oligopoly and of market structure theories in general. On the teaching side, multinational companies, their existence, growth and range of activities, are usually dealt with in a couple of lectures within a unit on industrial economics. This traditional approach can indeed be justified if one takes the view that the nationality of the investor and the transnationality of operations make no difference to the geographical pattern of investment and production or to the overall amount of production or to its impact on the country where the investment takes place.

Economists have traditionally looked into the identity of the investor, when analysing the investment by public versus private firms. The reason for this is clear: the public investor is assumed to have different *objectives* compared with the private one and therefore the private identity versus public does matter. However, this is not the case when the investor is a TNC. Whether the firm is foreign or domestic, whether it is a multinational or a uninational firm, the objectives are not different; they are profit or profit-related objectives.

In fact, the reason why in our case the uninational or multinational character of the investor matters, has nothing to do with objectives but with *strategies*, as will be argued later in the book and particularly in Chapter 14. The argument for specific studies of the TNCs and for their incorporation into the main body of the economics curriculum is that the existence of nation-states has a bearing on firms' strategies. Such strategies affect the levels and patterns of world investment and production, and they affect the economic and social context in which other agents – such as labour, uninational firms or governments – operate. They do, in particular, affect the context of government policy. This is the main reason why a study of TNCs and their activities is important, and indeed basic, for an understanding of the activities of firms, industries and national economies in the global context.

Notes

* The italics used in passages quoted from other authors throughout the book should be understood to be in the original text, unless specified otherwise.
1 The arguments in this section are further developed in Ietto-Gillies (2004).

PART I · EVOLUTION AND CONCEPTS

1 Evolution and concepts

* *

PUCK: How now, spirit; whither wander you?
FAIRY: Over hill, over dale,
           Thorough bush, thorough briar,
           Over park, over pale,
           Thorough flood, thorough fire –
           I do wander everywhere . . . (Shakespeare, *A Midsummer Night's Dream*, II.1)

I Historical antecedents

The modern multinational or transnational company (MNC or TNC) has developed and grown in the decades after the Second World War (WWII). However, its distant antecedents go much further back. Transborder direct business operations have existed for many centuries, indeed before the existence of nation-states: the Medici bank – in fifteenth-century Florence – can be considered a company with such business activities.

More recently-established companies, such as the East India Company, the Royal African Company and the Hudson Bay Company, and others dating back to the seventeenth and eighteenth centuries, are sometimes considered to be the forerunners of the modern TNC. However, these companies were chartered by governments to carry trading business operations in colonies. The specificity of their operations and the fact that the charter was for business in the colonies – which were considered part of the country whose government had granted the charter – make these companies substantially different from the modern transnational corporation.

Steven Hymer – the father of the theory of the transnational corporation whose works are presented in Chapter 4 – focuses on the organizational ability of these early companies or rather on the paucity of it. He writes with regard to the above companies:

> But neither these firms, nor the large mining and plantation enterprises in the production sector, were the forerunners of the multinational corporations. They were like dinosaurs, large in bulk, but small in brain, feeding on the lush vegetation of the new worlds (the planters and miners in America were literally *Tyrannosaurus rex*). The activities of these international merchants, planters and miners laid the groundwork for the Industrial Revolution by concentrating capital in the metropolitan centre, but the driving force came from the small scale capitalist enterprises in manufacturing. . . . It is in the small workshops, organized by the newly emerging capitalist class, that the forerunners of the modern corporation are to be found. The strength of this new form of business enterprise lay in its power and ability to reap the benefits of cooperation and division of labour. (Hymer, 1971: 115–16)

Hymer as well as business historians (Cox, 1997; Jones, 2002) sees the real fore-runners of the transnational companies in the early joint stock companies established from the mid-nineteenth century onwards.

But what is specific to the transnational corporation compared to other companies? The immediate response might be that the specificity lies in doing business across frontiers. However, there are many ways of doing business across borders. The most ancient method is trade, that is, the importation or exportation of goods between enterprises or people located in different countries. But trading activities are not the defining characteristic of transnationals. Nor are the lending and borrowing of money across frontiers.

The distinguishing way of doing business abroad, the one that characterizes the transnationals compared with other companies, is *direct* production and generally direct business activities abroad. In order to engage in these direct activities, the TNCs establish affiliates abroad and acquire the ownership and control of their assets. This gives them a long-term interest in the strategies and management of the foreign enterprises which they control. But what do we mean by control?

2 Control

In the context of direct activities abroad by transnational corporations, control has two connotations. First is its relationship with the equity stake in the foreign enterprise (Box 1.1). What percentage of the foreign assets must be owned by the main company for the latter to have control? This issue is far from clear-cut because there is no single percentage of ownership – below the 50+ percentage – that can definitely ensure control to a single owner or a group of associate owners over the company whose shares are being acquired. If the ownership of the company is very widespread among many shareholders, a relatively small amount of equity ownership may suffice to exercise control. Conversely, if ownership is very concentrated and a few large share-holders already possess considerable percentages of equity, an even larger percentage of shares is necessary to gain control. The International Monetary Fund (IMF) guide-lines set a minimum of 10 per cent of share ownership for the main company to be considered to have control.

Second, is any required controlling share of the equities enough for the main company to exercise control? In other words, *the equity control* is a *necessary condition*, but is it sufficient to ensure control? The answer is negative for the following reasons.

Equity control by itself does not lead to strategic managerial control if the means of exercising such control are not available, in particular, if the system of communications and the organization of the business across countries are not suitable for the exercise of managerial control. This was indeed the case of much foreign business prior to the First World War (WWI).

Economic and business historians noted that there was indeed a very consider-able amount of foreign investment prior to WWI (Cox, 1997; Tiberi, 2004). There were a number of enterprises whose assets were owned wholly or in large part by a person or groups or companies in foreign countries (usually in Britain or Holland or the USA). However, though these owners from foreign countries had controlling stakes in the business, they were not in a position to exercise managerial control because of the large distance between the home and host countries under conditions of poor communication and transportation systems. The business historian Mira Wilkins (1988) has termed these businesses '*free-standing enterprises*' to highlight the fact that though they were owned wholly or partially by foreign nationals (whether individuals or groups or companies), they were managed and developed as independent concerns (Cox, 1997).[1]

The modern transnational corporation is characterized by both the equity ownership and the ability to manage[2] strategically the foreign affiliates at a distance (Box 1.1). The latter characteristic is the product of two relevant and interconnected innovations, both of which form the *sufficient conditions* for the exercise of control: first, the technological innovation in personal communications which started with the telegraph and telephone and, more recently, with electronic communications; and second, organizational innovations which were made possible (and/or strongly facilitated) by the communication technologies as well as by the experience of firms operating large manufacturing projects – particularly the building of railways – during the nineteenth century. To this second condition – organizational innovation – we now turn.

Box 1.1   *The transnational corporation and control*

Two key conditions for the exercise of control

1 Ownership of sufficient equity stake in the foreign enterprise

2 Ability to manage strategically at a distance which depends on:

   • systems of transportation and personal communications;

   • internal organization of the firm

---

3   Evolution in the internal organization of firms

In the relevant literature, developments in the internal organization of companies have been analysed under several paradigms and particularly: the 'strategy', the 'efficiency', and the 'institutionalist' paradigms. Penrose ([1959] 2009) sees the boundaries of the firm and its internal organization changing as the firm grows. Growth and growth strategies lead to changes in the internal organization and the latter facilitates further growth. On a similar vein Chandler's (1962) historical narrative sees the internal organization of corporations evolving mainly in response to strategic objectives, in particular, growth strategies.

Williamson (1975; 1981; 1984) sees changes in the internal organization as driven by efficiency objectives; specifically, by the desire to economize on transactions costs (that is, on costs of organizing the business transactions with units external to the firm) as well as to minimize the pursuit of individual goals within the organization.[3]

The institutionalist school sees the internal structure of companies – and of organizations in general – as evolving in response to the institutional environment in which they operate. The relevant institutional environment is delimited by the organizational field(s) of the company. The organizational field of reference is loosely defined to include all agents who have some form of business interaction with the company, from suppliers to consumers to rival firms to regulatory agencies (DiMaggio and Powell, 1983). Companies may straddle different organizational fields (Westney, 2005). This is the case of diversified companies as well as of transnational companies. The former straddle several fields because of the different products they are involved in; the latter straddle different fields in relation to the different countries in which they operate. Diversified TNCs will have scope for interaction with a variety of fields connected with both their different products and the different countries in which they operate.

Hymer follows Chandler in his analysis of the relationship between the evolution in the internal structure of the firm and multinationality and, in particular, considers how the former facilitated the latter. He distinguishes: 'three major stages in the development of corporate capital. First, the Marshallian firm, organized at the factory level, confined to a single function and a single industry, and tightly controlled by one or few men, who, as it were, see everything and decide everything' (Hymer, 1970: 42). The second stage sees large corporations, vertically integrated and increasingly moving towards mass production, develop a new type of business organization. The crucial element in the development of the new internal organization was the experience of managing the building and running of railways, with their widely dispersed operations and their need for commitment and coordination of vast resources. The new organization was based on the separation of different administrative functions such as finance, personnel, purchasing, engineering and sales. The new structure was referred to as the *'unitary'* (*U-form*) or *'central office functionally departmentalized'* (*COFD*) structure.

The twentieth century saw further economic developments. Industry became more concentrated, large corporations followed diversification strategies which involved production of several products or/and production in several countries. These corporations needed a new, more flexible organization, one which could cope with its product and geographical diversification. The *'multidivisional form'* of internal organization (*M-form*) emerged; it was first introduced by General Motors and Du Pont after WWI. It soon spread to other US corporations and, after WWII, to European ones.

The M-form was first tried in order to face the challenge of multi-product companies. In the new structure the corporation was organized into divisions, each dealing with a product. It differed from the U-form in three main aspects:

- It centred on products rather than functions.
- It focused on the establishment of a central office.
- It relied on 'information' for its centralization/decentralization scheme to work.[4]

The new structure proved flexible as new divisions could be added alongside the expansion of the whole business. Moreover, it proved very useful in the internation-alization of business. The organization of business internationally could be done along the pattern of different divisions for different countries or regions with the additions of new divisions as operations spread into new countries. In some cases the conflict-ing demands of product and geographical diversification led to '*grid structures*' which exhibited mixed product/geography features.[5]

In the divisional structure each division is a profit centre and its performance is assessed independently of the others. The central office receives profits from the vari-ous divisions and allocates capital and other resources to them, thus exercising its strategic role.

Parallel to the evolution of the internal organization, there also took place an evolution in the division of labour within each division and within the corporation across different countries. In the last analysis, growth strategies (mass production, product diversification and internationalization) led to changes in the internal organiz-ation and this, in turn, brought a sharper internal division of labour. It also had an impact on the international division of labour. At the same time the evolution in the structure of companies in general, paved the way for the evolution of the transnational corporation and the massive growth in its activities as we have seen in the post-WWII decades.

In summary, for the transnational company to exist and grow it must be able to plan, organize, coordinate and control production[6] in many countries from a centre and under common objectives and strategies. This also requires the ability to monitor the performance of the various business units wherever they are located. The ability to perform all these functions is currently very well developed owing to two types of innovation which have occurred in the last few decades: (1) technological innovation in the transportation and communication systems; and (2) organizational innovation with regard to the internal structure of companies.

4   The modern transnational company and its enterprises

The transnational is a corporation that owns assets and operates direct business activ-ities in at least two countries.[7] Several adjectives and nouns are used in the literature to identify the institution we are dealing with. The nouns (corporation, company,[8] firm or enterprise) are used interchangeably and so are the adjectives multinational or transnational or international. The term multinational corporation/company (MNC) is the most widely used in everyday language.

The term transnational corporation (TNC) is used by the United Nations Conference on Trade and Development (UNCTAD). It is the term which we shall normally use in this book. Exceptions are made whenever we discuss the works of authors who use different names. In this case I shall follow the author's terminology. I prefer the adjective 'transnational' to 'multinational' because it best represents one of the characteristics of this modern corporation: the ability to operate *across* countries and not just in many of them independently and autonomously. It is their ability to manage, control and develop strategies across and above national frontiers that distinguishes them from other actors in the economic system, as will be further argued in Chapter 14. Some authors (Bartlett and Ghoshal, 1991) distinguish between transnationals and multinationals on the basis of the companies' internal organization and control and, therefore, on the basis of the amount of independence that the subsidiaries have in reality.

The TNC is a company that operates *direct* business activities abroad. As already noted, it is not enough for the company to engage in general international business activities abroad to be classified as transnational or multinational. A company that engages in international business via exports and/or import of goods and services or via non-equity collaborative agreement, or that engages in international portfolio investment – i.e. investment undertaken for purely financial reasons – does *not* become a TNC by virtue of these business activities. To be a transnational, the company must operate *directly* in the foreign country via the setting up of affiliates, and therefore through the ownership of assets located abroad.

Within the transnational corporation as a whole we can identify various types of enterprises as in Box 1.2 and further highlighted in the Appendix to this chapter.

Box 1.2   *The TNC and its enterprises*

Various types of enterprises

Parent enterprise
An enterprise that controls assets of affiliates in foreign countries. The country it is located in is the *home country* of the TNC. The countries where the foreign affiliates are located are the *host countries*.

Foreign affiliates

1 Incorporated enterprises include:

   • *associates*: affiliates with equity involvement between 10 and 50 per cent;
   • *subsidiaries*: affiliates with equity involvement in excess of 50 per cent

2 Unincorporated enterprises or *branches* that may be wholly or partly owned

---

The setting up of affiliates can be the result of acquisitions of pre-existing business or of the creation of new businesses. An affiliate can be a large enterprise with assets and resources of considerable value, or with very few resources.

The country in which the TNC as a whole is legally registered is considered its *home country*; this is also the country where the main headquarters are located. Some companies may have more than one home country; for example Unilever is registered in both the UK and the Netherlands. *Host countries* are the foreign countries in which the company invests and owns affiliates.

5   Growth, characteristics and patterns

The growth in the number of TNCs worldwide and in their operations has progressed steadily after WWII. The increase has been very considerable since the mid-1970s. Ietto-Gillies (2002a: 12, Table 2.1) shows that in 1968–69 the number of TNCs originating from 14 developed countries was 7276. This figure is likely to be very close to the total number of world TNCs at the time. The *World Investment Report 2011* (UNCTAD, 2011) estimates the total number of TNCs worldwide for 2010 to be 103 786.

Various elements have contributed to the growth of TNCs and specifically:

*   The technological and organizational innovations mentioned in section 3, in particular the development in communication and transportation technologies and the organizational innovation within companies.
*   The favourable political environment after the Second World War. Under the new global order and the auspices of international institutions such as the International Monetary Fund (IMF) and the General Agreement on Tariffs and Trade (GATT),[9] governments in western countries became less protectionist and less hostile to both international trade and international direct production activities by companies.
*   The liberalization and privatization programmes of many developed and developing countries in the last 30 years. They have facilitated and encouraged companies to invest abroad.

Developments of favourable conditions explain why internationalization via direct activities of TNCs was possible on the scale we witnessed in the last 60 years. However, it does not, by itself, explain why companies wanted and, indeed, want to take the international route to growth. This is the subject of the theories presented in Part III and – to some extent – in Part II.

What characteristics and patterns do the TNCs as a whole exhibit? The media image of TNCs is of huge corporations in charge of the world's business and with a tremendous amount of power. This view is fairly correct but not exhaustive. Most large corporations do indeed operate transnationally and most TNCs are very large. However, transnationality of business operations is gradually becoming a feature of smaller companies as well as of the largest ones. This has been the case particularly in the last three decades.

The new information and communication technologies (ICTs) have made it easier to operate internationally for both large and smaller firms. With the increase in the degree of internationalization, smaller companies have been learning from larger ones and from the more internationalization-friendly environment. More and more firms which are not very large are branching out into direct operations abroad. Many may have been operating other forms of international business, particularly exports, and are now moving into the next mode: direct production abroad. The learning process for international business can therefore take place through different modes. It can also take place via direct contact with larger TNCs. A smaller company may start working as supplier or distributor to a large TNC and then branch out independently into direct operations in another country.

In terms of the regional pattern, over 70 per cent of these companies originated from developed countries at the end of the first decade of the twenty-first century. However, the developing countries are slowly increasing their participation. In the early 1990s they were contributing less than 10 per cent to the world population of TNCs (UNCTAD, 1995: 8–9, Table I.2) while the figures for 2010 show a contribution of some 29 per cent. The participation of developing countries to the location of affiliates is considerably higher than their participation as home country. The *World Investment Report 2011* reports that the developing countries were host to over 57 per cent of foreign affiliates with China accounting for almost 49 per cent. Some of these affiliates may not, however, incorporate large amounts of capital assets.

There has also been an evolution in terms of sectors of operation. Prior to WWII most corporations invested abroad to acquire resources, specifically raw materials. The first decades after WWII saw the growth of foreign direct investment in manufacturing. More recent decades have seen an acceleration of foreign activities in the service sector. We should, however, note that many large TNCs are diversified and may, therefore, operate in both manufacturing and services.

The geographical scope of TNCs' direct operations has also been expanding. There is evidence that companies have extended their internal networks of affiliates abroad in more and more countries (Ietto-Gillies, 2002a: ch. 5).[10]

A further feature of the modern TNC is its operations via external networks, i.e. via a variety of arm's-length contractual arrangements with other firms, be these suppliers or distributors

The main stylized features of TNCs and their evolution are highlighted in Box 1.3.

Box 1.3   *Transnational corporations: some stylized facts*

TNCs' growth pattern worldwide

- Considerable increase in the number of TNCs worldwide since WWII.

- Most large companies operate transnationally.

- Increasing participation by smaller companies to the population of TNCs.

- Most TNCs originate from developed countries; however, there is increasing participation by companies from developing countries.

- Developing countries have a large share of affiliates of foreign TNCs located in them.

- The large TNCs have direct operations in many countries.

- The main sector of operations has evolved from resources to manufacturing to services.

- International business networks via internal networks of affiliates as well as via external contractual networks.

6   Foreign direct investment (FDI)

International portfolio and direct investment

International investment falls into two categories: international portfolio investment and foreign direct investment. International financial investment – or *international portfolio investment* – is investment undertaken for purely financial reasons, often on a short-term basis. It includes loans as well equity investment, i.e. the acquisition of shares in a foreign company. In the latter case what we mean by financial or portfolio reasons is that the equity share is not substantial enough to give the investors control or a long-lasting interest in the management of the company they have invested in. Portfolio investment may be undertaken at the national or international level according to whether the equity acquisition or the loans are between institutions/people belonging to the same country or to different countries.

Whenever the investment is large enough to give a *controlling and long-term interest* in the acquired company, we consider it to be direct investment and we refer to it as *foreign direct investment* (FDI). This is the type of investment that companies use to acquire assets abroad. FDI is therefore the defining modality of TNCs. The demarcation between international portfolio and direct investment based on the criterion of *control* goes back to the seminal work by Steven Hymer (1960), on which more in Chapter 4.

How do central statistical offices of various countries decided to apportion international investment between the two categories? The IMF gives the guideline of a 10 per cent ownership for the investment to be included into the FDI statistics as highlighted by the Appendix to this chapter. This is the same issue we encountered in section 2 when discussing control of assets by transnational corporations. We then stressed two types of control: ownership control and managerial control. For the demarcation between portfolio and direct investment the relevant type of control is the equity control.

In principle, all international investment – whether portfolio or direct – can be made by private or public institutions and by individual or corporate actors. Individual investors may engage in the acquisition of controlling shares in foreign companies. However, in practice, most international investment is made by the corporate sector and the TNCs are responsible for most FDI worldwide. They are also responsible for the majority of portfolio investment and indeed of other international transactions, including trade.

The growing relevance of FDI for the world economy can be highlighted by the following statistics. In 1960 the ratio of world inward FDI stock to GDP was 4.4 per cent; by 1990 it reached 9.6 and in 2010 it was 30.3 (UNCTAD 2011, Statistical Annexes). The developed countries play the key role in both outward and inward FDI stock with percentages of the total world FDI of, respectively, 82.3 and 65.3 in 2010.

The developing countries' contribution to outward FDI has been increasing in the last couple of decades. Most of it is directed to other developing countries and tends to be of the greenfield modality. However, in recent years we have seen a growing amount of outward FDI by MNCs from developing countries directed towards developed countries; it usually takes the acquisition modality. The home countries most involved in the latter pattern are: Brazil, China, India, South Africa, South Korea and some Eastern European countries.

Greenfield versus mergers and acquisitions

The controlling share in a business enterprise through foreign direct investment can be obtained via *mergers and acquisitions* of an existing company in a foreign country or via the setting up of a completely new business establishment (see Box 1.5). The latter is referred to as *greenfield* direct investment and is the result of organic growth within the company. Some authors distinguish between greenfield and *brownfield* investment. The latter denotes that investment which adds to capacity in a situation in which some established fixed capital (brownfield) already exists. Greenfield investment implies that a new plant, building or other fixed capital is built where none existed at all. Many authors use the term greenfield for both situations. This convention will be followed in the rest of this book. The effects of greenfield versus M&As on employment will be considered in Chapter 18.

The official statistics on foreign direct investment do not usually distinguish between greenfield and M&As FDI. Databases on M&As are often supplied by private research businesses that collect the data on the basis of stock exchange selling and purchasing deals. They are not directly comparable with overall FDI data and this is a source of difficulty for researchers into the field.

FDI data issues

Data on FDI is available as *flows* or *stocks*. Flow concepts refer to a period of time, whether they are in relation to an economic/business concept or not (see examples in Box 1.4).

Box 1.4   *Flow and stock concepts and their relationship: two examples*

Example A: Population changes
Let us assume that the total population in a country at the beginning of January 2005 is 100 million people; this is a *stock* concept. Let us now assume that a year later at the beginning of January 2006 the total population is 110 million. This is also a stock concept. The difference between the two stocks (10 million) is due to a variety of population *flows* that take place *during* the year 2005. In particular: the positive flow of births and the negative flow of deaths during the year plus the positive flow of immigrants and the negative flow of emigrants during the year.

Example B: Foreign direct investment: flows and stocks
As regards FDI, flows data record the year to year value of investment, that is, the value of investment undertaken *during* a specific year. Stock data represent the net accumulated value resulting from past flows; they give us the value of accumulated stock *at a point in time* such as the end of the year.

Each country's central statistical office collects data for both *inward* and *outward* FDI. *Inward* foreign direct investment for a specific country is the direct investment by foreign companies into that country. *Outward* foreign direct investment is the investment abroad by companies whose nationality is in the specific country under consideration.

At the world level, the total value of inward and outward data should coincide. They usually do not for statistical reasons related to lack of consistency in the methods of measurement and data collection in various countries (OECD, 1994: 102). The data is usually broken down by country of origin (for inward investment) or destination (for the outward investment). It is also broken down by sector of investment. Detailed statistics are made available by UNCTAD via its annual *World Investment Report* and related Statistical Annexes.

The data on FDI flows record the year-to-year value of investment on the basis of the balance of payments statistics, therefore on the basis of records of currency movements for investment purposes. This means that the records are made on the basis of how the investment is funded. Specifically, foreign direct investment statistics record that part of investment abroad that is funded in one of the following forms (OECD, 1994: 100):[11]

- net capital contribution by the direct investor in the form of purchases of corporate equity, new equity issues or the creation of companies;
- net lending, including short-term loans and advances by the parent company to the subsidiary;
- retained (reinvested) earnings.

However, investment projects could also be funded by loans taken by the foreign enterprise in the country in which it operates. In such a case no funds cross borders and the relevant amount of investment will not be included in the FDI statistics. Foreign direct investment data only record that investment funded via retained profits or net equity acquisition or loans directly made by the parent company to the subsidiary. This means that the total amount of investment by the foreign affiliate, may be grossly underestimated (UNCTAD, 1997: ch. 1).

As regards the funding via net equity acquisition or retained profits, the former is likely to involve movements of funds – i.e. intra-company flows – from headquarters to the foreign affiliate. The latter – retained earnings – does not involve movements of funds, because the affiliate utilizes past profits,[12] though the company as a whole is legally entitled to the profits of the affiliate.

Foreign direct investment and domestic capital formation

It is important to bear in mind that foreign direct investment is not fully analogous to the concept of capital formation, i.e. to the concept of investment with which economics and business students are familiar. The gross (or indeed net) domestic fixed capital formation (GDFCF or NDFCF) gives an indication of *new capacity* that is formed in the country through the investment. The data are *independent of the nationality* of the investor, though they are often broken down by whether the investment is made by a private or public investor.

Foreign direct investment data differ from GDFCF (or indeed NDFCF) in two respects: first, because they refer to the nationality of the investor, which is key to the whole concept; and, second, because, within this key perspective, the *capacity form-ation refers to the company which is investing and not to the country where the invest-ment takes place*. This means that in FDI we have the inclusion of two types of investment: the investment that refers to the establishment of, for example, a new plant via greenfield investment, and that resulting from the company's acquisition of controlling shares in an existing company in the host country (cross-border mergers and acquisitions).

These two forms of company's foreign direct investment both lead to an *increase in productive capacity for the company*. However, only the former (green-field) leads to *new productive capacity for the host country*. The latter (M&As) only leads to a change in ownership of the acquired company in toto or in part. These are not just statistical issues and demarcation problems. Essentially, in the collection of data on GDFCF, statistical offices take a macro perspective in which the relevant issue is whether the investment adds to the country's capacity, not whether the nationality of the investor is foreign or domestic. In the statistics on FDI, the perspective is micro and, in particular, the key issue is the nationality of the investor. Therefore, the investment is included if it adds to the capacity of the investor, independently of whether it may or may not add to the productive capac-ity of the host country.

Box 1.5   *Foreign direct investment (FDI)*

Modality
Greenfield vs mergers and acquisitions (M&As)

Data issues

- Stocks and flows

- Inward: host country perspective

- Outward: home country perspective

Funding of FDI via

- equity purchases;

- net lending by parent to affiliate;

- retained profits

7 International production

Foreign direct investment – whether by greenfield or M&As – leads to international production, of which it is usually considered the main indicator. International production includes all the foreign value-added activities by TNCs. These business activities may involve material goods or immaterial services. The general term 'international production' is used to signify value-added activities under the control of a foreign company.

The capital injected through FDI is, of course, the essential element both in terms of capacity formation and in terms of the technology embodied in it. However, FDI is not the only injection of capital that contributes to international production. As discussed in section 6 (FDI data issues), the investment into a foreign affiliate is much wider than FDI because the latter does not include that investment funded via loans raised directly by the affiliate in the host country in which it operates. Therefore, while FDI is essential to international production and is indeed its largest source of funding, it is not the only capital resource contributing to it.[13] This means that international production can be considerably larger than the amount/value warranted by the FDI stock.

Moreover, there are wider resources made available by the TNC for international production alongside capital: many of these resources are in the nature of services to which it may or may not be possible to attach a specific monetary value. The individual items range from equipment to technology, to skills and to know-how. The latter includes technological as well as organizational and managerial knowledge. It also includes knowledge about markets, suppliers, distributors or competitors in countries other than the one in which the international production takes place.

The end result is that international production is best seen as a 'bundle' or 'package' in which the overall contribution of the 'package' is more than that possible by the sum of the contributions of each item considered separately. Moreover, the items cannot easily be 'unbundled': they are often inextricably linked together in the 'package'.

Nonetheless international production and related FDI is only one of the modalities of operation of TNCs. The corporations can use exports to source markets as well as a variety of other modalities to either source markets or secure supplies.

8 Alternative modalities of TNCs' business operations

While FDI – and the international production it leads to – are the distinguishing features of the TNC compared with other companies, they are not the only form of international business that the TNC is involved in. The following are all possible modalities of market sourcing or supply channels in foreign countries:

- foreign direct investment and international production;
- exports;
- franchising;

- licensing;
- setting up inter-firm partnerships such as alliances and joint ventures;
- outsourcing of parts of production through arm's-length contracts with external firms via subcontracting arrangements.

Exports are the best known mode of market penetration and sourcing across frontiers. Exports by one country imply imports by other(s). International trade refers to both the importation and exportation of goods and services across frontiers. Historically, trade is the most ancient mode of transborder business operations. It is only with the birth of the nation-states that we can appropriately talk of 'international' in the context of trade or indeed of other business transactions. Worldwide, international trade is still the most relevant business transaction mode across frontiers, though it is declining in relative terms, that is, as a percentage of the total value of world transactions.

The activities of transnational corporations have a considerable impact on both the volume and pattern of trade as will be argued in Chapter 19. In particular we have seen an increase in the so-called *intra-firm trade*, that is, in trade that is external to the country (and therefore forms part of international trade) but internal to the firm. The latter characteristic means that the trade takes place between parts of the same company located in different countries (parent to affiliate or affiliate to affiliate). Over three-quarters of world trade originates with TNCs and, indeed, over a third of world trade is estimated to take place on an intra-firm basis (UNCTAD, 1996).

Another emerging pattern of international trade is the so-called *intra-industry trade* by which expression we denote that part of trade that results in the imports and exports – for the same country – of products belonging to the same industrial category. Examples of intra-industry trade are: imports of motor cars and exports of parts and components of motor cars; exports of leather bags and imports of leather shoes; or exports of leather handbags and imports of textile bags. As we shall argue in Chapter 19, the activities of TNCs have also an impact on this type of trade.

The last four modalities (*franchising, licensing, alliances/joint ventures and subcontracting*) involve contracts between our firm in the home country and a host country enterprise.[14] They all involve, therefore, a certain degree of externalization of activities, that is, a degree of involvement by enterprises that are external to the firm. Licensing, franchising and some types of joint ventures/partnerships are seen, from the point of view of the principal company, as modes of market entry alongside direct production and exports. Joint ventures are, sometimes, the only entry mode allowed into specific host countries, such as China for many years. The rationale for this restriction is to facilitate the involvement and learning process of local businesses. However, joint ventures can also be developed for other strategic purposes such as sharing the costs and risks of innovation.

Outsourcing – via subcontracting – is mainly a supply channel mode rather than a market sourcing mode.[15] It creates a backward linkage in the supply chain. Arm's-length contracts can also be used in forward linkages such as distribution (UNCTAD, 2001: chs IV and V).

Outsourcing has been defined as: 'the act of transferring some of a company's recurring interval activities and decision rights to outside providers, as set in a contract' (Greaver,1999 reported in WTO, 2005: 266). It is part of the make-or-buy strategic decision. The two parties to the outsourcing contract can be located in the same country or in different ones. There is evidence that international subcontracting has been increasing in the last 25 years and is now very large (WTO, 2005: section 4). Whether there is ownership control or not, the principal is likely to exercise strategic control over the subcontractor as argued in Chapter 13.

If the contractual agreement – be it for subcontracting or licensing of franchising – leads to substantial equity ownership between the two parties located in different countries, the value of the ownership stake is recorded under foreign direct investment. In this case the partnership between the two enterprises involves 'ownership control'. However, usually no such equity arrangements and thus control exists.

The conclusion is that, though FDI (and international production) is the main and defining modality of TNCs' operations, the companies can – and do – operate with many other modalities. Hard statistical evidence on the weight of various modalities – other than exports and FDI – is difficult to gather. We should therefore bear in mind that the overall relevance of TNCs to the world economy and their overall power go well beyond what we can infer from data on FDI.

9   Impact on wider cross-border transactions

The activities listed in section 8 – as well as FDI – are direct modalities of business used by TNCs to operate in their markets and/or to organize their production activities. All these activities together give, directly, rise to considerable flows of resources and products across borders. In addition there are also flows of resources *indirectly* related to those business activities. Among the latter it is worth mentioning the following.

Earnings from portfolio and direct investment

Both portfolio and direct investment give their investors returns in the form of interest or dividends or profits. The flow of earnings travels in the opposite direction to the flow of funds for the original investment.[16] Moreover, a given investment in a particular period is likely to produce earnings for several subsequent years. This issue is discussed further in Chapter 20.

Movements of people across borders

International business generates large movements of people across frontiers. Such movements may, at times, be the direct result of specific types of international business, as in the case of tourism or international transport business. It can also relate to the exchange of labour services between business units located in different countries. Employees of large companies are sent on international assignments to other parts of the company operating abroad or to independent companies with which the TNC has collaborative agreements, which include the exchange of personnel. Such movements may also originate with governmental and international institutions. The movements of people can be for very short periods or for longer terms; the people who work abroad while retaining their original nationality are considered *expatriates*. There is evidence that movements of highly skilled labour, for short or long assignments, have been increasing (Salt, 1997), in line with the increased cross-border business activities and, in particular, with those originating with transnational corporations.

SUMMARY BOX I

Key concepts on TNCs and their activities

Historical antecedents

Control of foreign assets by TNCs

- Equity control
- Managerial control: relevance of technological and organizational innovations
- Evolution in the internal organization of companies

Transnational companies

- Terminology issues
- Enterprises: parent companies, associates, affiliates, subsidiaries

The population of TNCs

- TNCs' size and growth
- Location in developed and developing countries
- Geographical spread of affiliates
- From resources to manufacturing to services
- Increase in operations via external networks

International investment

- Foreign portfolio investment
- Foreign direct investment (FDI): greenfield versus mergers and acquisitions (M&As)
- Inward and outward FDI
- Stocks and flows of FDI
- Funding sources for FDI

Alternative modalities of international operations

Market sourcing, supply and distribution channels

Relevant chapters

Appendix to this chapter
Chapters 4, 18 and 19

Today, as in previous centuries, we see also more traditional migration, usually – though not always – of unskilled labour. All these movements of people are likely to give rise to movements of funds across frontiers. Tourists spend their money abroad and migrant labourers remit part of their wages to their families and relatives in their own country.

Indicative further reading

Buckley, P.J. and Ghauri, P.N. (1999), *The Internationalization of the Firm: A Reader*, London: Thomson Business Press, parts III and IV.

Cox, H. (1997), 'The evolution of international business enterprise', in R. John et al., *Global Business Strategy*, London: ITBP, ch. 1, pp. 9–46.

Dicken, P. (2003), *Global Shift: Reshaping the Global Economic Map in the 21st Century*, 4th edn, London: Sage Publications, chs 2 and 3.

Hymer, S. (1970), 'The efficiency (contradictions) of multinational corporations', *American Economic Review*, **60** (2), 441–8.

Ietto-Gillies, G. (2002), *Transnational Corporations: Fragmentation Amidst Integration*, London: Routledge, ch 2, pp. 11–36; chs 4 and 5, pp. 63–104.

Jones, G. (2002), *Merchants to Multinationals: British Trading Companies in the Nineteenth and Twentieth Centuries*, Oxford: OUP.

OECD (1994), *The Performance of Foreign Affiliates in OECD Countries*, Paris: OECD, pp. 100–104.

UNCTAD (2001), *World Investment Report, 2001: Promoting Linkages*, Geneva: United Nations, chs IV and V.

UNCTAD (various years) *World Investment Report*, Geneva: United Nations.

Wilkins, M. (1988), 'The free-standing company, 1870–1914: an important type of British foreign direct investment', *Economic History Review*, 2nd series, **41** (2), 259–82.

Notes

1 For further details on the historical evolution of TNCs the reader is advised to read the whole chapter by Cox.

2 The relevant type of management in our context is the one related to the setting of strategic goals and the monitoring of performance, rather than the day-to-day operational management.

3 More on transaction costs in Chapter 8.

4 An analysis of theoretical and historical issues of the U- and M-forms is in Auerbach (1988).

5 On the various organizational structures see Westney and Zaheer (2001).

6 Forsgren et al. (2005) argue that the headquarters of a TNC may not be able to exercise influence in spite of equity and organizational control whenever its subsidiaries are very highly embedded. See Chapter 17 on this.

7 The Harvard Multinationals Project developed in the 1960s under the direction of Raymond Vernon, places a cut-off point for a multinational as direct operations in at least six countries. Details of the results of the project were published in Vaupel and Curhan (1974).

8 The term company tends to be used in the British literature, while corporation is more used in the North American literature. I use both expressions interchangeably.

9 The GATT has been restructured and is now known as the World Trade Organization (WTO), which was established in 1995. The GATT and the IMF were established immediately after WWII.

10 Further information on the geographical spread of TNCs' direct activities is in work by this author and Marion Frenz for UNCTAD (UNCTAD, 2004) on the basis of the Dun and Bradstreet 'Who Owns Whom' (2002) database on companies' ownership trees.

11 See also Appendix to this chapter, section 2.

12 Kogut (1983) analyses the time sequence in the funding process of FDI. He points out that the first investment in a foreign country is likely to be funded via inter-company flows/equity acquisition. The later additions to foreign direct investment in the same foreign affiliate are likely to take place via reinvested profits.

13 It is nonetheless not unusual to identify FDI with international production. Dunning (2000b: 119) defines international production as 'the production financed by foreign direct investment'.

14 These are general types of arm's-length contractual arrangements between companies and other partners. They are liable to manifest in a variety of specific forms and have given rise to refinements in the terminology (Inkpen, 2001; McDonald and Burton, 2002: ch. 9; Narula and Duyster, 2004: ch. 10).

15 The distinction between market sourcing, supply and distribution channels is not sharp. A market sourcing mode can facilitate supply or distribution channels and vice versa.

16 However, bear in mind that FDI is not always financed via funds from the home country as discussed in section 6.

Appendix to Chapter 1: definitions and data issues

I Transnational corporations[1]

Transnational corporations (TNCs) are incorporated or unincorporated enterprises comprising parent enterprises and their foreign affiliates. A *parent enterprise* is defined as an enterprise that controls assets of other entities in countries other than its home country, usually by owning a certain equity capital stake. An equity capital stake of 10 per cent or more of the ordinary shares or voting power for an incorporated enterprise, or its equivalent for an unincorporated enterprise, is normally considered as a threshold for the control of assets. A *foreign affiliate* is an incorporated or unincorporated enterprise in which an investor, who is resident in another economy, owns a stake that permits a lasting interest in the management of that enterprise (an equity stake of 10 per cent for an incorporated enterprise or its equivalent for an unincorporated enterprise). In the *World Investment Report*, subsidiary enterprises, associate enterprises and branches – defined below – are all referred to as *foreign affiliates* or *affiliates*:

- A *subsidiary* is an incorporated enterprise in the host country in which another entity directly owns more than a half of the shareholder's voting power and has the right to appoint or remove a majority of the members of the administrative, management or supervisory body.
- An *associate* is an incorporated enterprise in the host country in which an investor owns a total of at least 10 per cent, but not more than half, of the shareholders' voting power.
- A *branch* is a wholly or jointly owned unincorporated enterprise in the host country which is one of the following: (i) a permanent establishment or office of the foreign investor; (ii) an unincorporated partnership or joint venture between the foreign direct investor and one or more third parties; (iii) land, structures (except structures owned by government entities), and/or immovable equipment and objects directly owned by a foreign resident; or (iv) mobile equipment (such as ships, aircraft, gas- or oil-drilling rigs) operating within a country, other than that of the foreign investor, for at least one year. (UNCTAD, 2001: Annex B, 275)

2 International investment

The IMF *Balance of Payments Manual* (1977) includes, in the category of *portfolio investment*, 'long-term bonds and corporate equities other than those included in the categories for direct investment and reserves' (ibid.: 142). Thus, portfolio investment is defined by default – as a residual – from FDI. On foreign direct investment the manual reads: 'Direct investment refers to investment that is made to acquire a lasting interest in an enterprise operating in an economy other than that of the investor, the investor's purpose being to have an effective voice in the management of the enterprise' (ibid.: 136). The IMF guidelines on this demarcation sets a minimum of 10 per cent share ownership or voting power for the investment to be included in the FDI.

Central statistical offices in some countries set their actual demarcation percentage at the minimum level of 10 per cent; others go well above it. The IMF (ibid.: 137) acknowledges that the percentages considered relevant for control and thus inclusion into the FDI category can vary from country to country. In general it sees that: 'the percentage chosen as providing evidence of direct investment is typically quite low – frequently ranging from 25 per cent down to 10 per cent'.

UNCTAD (2001) follows the IMF closely and thus qualifies FDI and its various components:

> *Foreign direct investment* (FDI) is defined as an investment involving a long-term relationship and reflecting a lasting interest and control by a resident entity in one economy (foreign direct investor or parent enterprise) in an enterprise resident in an economy other than that of the foreign direct investor (FDI enterprise or affiliate enterprise or foreign affiliate).[2] FDI implies that the investor exerts a significant degree of influence on the management of the enterprise resident in the other economy. Such investment involves both the initial transaction between the two entities and all subsequent transactions between them and among foreign affiliates, both incorporated and unincorporated. FDI may be undertaken by individuals as well as business entities.
>
> *Flows of FDI* comprise capital provided (either directly or through other related enterprises) by a foreign direct investor to an FDI enterprise, or capital received from an FDI enterprise by a foreign direct investor. FDI has three components: equity capital, reinvested earnings and intra-company loans:
>
> • *Equity capital* is the foreign direct investor's purchase of shares of an enterprise in a country other than its own.
> • *Reinvested earnings* comprise the direct investor's share (in proportion to direct equity participation) of earnings not distributed as dividends by affiliates, or earnings not remitted to the direct investor. Such retained profits by affiliates are reinvested.
> • *Intra-company loans* or *intra-company debt transactions* refer to short- or long-term borrowing and lending of funds between direct investors (parent enterprises) and affiliate enterprises.
>
> FDI stock is the value of the share of their capital and reserves (including retained profits) attributable to the parent enterprise, plus the net indebtedness of affiliates to the parent enterprise. FDI flow and stock data used in the *World Investment Report* are not always defined as above, because these definitions are often not applicable to disaggregated FDI data. For example, in analysing geographical and industrial trends and patterns of FDI, data based on approvals of FDI may also be used because they allow a disaggregation at the country or industry level. Such cases are denoted accordingly. (UNCTAD, 2001: Annex B, 275–6)

Both flow and stock statistics are 'current prices' data; for 'stocks' the prices are those of the year in which the investment was made. Attempts to calculate 'real' values flows and stocks FDI data are fraught with considerable difficulties as noted by UNCTAD (1997: ch. 1).

Estimates of stock data are based on the historic value of the investment and are not updated. This grossly underestimates the value of the capital assets owned by foreign companies in any particular country. It also leads to distortions in the comparative position of countries because it undervalues the capital stock of countries with a longer history of FDI compared to those that are relatively new to such activities. Recent re-estimates of FDI stocks at replacement values for Japan, Germany, the USA and the UK by Cantwell and Bellak (1998) find many distortions.

3   Non-equity forms of investment

Foreign direct investors may also obtain an effective voice in the management of another business entity through means other than acquiring an equity stake. These are non-equity forms of investment, and they include, *inter alia*, subcontracting, management contracts, turnkey arrangements, franchising, licensing and product sharing. Data on these forms of transnational corporate activity are usually not separately identified balance-of-payments statistics. These statistics, however, usually present data on royalties and licensing fees, defined as 'receipts and payments of residents and non-residents for: (i) the authorized use of intangible non-produced, non-financial assets and proprietary rights such as trademarks, copyrights, patents, processes, techniques, designs, manufacturing rights, franchises, etc., and (ii) the use, through licensing agreements, of produced originals or prototypes, such as manuscripts, films, etc.' (UNCTAD, 2001: Annex B, 276)

4   Inter-firm collaborative agreements

Licensing

This is a contractual arrangement by which the licensor allows the licensee to utilize intellectual property in return for financial or other rewards. The utilization of intellectual property may refer to brand name or trademark or patents or design or technology or whole products. There may also be the transfer of collateral services to allow the proper exploitation of the licence. For the licensor the danger may be that its knowledge may leak to competitors or that, in time, the licensee may become a competitor.

Franchising

This is similar to licensing. The related contract allows the franchisee to undertake business activities in a certain domain (in relation to a product and/or a geographical territory). The activities are to be carried on in specified ways and involve the use of the franchisor's trade mark or design or business formula. The franchisee will pay financial compensation and will bear the risks of the business. One risk for the franchisor is that, if the quality of the franchisee's business is poor, it will debase the overall brand name.

Alliances and joint ventures

These are forms of inter-firm collaboration and the two expressions are often used interchangeably. Nonetheless, 'joint ventures' is more often reserved for those collaborations that involve equity ownership. The venture may sometimes result in the birth of a new business entity. An alliance is usually set up to carry out specific business activities such as joint research or product development. The contracts are usually for specified periods and they often are dissolved earlier because of difficulties in the relationship. Such difficulties arise from having to balance the separate objectives of each firm with the stated objectives of the alliance.

Subcontracting

The UNIDO group of experts defines this contractual arrangement as follows:

> a sub-contracting relationship exists when a firm (the principal) places an order with another firm (the sub-contractor) for the manufacture of parts, components, sub-assemblies or assemblies to be incorporated into a product which the principal will sell. Such orders may include the treatment, processing or finishing of materials or parts by the sub-contractor at the principal's request. (Michalet, 1980: 40)

Notes

1 Large parts of this Appendix are reproduced from UNCTAD (2001: Annex B, 275–7). Notes 2, 3 and 4 are also from the same source. The UNCTAD Annex also contains very useful details on sources and data consistency, not reproduced here. Very detailed information about the statistics on TNCs and on FDI are in OECD (2008) and UNCTAD (2009b), both available online.
2 This general definition of FDI is based on IMF (1993) and OECD (1996).

PART II · PRE-WWII APPROACHES TO INTERNATIONAL INVESTMENT

Introduction to Part II

> per che una gente impera ed altra langue [so that one people rules and another languishes]
> (Dante, *La Divina Commedia, Inferno*, VII.82)

The two chapters in this part both deal with theories developed before the Second World War (WWII). The theories are grouped into Marxist and neoclassical approaches. The treatment of the theories is kept deliberately short. While recognizing that the contemporary reader may be less interested in these pre-WWII developments, I consider these approaches to have great historical relevance and, in some cases, to be also relevant to a wider interpretation and understanding of modern social, political and theoretical developments.

All the theories presented deal with foreign investment in general. The Marxist writers analyse it in relation to its role in imperialism in its colonial phase. Many of the issues they consider are of great relevance for the relationship between developed and developing countries today, and for an understanding of the modern non-colonial brand of imperialism.

None of the theories presented deals specifically with transnational companies as such or with international production and foreign direct investment. Indeed some of these concepts had not yet been developed.

In general, many concepts used by economists in the period covered in this part are different from concepts and issues of interest to more modern economists. Nonetheless, many of the issues raised by classical Marxist writers have also been the concern of many writings in the last 60 years, for example: the concentration of production; the integration of production and its organization across countries; underconsumption and lack of effective demand; the role of international finance in underdevelopment; the coexistence of development with some backward sectors/areas; the linkages between finance and industrial capital. The latter issue is indeed very relevant in the current globalization phase of capitalism.

One of the main issues of interest to pre-WWII Marxist as well as neoclassical economists – namely, the large flow of financial investment across countries – is very relevant today. Moreover, the financial crisis of 2008 has brought into a sharper focus issues of international finance, lack of effective demand and maldistribution of income and wealth; these are issues at the centre of the Marxist writings presented in Chapter 2. As I revise the book the turmoils in North Africa are bringing to our attention the high level of integration between developed and developing countries as well as the high risks for international investment of sudden political events.

Readers interested in the book as a whole may find it useful to revisit some of the material in this second part after they have reached the end of the book. It may allow them to see some points of analogy between old and new theories or both these groups of theories and the effects of international production (Part IV). Readers uninterested in these pre-WWII writings, may, of course, skip this part altogether. None of the material in it is essential to the understanding of Parts III and IV. Nonetheless, reference to the writings presented in this part will, occasionally, be made later in the book. The summary boxes give pointers to possible linkages between chapters. No key reading is given for these two chapters, as no recent specific literature exists – as far as I know.

2 Marxist approaches

I Hobson's analysis of imperialism[1]

John Atkinson Hobson's book *Imperialism*, first published in 1902, contains a very clear analysis of the economic and political implications of the growing imperialist tendency of developed countries in the nineteenth century, and particularly of Britain.

He starts his analysis by giving an assessment of the magnitude and growth of imperialism in terms of size of colonized territories and populations; these measures are set against comparative data for the related developed imperialist country. The main focus of the study is Britain: its very considerable expansion in the last 30 years of the nineteenth century is emphasized.

Does the nation as a whole need imperialism and does it benefit from it? Hobson asks and analyses this question in relation to:

*   the need to generate exports to sustain domestic activity and employment; and
*   the need to expand territorial areas in which the growing population of Britain can find settlement.

He considers both of these 'needs'. In particular the 'need' for colonial trade is discussed and queried for the following reasons:

1   A possible cut in colonial exports could be counterbalanced by increased domestic demand for consumption provided the 'appropriate' distribution policies on income and wealth were followed.
2   Trade with the colonies was becoming a decreasing proportion of total trade at the time.
3   Moreover, political annexation and subjugation are not necessary to the generation of trade. Indeed, he points out the inconsistency between the free trade doctrine of British economists and politicians and the imposition of 'protected' trade via colonialism[2] when he writes: 'In total contravention of our theory that trade rests upon a basis of mutual gain to the nations that engage in it, we undertook enormous expenses with the object of "forcing" new markets, and the markets we forced were small, precarious and unprofitable' (Hobson, 1902: 65–6).

His conclusion is, therefore, that 'imperialism' is not needed by the British nation as a whole. Indeed, when the economic and human costs of imperialism and the related distortions in the structure of public expenditure are considered, one is led to conclude that the nation as a whole does not benefit from imperialist expansion.

Why, then, is it done? The answer is that although the nation as a whole may lose out from imperialism, a section of the population benefits from it. Hobson spells this out clearly when, in answer to his own question, 'How is the British nation induced to embark upon such unsound business?' he writes: 'The only possible answer is that the business interests of the nation as a whole are subordinated to those of certain sectional interests that usurp control of the national resources and use them for their private gain' (ibid.: 46). The sections of the population that benefit comprise a variety of people drawn from the educated middle and upper classes: engineers, people working in armaments, planters, missionaries etc. However, the prime movers and instigators are the financial investors.

One of Hobson's best insights is to realize that imperialism has little or nothing to do with trade and more to do with investments as prime motivators: 'By far the most important economic factor in Imperialism is the influence relating to investments' (ibid.: 51). This is made clear, among other things, by looking at data on incomes from foreign investment and profits from exports; the first set of incomes has grown much faster than the second. Hobson's own words on the relevance of investment and the interests of investors are very clear:

> It is not too much to say that the modern foreign policy of Great Britain has been primarily a struggle for profitable markets of investment . . . If, contemplating the enormous expenditure on armaments, the ruinous wars, the diplomatic audacity or knavery by which modern Governments seek to extend their territorial power, we put plain, practical question, *Cui bono?* the first and most obvious answer is, the investor. (Ibid.: 53, 55)[3]

The financiers manage to impose their line by control of the press and by their manipulation of political power. Why are financiers seeking investment abroad, why not in their own country? Is the country generating more savings than it can absorb? The answer is affirmative and this is connected with the tendency of the economic system towards overproduction, glut and under-consumption, and generally towards a lack of what we now call 'effective' demand, that is, demand for goods and services supported by adequate purchasing power:[4] 'Everywhere appear excessive powers of production, excessive capital in search of investment . . . the growth of the powers of production . . . exceeds the growth in consumption . . . more goods can be produced than can be sold at a profit, and . . . more capital exists than can find remunerative investment' (ibid.: 81).

This tendency to under-consumption or over-saving increases with improvements in methods of production and concentration of ownership and control as these lead to higher profits and to concentration of incomes. The question now is, to what extent is this over-saving and over-production the inevitable outcome of progress and improvements in the economic system? Hobson vehemently rejects this line and explains over-saving and under-consumption through the distributional structure, which favours the wealthy classes against those classes that have a greater need and ability for consumption, but are denied 'consuming power' by the unfair distribution of income: 'The over-saving which is the economic root of Imperialism is found by analysis to consist of rents, monopoly profits, and other unearned or excessive elements of income, which, not being earned by labour of head and hand, have no legitimate *raison d'être'* (ibid.: 85). So the 'taproot' of imperialism is under-consumption and this is generated by maldistribution of income: the remedy is to move towards substantial reforms which distribute more income to the working classes and shift public expenditure from armaments towards public and social/community projects.

The economic system is condemned for the political and economic distortions it causes and for generating 'an economic waste which is chronic and general through-out the advanced industrial nations, a waste contained in the divorcement of the desire to consume and the power to consume' (ibid.: 87). Box 2.1 summarizes Hobson's key points.

Box 2.1   *Key points in Hobson's theory*

- Imperialism benefits only a section of the population and particularly the financial investors.

- Foreign investment is needed to counteract the under-consumptionist tendency in capitalist economies.

- Under-consumption is due to the maldistribution of income and wealth.

- If a fairer distribution of income could be achieved, the need for imperialism would diminish or disappear.

---

2   Lenin's theory of imperialism

In 1916, while in exile in Switzerland, Vladimir Ilyich Lenin wrote his 'pamphlet' *Imperialism, the Highest Stage of Capitalism*, which was first published in 1917. The work takes account of the books by Hobson (1902) and Hilferding (1912).

Lenin sees the economic, social and political situation at the beginning of the twentieth century as *a new stage in capitalist development*, with the characteristics highlighted in Box 2.2. This state of affairs led to capitalism reaching its highest stage: that of imperialism, characterized by the features in Box 2.3. The effects of the new stage of capitalism according to Lenin are shown in Box 2.4.

Imperialism is the *inevitable* consequence of the development of capitalism. Competition inevitably leads to monopolies in banking; this furthers the tendency towards monopolistic production and creates a subjection of production and indus-try to finance. Monopoly leads to a decrease in profitable opportunities at home; this leads to colonization, which in itself creates further monopolies in terms of markets and investment opportunities. Throughout his pamphlet, Lenin stresses the role of 'finance capital' in imperialism, in terms of its role in the developed countries and the need to search for outlets for the surplus finance capital, and in terms of the colonies' ability to offer investment opportunities to surplus capital.[5] Any issues of annexation of land for the benefit of the people from the developed countries, or for the appropriation of sources or raw materials, becomes therefore of secondary importance in relation to the role of finance capital. In this, Lenin's analysis is very close to that of Hobson, who also sees the push towards imperialism as coming from surplus finance (over-saving in Hobson's terminology) and monopolistic finance capital (in Lenin's scheme) rather than from any need to secure raw materials: the raw materials could, after all, be bought on the open market.

This state of affairs led to capitalism reaching its highest stage: that of imperialism, characterized by the features in Box 2.3.

Box 2.2   *Characteristics of the 'new stage of capitalism'*

- There is very considerable and increasing concentration in production: an increase in 'combination'[6] of production or in what we would now call degree of integration, both horizontal and vertical. 'Combination' or integration gives firms various advantages, among which are: elimination of costs of market transactions; evening out of the trade cycle; scope for further technical advances; and a stronger monopolistic position vis-à-vis competitors or rivals. All these lead to an increased monopolization of production.

- Monopolies are spreading in the sphere of banking and finance as well as in other sectors.

- Finance capital and banks in particular are increasingly exercising power and hold over production and industry.

- A vast increase in colonization, and 'partition' of the world among the great powers.

- Large exports of surplus finance capital from developed countries.

Box 2.3   *Lenin's definition of imperialism includes five basic features*

1 The concentration of production

2 'The merging of bank capital with industrial capital, and the creation, on the basis of this "finance capital", of a financial oligarchy'

3 'The export of capital as distinguished from the export of commodities'

4 'The formation of international monopolist capitalist associations which share the world among themselves'

5 The complete 'territorial division of the whole world among the biggest capitalist powers' (Lenin, 1917: 86)

Box 2.4   *Effects of the new stage of capitalism according to Lenin*

- Capitalism spreads its net. Capitalist relations are introduced into larger parts of the world. Development in these countries spreads while growth in industrial countries is retarded. Investment in the host countries (colonies) adds to their total investment while detracting from the investment in the home country (motherland).

- Capitalism in industrial countries becomes parasitic as the *rentier* capitalists live by 'clipping coupons' and thus become more and more divorced from production (Lenin, 1917: 96).

- The profits from foreign investments are only part of the total profits flowing from the colonies to the advanced countries. Investments in railways, general infrastructures, etc. are likely to require imports of products from the motherland into the colonies, thus creating extra profits for the manufacturer and exporter. Lenin therefore sees investments and exports as complementary.

- Imperialism allows the bourgeoisie to give the upper stratum of the working class in industrialized countries special concessions and a share of the profits, thus 'bribing' them into acquiescence and opportunism.

- The monopolization of production leads to its increasing socialization. 'When a big enterprise assumes gigantic proportions, and, on the basis of an exact computation of the mass data, organises according to plan the supply of primary raw materials . . .; when the raw materials are transported in a systematic and organised manner to the most suitable places of production . . .; when a single centre directs all the consecutive stages of processing the material right up to the manufacture of numerous varieties of finished articles; when these products are distributed according to a single plan among tens and hundreds of millions of consumers . . . then it becomes evident that we have socialisation of production' (ibid.: 121–2).

- The socialization of production combined with the private appropriation of its fruits, will, increasingly, create further and further conflicts and will lead to the ultimate demise of capitalism.

---

3   Bukharin on imperialism and the world economy

In 1917 Nikolai Bukharin published an essay (*Imperialism and World Economy*) that had been completed for two years. In it, he attempted to place imperialism in the context of changes in the overall world economy and of the historical development of capitalism.

Bukharin (1917) starts his work with a disquisition on the division of labour and particularly on the *international division of labour*; this is, in his view, based on two kinds of prerequisites: natural and social.

- Natural conditions lead to the production of different products in different countries and thus give scope for trade and division of labour at the international level.
- However, division of labour and trade between different countries can also be the result of 'differences in the cultural level, the economic structure, and the development of productive forces in various countries' (ibid.: 18) and hence of social conditions.

The scope for international exchanges is very wide as 'Countries mutually exchange not only different products, but even products of the same kind' (ibid.: 24). Trade and the international division of labour lead to strong connections between capitalists and workers in the two countries. The growth of the world economy is accompanied by growth of migration, trade (in both raw materials and products) and movements of capital. The capitalist economic system has moved more and more away from competition into monopolization, which is, however, a natural, logical development from competition itself.

Bukharin gives pages of examples of the growth of cartels and trusts in various advanced countries. He notes that concentration of production can take a horizontal or vertical form; but whichever the form, increased monopolization leads to conflicts among the different cartels. The 'process of binding together the various branches of production' and 'transforming them into one single organization' goes hand in hand with a similar process between banking and industry: 'banking capital penetrates industry, and capital turns into finance capital' (ibid.: 70). The binding process also links together private enterprises and the state in capitalist systems:

> Thus various spheres of the concentration and organisation process stimulate each other, creating a very strong tendency towards transforming the entire national economy *into one gigantic combined enterprise under the tutelage of the financial kings and the capitalist state, an enterprise which monopolises the national market and forms the prerequisite for organised production on a higher non-capitalist level.* (Ibid.: 73–4)

As monopolization increases, capitalists look for new markets and for higher profits: 'the motive power of world capitalism' is 'the race for higher rates of profit' (ibid.: 84). Imperialism is then needed to secure raw materials and to secure markets for products. This second motive becomes more and more pressing with the advent of mass production and with the increasing protectionist policies of many countries that rely on high tariffs to protect their own industries.

The struggle for sources of raw materials and for markets is accompanied and greatly enhanced by the struggle for investment opportunities abroad. Capital is exported in order to gain higher rates of return abroad than could be realized at home. The export of capital is enhanced by the increasing monopoly profits and by the difficulties in exporting products because of protectionist policies; hence one of the motives given for the export of capital is the avoidance of tariffs in the host country.

The export of capital is more likely to lead to struggles for annexation and wars than the export of commodities. This is because with commodity export 'the exporters risked only their goods, i.e., their circulating capital', while with export of capital and the investment 'in gigantic constructions: railroads stretching over thousands of miles, very costly electric plants, large plantations etc., etc.' the capitalists have their 'fixed capital' at stake and want to guard it closely (ibid.: 101).

The seeds of discord, wars of annexation and wars for the division of colonies are therefore sown: finance capitalism and imperialism are inevitably linked together. Imperialism is the product of monopolization and finance capital and at the same time 'finance capital cannot pursue any other policy than an imperialist one' (ibid.: 140). In a clear concise chapter (IX) Bukharin strongly criticizes other theories of imperialism which do not stress the historical character of this particular stage of capitalism and do not link it to finance capital. Similarly the 'necessity' and inevitability of imperialism are asserted as part of a strong critique of Kautsky's theory in a chapter (XII) devoted to this topic. Kautsky's mistake is in not seeing that imperialism is the logical, inevitable development of capitalism in its highest stage. According to Bukharin, Kautsky looks upon imperialism not as an inevitable accompaniment of capitalist development, but as part of the 'dark side' of capitalist development.

Bukharin also criticizes the view that wider markets could be found at home, since this could be achieved only via income redistribution. There is a major obstacle to this course as 'one cannot imagine that the big bourgeoisie would begin to increase the share of the working class, in order thus to drag itself out of the mire by the hair' (ibid.: 79). Here, of course, there is a criticism of Hobson's view and conclusion, though Hobson is not directly mentioned. The role of trade unions in forcing changes in income distribution seems to be ignored by both Hobson and Bukharin.

Bukharin, like Lenin and Engels before him, stresses the interest that some workers in advanced countries have in imperialism. He writes: 'Super-profits obtained by the imperialist state are accompanied by a rise in the wages of the respective strata of the working class, primarily the skilled workers' (ibid.: 165). See Box 2.5 for the key points of Bukharin's theory.

Box 2.5   *Key points in Bukharin's theory*

- The international division of labour is determined by natural and social conditions.

- Capitalists and their countries struggle to secure raw materials and investment opportunities abroad.

- The search for investment opportunities is likely to lead to wars of annexation.

- Extra investment opportunities and markets cannot be found at home, due to the maldistribution of incomes.

- The distribution away from wages is inherent in the logic of capitalism and cannot be easily corrected.

4   Rosa Luxemburg on imperialism

In section III of *The Accumulation of Capital* (1913) Rosa Luxemburg develops a theory of capitalism that binds together indissolubly capitalist societies with pre-capitalist ones. This is a completely novel approach and it starts with a critique of Marx on the following two points:

- Marx did not give sufficient weight to the problem of realization and therefore to the fact that, in a system where capitalists and workers are the only consumers, lack of effective demand prevents the full realization of the surplus value.
- Marx fails to see that pre-capitalist forces of organization of production are necessary for capitalism, and because his views are led by the principle of 'the universal and exclusive domination of capitalist production' (Luxemburg, 1913: 365).

The first point – the realization problem – is crucial to her overall approach. She starts from the observation that: 'The workers and capitalists themselves cannot possibly realise that part of the surplus value which is to be capitalised. Therefore, the realisation of the surplus value for the purposes of accumulation is an impossible task for a society which consists solely of workers and capitalists' (ibid.: 350). In order to solve the realization problem – 'a vital question of capitalist accumulation' – the system needs to find 'strata of buyers outside capitalist society' (ibid.: 351). The buyers from non-capitalist societies can absorb either consumer goods or means of production or both; the supply of products from the capitalist economy to the pre-capitalist one can take the form of sales from production in the capitalist centre or direct production in the pre-capitalist system. In practice, a combination of these various elements takes place, as the relationship between capitalist and pre-capitalist forces of organization unfolds. The capitalist system needs pre-capitalist organizations essentially for three reasons:

- to increase effective demand (for consumption goods or for means of production or as outlets for investments) and thus help to solve the realization problems;
- to secure the supply of raw materials needed for production; and
- 'as a reservoir of labour power for its wage system' (ibid.: 368).

The pre-capitalist organization needed by capitalism can be part of the same national identity and boundaries, or it can be geographically dispersed and part of a different national identity. No matter where they are geographically located, capital will struggle against societies with a 'natural economy', that is, an economy where 'there is no demand, or very little, for foreign goods, and also, as a rule, no surplus production, or at least no urgent need to dispose of surplus products' (ibid.: 368–9).

The struggle against pre-capitalist societies aims to:

- gain access to and possession of land and raw materials;
- gain access to labour and involve it in the wage system;

- introduce a commodity economy based on market exchanges;
- separate trade and agriculture.

Crafts are gradually wiped out and peasants are 'forced to buy' industrial products in exchange for agricultural ones. The struggle takes market forms as well as using coercion by force; Luxemburg gives many historical examples to substantiate her points. In all the examples, the building of a good network of communication and transport is essential to the destruction of the 'internal' national economy.

One immediate conclusion of her analysis is the *existence of a major contradiction in the relationship between capitalist and pre-capitalist forms of organization. Capitalism needs pre-capitalist forms but it also destroys them*; as the destruction proceeds and becomes accomplished, there arises the need for further expansion into other pre-capitalist systems. Luxemburg writes: 'Historically, the accumulation of capital is a kind of metabolism between capitalist economy and those pre-capitalist methods of production without which it cannot go on and which, in this light, it corrodes and assimilates' (ibid.: 416).

As time goes on, the struggle for access to, and domination of, pre-capitalist societies becomes more and more fierce with an increasing number of countries joining in (including those that are gradually moving from pre-capitalist to the capitalist stage) and with fewer and fewer pre-capitalist areas left. Eventually the systems will come to a standstill and 'For capital, the standstill of accumulation means that the development of the productive forces is arrested, and the collapse of capitalism follows inevitably, as an objective historical necessity' (ibid.: 417).

A major medium through which capitalism penetrates non-capitalist countries is international loans. Such loans are made for armaments and the building of infrastructure, particularly railways; they accompany all stages of capitalist penetration. The loan helps accumulation of capital in various ways; particularly it serves to:

- 'convert the money of non-capitalist groups into capital';
- 'transform money capital into productive capital by means of state enterprise – railroad building and military supplies';
- 'divert accumulated capital from the old capitalist countries to young ones' (ibid.: 420).

International loans are therefore the means by which 'capital accumulated in the old country' finds 'elsewhere new opportunities to beget and realise surplus value, so that accumulation can proceed' (ibid.: 427).

Capital makes it impossible to have a peaceful transition from the pre-capitalist stage for those areas and societies it involves in its sphere of influence. This means that armaments and militarism are necessary to subjugate new societies and territories, and to fight against rivals. However, military expenditure financed out of indirect taxes also has specific economic functions. First, indirect taxation lowers real wages without direct confrontation between capital and labour; second, and important, the support of the arms industry creates a stratum whose effective demand helps towards solving the realization problem.

5   Some comments

The classical Marxist writings considered in this chapter are concerned with explanations of imperialism in the colonialist form of the nineteenth and early twentieth
centuries. They are mainly concerned with the relationship between advanced capitalist economies and developing countries, mostly colonies. Political and economic
issues are very strongly interlinked in all the writings. Inter-disciplinarity goes even
further for authors such as Lenin and Luxemburg: the latter considers a variety of
social issues concerned with capitalist development. The former specifically considers the socialization of production that the monopolistic structure of advanced
economies brings with it. This is a theme of great relevance in today's world when the
activities of large TNCs lead to wide socialization of production across sectors, firms
and countries.

The authors are concerned with explanations of imperialism. They see the root
causes in the inner workings of capitalism and there are two main explanations in this
respect:

- The tendency of the rate of profit to fall in advanced capitalist countries causes
  capital to look for more lucrative investment for its financial capital. This is the
  basic explanation of Lenin or Bukharin.
- Hobson and Luxemburg explain imperialism in terms of under-consumption,
  i.e. the tendency of advanced capitalism to generate insufficient effective
  demand for its products. Expansion in underdeveloped countries (Hobson)
  and/or in pre-capitalist economic systems (within the advanced country or
  outside it) is a way of securing extra demand as well as resources including a
  large supply of cheap labour (Luxemburg). It is also a way of bringing more
  and more areas and sectors under the capitalist mode of production.[7] The
  under-consumptionist thesis is taken up by Marxist writers in the post-WWII
  decades and specifically by Baran and Sweezy (1966a; 1996b), on which more
  in Chapter 13.

Issues of distribution come in strongly in both Hobson and Luxemburg: the
former stresses distribution between different social classes. Hobson sees a shift in
distribution in favour of the working class as the solution to the under-consumption
problem and also as prevention to the further development of imperialism with its
own ills. The large incomes from foreign investment contribute to the distribution
of incomes in favour of capitalists. However, this maldistribution of income and
wealth can be reversed if the political will can be found. It is from this stance that
his reformist agenda unfolds. Luxemburg stresses the unequal distribution between
capitalist and pre-capitalist systems, which she sees as inevitable.

Most of the authors stress financial investment including loans. However,
Bukharin considers investment in fixed capital. He is also a precursor of some
modern approaches in considering horizontal and vertical integration of production.

The theories we have analysed are neither theories of the TNCs nor of foreign
direct investment. Neither concept had been fully developed at that stage. There was

no distinction between foreign portfolio investment and direct investment. In this sense the theories do not fall within the immediate scope of this book and within the study of international production. Nonetheless, they form a useful background to approaches of foreign investment, their motivations and effects.

The modern TNCs and their FDI span the whole world from developed to developing countries. The writings we have discussed in this chapter consider almost exclusively investment in the developing countries; nonetheless, they are still of great relevance for an understanding of the relationship between developed and developing countries in the contemporary world and in particular for the understanding of imperialism in its post-colonial phase. It should also be noted that the relevance of the role of finance and of maldistribution of income and wealth are points in common with the global economic system that has emerged in the last three decades.

SUMMARY BOX 2

Summary review of Marxist approaches

Main exponents and dates of relevant works

- John A. Hobson (1902)
- Vladimir Ilyich Lenin (1917)
- Nikolai Bukharin (1917)
- Rosa Luxemburg (1913)

Some key elements of the theories

- Explanations of imperialism in its colonial phase.
- Links between industrial and finance capital.
- Concentration of capital in fewer firms (Lenin and Bukharin).
- Capitalism generates lacks of effective demand because of its uneven distribution of income and wealth (Hobson, Luxemburg); imperialist expansion helps to reduce it.
- Economic, social, political analyses.
- Prominent role of finance capital in imperialism.

Level of aggregation of analysis

Firms, industries and national economies

Other relevant chapters

Chapter 4 (Hymer's later works)
Chapter 8 (Caves' analysis)
Chapter 13 (Under-consumptionist views after WWII)

Notes

1 Antonello Zanfei has pointed out to me that many Marxists may object to having Hobson's theory included in this section because he is not seen as a real Marxist. Nonetheless, I feel that the links with other works in this chapter are strong enough to warrant its inclusion.

2 Chang (2002) has recently reconsidered this issue and draws lesson for current trade policies.

3 *Cui bono?* means: 'in whose interest?' or 'who benefits?'.

4 The problem of under-consumption – or 'the realization problem' as it is sometimes called – is the fact that the economy does not have enough effective demand to generate a level of production that absorbs all the available productive capacity both in terms of capital equipment and labour. It also prevents the realization of potential profits and other surplus in the economy.

5 Here Lenin criticizes Kautsky for his stress on industrial capital from the point of view of both the colonizing and the annexed country. Other strong criticisms of Kautsky relate to the fact that Kautsky does not see imperialism as an inevitable phase of capitalism and its inner workings, and that he thus divorces politics from economics. Karl Kautsky (1854–1938) was a German theorist who started as a Marxist and then moved to a social democratic position. He wrote an influential history book, the *Foundations of Christianity* (1908).

6 Lenin takes the term 'combination' from Hilferding. This term is no longer used in economics writings.

7 There is an analogy here with the tendency towards privatization, as we have seen in the last three decades. This can be interpreted as a tendency to bring more and more public sector services under the capitalist mode of production.

3 Foreign investment within the neoclassical paradigm

I Background

Before Hymer's seminal thesis (1960) – which we shall consider in Chapter 4 – no theory of foreign direct investment as such existed. However, apart from the Marxist works reviewed in Chapter 2, a considerable amount of more traditional literature existed on foreign investment. Most of this literature was based on neoclassical assumptions and it ran mostly parallel to the neoclassical theory of trade developed by Eli Heckscher (1919) and Bertil Ohlin (1933).

The latter theory was developed on the basis of the classical theory of trade in which specialization and trade emerge as a result of differences in the costs of production of goods between two countries. Adam Smith in his book *The Wealth of Nations* published in 1776 argued for the benefits of trade in cases in which one country had an *absolute costs* advantage over the other. David Ricardo in his *Principles of Political Economy* published in 1817 extended the argument for specialization and trade to the case of differences in *relative costs* of production.

But how do differences in costs of production between countries emerge? This question forms the starting point of the neoclassical theory of trade, known as the factor proportions theory. According to Heckscher and Ohlin the differences in relative costs emerge from differences in the relative amounts of the factors of production with which the countries are endowed. A country abundant in labour and relatively poor in capital will specialize in labour-intensive products. A country relatively abundant in capital will specialize in capital-intensive products. The two countries will therefore both gain from trading their products.

This simple model is based on many strict assumptions presented in Box 3.1.[1] Given these assumptions, the two countries will specialize in one product each and trade with each other to offer the consumers both products at the lowest costs.

This model was the basic framework for the explanation of international investment between the two World Wars. We should first point out that the investment considered was general international investment and no distinction was made between portfolio and direct investment. The various models put forward are neoclassical and they, implicitly or explicitly, contain all the basic assumptions specific to the neoclassical paradigm, most of which are highlighted in Box 3.1.

Similarly to the neoclassical theory of trade, the neoclassical theory of foreign investment also assumes that countries are differently endowed with capital and labour; that there is mobility of products across frontiers, though immobility of labour. There is usually the assumption of capital mobility though, paradoxically, not always: a point on which more will be said later. The analysis is neoclassical also in that it, usually, considers movements from one equilibrium position to another and examines, comparatively, the effects of capital movements between the two equilibria.

Box 3.1   *Assumptions behind the neoclassical theory of trade*

- There are two countries each endowed with two factors of production (labour and capital) and each producing one product: a 2 x 2 x 2 model.

- Producers in both countries have access to the same technology, knowledge and information and produce with the same methods.

- The factors of production are mobile within the country but not between countries.

- Products are mobile within and between countries. Moreover, there are no transportation costs and no barriers to trade.

- The markets for products and factors of production are perfectly competitive in both countries and production takes place under constant returns to scale.

- Products are homogeneous: no product differentiation between various producers within and between countries.

- The preferences of consumers in the two countries are the same.

- There is no uncertainty on the part of consumers or producers.

---

2   Ohlin on foreign investments

Bertil Ohlin (1933) studied 'The mechanism of international capital movements' (Chapter XIX) using the same standpoint and type of analysis as in his neoclassical theory of international trade. He assumes all the above-mentioned neoclassical features. His analysis specifically refers to portfolio investment and no distinction is made with direct investment. Moreover, the capital movements considered are assumed to be 'autonomous' with reference to other variables related to the domestic economy; in effect the capital movements are seen as exogenous. This means that the movement of capital are not considered to depend on elements of the domestic or international economy(ies).

The movement of capital can, in his analysis, take place through 'reparations or gifts', and he refers, interchangeably, to 'borrowing country' and 'capital importing' country. The latter point is an indication that, for him, capital movements are due to borrowing and lending or similar reasons not directly linked to productive activities (ibid., 256). His analysis can, therefore, be said to contain the general assumption of capital immobility (as well as labour immobility) between two countries. However, there can be, now and then, capital movements due to entirely exogenous factors such as payments for gifts or for war reparations; these are the exception rather than the rule.

Ohlin's concern is to analyse the new equilibrium position following disturbances due to the capital movements. The analysis is extended to effects on exchange rates, terms of trade, imports and exports as well as variables related more specifically to the domestic economy. He also considers the issue of location of economic activity and production and the various elements affecting it. Besides the relative abundance of factors of production, other elements are considered in detail, such as: the relative mobility of raw materials and finished goods; the location of raw materials in markets; differences in transportation infrastructures and costs; and economies of scale in production.

Ohlin's book is about *interregional and international trade*. International trade is its main focus and capital movements must be seen in the context of his international trade theory in terms of both the assumptions and the effects considered. Similarly the elements which affect the location of production are considered to be more or less the same at both interregional and international level.

3   Nurkse's developments

Ragnar Nurkse (1933) took the analysis of capital movements a step further than Ohlin in that he made capital movements endogenous and dependent on the 'profit motive'.

The analysis is neoclassical and all the usual assumptions and features, already mentioned in section 1, apply. The foreign investment considered is still portfolio investment; however, the movements of capital are now prompted not by exogenous factors – reparations or gifts as in Ohlin's analysis – but by interest rate differentials. Interest rates are determined, like any other price, by demand and supply: a differential in interest rates can come about because of demand or because of supply conditions.

A change in savings in one or both nations – whether spontaneous or induced by credit creation – would lead to changes in the supply conditions and hence affect, ceteris paribus, the interest rates and thus the differentials between the two countries. Similarly, technical changes in production methods that affect costs and profits, or changes in consumers' tastes that affect production and the amount of capital attracted to the various industries, might lead to changes in demand for capital and hence to interest rate differentials which will cause international capital movements.

In the final analysis Nurkse, like Ohlin, is interested in movements from one equilibrium position to another and in the effects on international variables, such as terms of trade, exchange rates, imports and exports, as well as in the effects on variables related to the domestic economy.

4   Iversen's analysis

Carl Iversen (1935) presents us with a long and detailed analysis of *international capital movements* based on most of the assumptions and features of neoclassical economics. Again no distinction is made between portfolio and direct investment.

In analysing geographical mobility, Iversen sees that what is moving is '*not the capital goods, but something else*' (ibid.: 21). He sees capital and its services in terms of 'waiting'. What this means is that capital is the result of saving, and therefore is the result of abstaining from consumption in the short term and waiting to have larger incomes and therefore greater consumption in the future. He writes on this point: 'The new elementary productive service, a supply of which is required in order to obtain greater future satisfaction, is waiting' (ibid.: 22). It follows from his analysis that 'when capital moves from country to country . . . that *part of the supply of waiting or capital disposal in one country is put at the disposal of people in another*' (ibid.: 23). As in previous analyses, capital movements are motivated by interest rates differentials. One of the elements that affects the level of interest rates is the risk involved in the operations: as the estimated or objective risk may be different in different sectors, we could, in fact, have different interest rate differentials between countries in different sectors and hence we might witness a two-way flow of capital between countries and according to sectors.

On the whole, *foreign investment involves higher risks than domestic investment, so lenders expect higher interest abroad than at home*. The difference in interest rates needed to set in motion international capital movements can be taken as a measure of the cost and the extra risk of capital transfer between countries. Iversen gives us a detailed analysis of why interest rates differ between countries and sectors.

As with previous authors, we are presented with an analysis of the effects of capital movements on various international and domestic variables. The analysis is, again, equilibrium analysis of the comparative static type; this means that comparisons are made between the equilibrium situation before and after the capital movements but there is no analysis of the 'interim' situation, of what goes on before the final equilibrium is reached. And, of course, equilibria may never be reached.

5   Some comments

The neoclassical theory of foreign investment has been developed mainly as a by-product of the theory of international trade; thus some of the developments and refinements of the neoclassical theory of trade have bearings on the theory of foreign investments.[2] Methodologically, a marginalist analysis with its emphasis on marginal changes in one variable at a time can be, and has been, useful in the study of effects.

The main problem in the neoclassical analysis is linked to the unrealistic assumptions of perfect competition.[3] A perfectly competitive environment may have been not too unreasonable as an approximation of reality when the neoclassical theory was first applied to the international trade. It is, however, completely at variance with reality to apply such an assumption to the activities of TNCs, in terms of both FDI and trade, of which they now control a large share, as mentioned in Chapter 1.

It may be arguable whether the neoclassical theory of foreign investment would, in modern economic systems, apply to portfolio investment; it is out of the question that it could possibly have either explicative or predictive power when applied to foreign direct investment. For a start, the transition from a theory of portfolio investment to one related to direct investment would imply that interest rates and profit rates can be used interchangeably, an assumption that may only hold in the long run under perfectly competitive markets.

The difficulty of the neoclassical theory in explaining portfolio investment and in its application to direct investment has been highlighted by Hymer (1960). Hymer points out that the neoclassical theory of portfolio investment does not provide a clear-cut answer to which way capital would flow and by what amount, because of the elements of risk and uncertainty involved as well as the costs of gathering information.

Hymer's point can be strengthened with reference, for example, to Iversen's claim (mentioned in section 4) that the cost and risk of capital transfers can be assessed with reference to the difference in interest rates, while the theory which he is presenting would claim that the differentials in interest rates depend, among other things, on the risk involved. An independent assessment of costs and risks of transaction thus becomes necessary for the theory to have predictive and explanatory power. Hymer concludes that it is imperfections in the market that make difficult the explanation of portfolio foreign investment in the context of the neoclassical theory. However, these are the factors that make the study of foreign direct investment relevant.

In analysing the applicability of neoclassical portfolio investment to foreign direct investment, Hymer brings in some very convincing arguments and evidence to show the poor predictive power of such a theory. For example, the neoclassical theory based on interest rates differentials would predict that financial capital moves from the investing country to the countries where investment takes place; however, this is often not the case as companies involved in direct investment can raise the capital somewhere else, including the same country in which they invest, as noted in Chapter 1, section 6. Similarly, the neoclassical theory would predict that capital moves from a country with low interest rates to a country with high interest rates. In reality, foreign direct investment seems to follow the industry lead rather than the country lead: according to Hymer, foreign direct investment tends to concentrate in certain industries across countries, rather than in some countries across industries.

It would be difficult to explain the present, and increasingly relevant, situation of countries that are involved in both inward and outward direct investment (such as the UK).

Iversen's hypothesis that industries' differentials can be explained by different risks is difficult to test; his argument is indeed circular as he implies that interest rates depend on different risks (and their estimates) while, at the same time, he seems to argue that movements of capital and differentials in interest rates are indicators of the amount of risk involved.

All in all, the standard neoclassical assumptions are clearly unsuited to dealing with the activities of transnational companies.

SUMMARY BOX 3

• •

Summary review of the neoclassical theories of foreign investment

Main exponents and dates of their relevant works

- Bertil Ohlin (1933)
- Ragnar Nurkse (1933)
- Carl Iversen (1935).

Some key elements of the theories

- Developed, mostly, as a by-product of the theory of international trade (Ohlin's in particular)
- No distinction between international portfolio and direct investment
- Neoclassical assumptions on the economic systems
- Assumptions of mobility of products and capital and immobility of labour
- Movements of capital determined by differentials in interest rates between countries

Level of aggregation of analysis

Mainly the macroeconomy

Other relevant chapters

Chapter 4 (Hymer's theory and his critique of the neoclassical approach)
Chapter 7 (Aliber and flows of financial capital between countries)

Notes

1 More on classical and neoclassical theories of international trade can be found in Grimwade (2000).
2 See, in particular, Stolper and Samuelson (1941), Samuelson (1948; 1949) and Rybczynski (1955).
3 Not all economists consider unrealistic assumptions to be a problem. Friedman's (1953) instrumentalist position leads him to write: 'the relevant question to ask about the "assumptions" of a theory is not whether they are descriptively "realistic", for they never are, but whether they are sufficiently good approximations for the purpose in hand' (ibid.: 15). According to Friedman, we should accept unrealistic assumptions provided the real world behaves '*as if*' these assumptions were correct. He writes that: 'The decisive test is whether the hypothesis works for the phenomena it purports to explain' (ibid.: 30). Many authors have criticized Friedman's instrumentalism, including Samuelson (1963) and the philosopher of science, Alan Musgrave (1981).

PART III ● MODERN THEORIES

Introduction to Part III

I have always been in favour of a little theory: we must have Thought
(George Eliot, *Middlemarch*, Penguin, 1965 edition, p. 39)

This part deals with the theories of the transnational corporation and its main international activities. The theories are presented in their historical development starting with Hymer's seminal work in 1960 through to the present times. The last 60 years are the period during which the main theories of the modern TNC have been developed.

Hymer's early research came out of a critique of some pre-WWII analyses of foreign investment which we saw in Chapter 3. After that, the theories have taken a momentum of their own, which can be traced to attempts to overcome problems of previous theories, or to deal with other aspects of TNCs' activities or attempts to take account of further developments in the economic basis at the firm or industry or macro levels.

As we shall see later in this part, there is now a large body of literature on theories of direct business activities across frontiers. However, the specific subject matter of the various theories can vary considerably. Many theories deal with the transnational company as a whole. The studies may relate to its organizational structure or its behaviour. The research works may consider these elements of the company in their historical development or at a point in time. Moreover, the organizational issues are, at times, part and parcel of the entry mode as in the case of theories dealing with inter-firm collaborations or of the internalization theories (Chapters 8 and 9).

More often the researchers focus on the activities of the company and specifically its international activities. Here again we may have several possible foci: the studies may relate to a variety of entry modes – and their relationship with each other – or it may refer to the TNCs' most specific and defining international activity: international production and foreign direct investment. Sometimes TNCs' activities and strategies are linked to the organizational structure of the companies.

The demarcation between theories that focus on the transnational company and those that focus on international production is not always clear-cut. Given the subject matters and the links between them, many theories straddle between the two. Moreover, the specific issues with which theories are concerned vary and they range from: explaining why firms become transnationals (Chapters 4, 5, 9, 13 and 14) to explanations of the boundaries of the firm and modalities of internationalization (Chapters 8, 9, 10, 11 and 15) to concerns with issues of organization and control and value creation (Chapters 8, 9, 10 and 15).

The overall perspective of the theories can be the firm and its activities or the industry or the country(ies), thus leading to micro, meso or macro perspectives. Some works may, of course, deal with more than one level of aggregation.

While theories of international production are relatively recent, macroeconomic theories of international trade have a long tradition going back to the classical writings of Adam Smith and David Ricardo. The theoretical tradition of international trade filters thorough the theories of international production or the theories of the transnational company in a variety of ways in many of the theories presented. Whenever this is the case it will be pointed out in the critical analysis of the theory.

In terms of general theoretical perspectives we can group the theories according to whether they are led by the assumption of efficiency or strategic behaviour on the part of the TNC (see Ietto-Gillies, 2007 for more on this point). To the first category belong those theories particularly concerned with costs and the efficient use of resources such as the theories considered in Chapters 7, 8 and 12. To the second category belong those theories that see the behaviour of TNCs dominated by strategic elements such as the theories considered in Chapters 4, 5, 6, 11, 13 and 14. However, the distinction between efficiency and strategic behaviour is not clear-cut and many theories can be seen as possessing elements of both categories as those in Chapters 4, 9 and 15.

Moreover, strategic behaviour begs the question of 'strategies towards whom?'. Most theories with strategic elements focus on strategies towards rival firms and market shares (Chapters 4, 5, 6, 9, 11 and 13). The theory expounded in Chapter 14 focuses on strategic behaviour towards labour and governments.

Another key element of the theories is their degree of dynamicity. Some theories are definitely about dynamic processes and changes through time (Chapters 5, 6, 10, 11 and 15). Others deal more with static conditions. Nonetheless, the demarcation is not sharp and whether a theory is dynamic or not is often a matter of degree.

The theories are presented in 12 chapters in which a similar structure is followed. Each chapter first gives the background to the theory and then an exposition of the same as presented in the original literature. The chapters end with a critical analysis deliberately kept separate from the exposition sections. The following elements are considered in the critical comments: the strong points of the theory; the antecedents of the theory; the linkages with earlier or later theories; the level of aggregation dealt with in the theory; the type of activity considered, such as mode of entry or organizational issues; the extent to which the existence of national frontiers is an important feature of the theory; and the possible difficulties of the theory in explaining salient features of TNCs' activities. The critical comments are not meant to be a definitive assessment of the theory. Quite the contrary. They are meant to aid the readers – particularly students and young researchers – in sharpening their own critical sense and developing their own criticisms. Critical comments may also suggest possible avenues for future research.

Each chapter ends with suggestions for further reading and with a summary box. The last item in this box is usually devoted to highlighting the linkages between the specific chapter considered and others in the book. Chapter 1 and its Appendix are relevant for all the subsequent chapters and, therefore, they will not be cited in the summary boxes.

4 Hymer's seminal work

I Background to the theory

Stephen Hymer in his doctoral dissertation of 1960 put forward the first modern theory of 'international operations' by large companies. He was a Canadian economist doing research at the Massachusetts Institute of Technology in Cambridge, Massachusetts. He became intrigued by the motivations behind the large foreign investment by US corporations in a growing number of countries including his own. He died in a car accident in 1974, aged 39. His dissertation was published posthumously in 1976.[1]

Hymer's work constitutes a radical departure from the conventional neoclassical approach of the time. It opened a whole new research programme in the area of international production. Follow-ups, refinements and new twists to the theory are continuously coming out.[2]

In order to understand the relevance of Hymer's contribution as well as the novelty of his approach, we must remember that, when he was writing, there was no theory of foreign direct investment as such. There were theories of capital movements across borders and these were widely assumed to extend and apply to all types of investment as we saw from Chapter 3. There was no perceived need to consider direct investment as a special case; indeed the concept of foreign direct investment had not been developed before Hymer's breakthrough.

Hymer starts his research by analysing financial investment and the then prevalent neoclassical theory. As we saw in Chapter 3, in this theory the main determinant of movements of funds across frontiers is the difference in interest rates, with other elements, such as risk and uncertainty, playing a subsidiary though sometimes important role.

Hymer then goes on to consider the peculiarities of foreign investment by large companies for production and direct business purposes: what he called foreign direct investment. Hymer saw the need to differentiate this type of investment from purely financial investment, i.e. from portfolio investment. The two types of investment differ in terms of motivations behind them and in terms of consequences for the firm and the macroeconomy. Hymer's demarcation criterion between foreign direct investment and portfolio investment is *control*. Direct investment gives the firm control over the business activities abroad; portfolio investment does not.

He felt that the neoclassical theory based on interest rate differentials could not possibly explain foreign direct investment and its motivations. In particular, he emphasized the problems shown in Box 4.1.

The conclusion is that, although direct investment may involve capital movements, it cannot just be equated with capital movements in its significance or effects or determinants.

Box 4.1   *Hymer's reasons for his critique of the neoclassical approach*

Foreign direct investment

- Does not necessarily involve movement of funds from the home to the host country. In fact, direct investment is, at times, financed by borrowing in the host country or using retained profits or by payments in kind (involving patents, technology or machinery) in exchange for equity in a host country enterprise.

- Often takes place both ways so that both countries involved are originators and host to FDI.

- Tends to be concentrated in particular industries across various countries, rather than in a particular country across various industries, as one might expect if the main determinant were interest rate differentials between countries.

One explanation for firms' direct investment abroad[3] relates to the growth of the firm. There are two strands to this view. The first stresses the search for markets and hence considers foreign direct investment as demand led; it is, however, difficult to explain why the extra markets cannot be sourced through exporting output produced in the home country. The second strand emphasizes the role of internal finance; retained profits from foreign subsidiaries are best used for reinvestment in the host country. This view gives direct investment a passive role quite at variance with the large expansion witnessed after the Second World War. Therefore this explanation is rejected by Hymer.

2   The determinants of FDI

Hymer assumes that direct production abroad involves *extra costs and risks* due, in particular, to the following:

1   Costs of communication and of acquisition of information in general. These costs are linked to the different cultural, linguistic, legal, economic and political environments in which the firm will have to operate in the host country.
2   Costs due to less favourable treatment given by host countries' governments.
3   Costs and risks of exchange rate fluctuations.

Hymer dismisses the argument that FDI is motivated by search for low costs of production in foreign locations. He argues that if this were the main reason for investment we would find it difficult to explain why the local firms do not compete successfully with the foreign ones. After all, they would face similar low production costs and would have none of the costs and risks associated with investing in a foreign country as listed above.

Firms are prepared to meet the costs and risks associated with foreign production

because of the expected increase in their market power and thus expected extra profits. Hymer's key element in the search for determinants of international production –
and a key assumption in Hymer's theory – is the existence of *market
imperfections/failures*. The type of imperfections he considers are structural ones, that
is, those imperfections arising from the market structure, for example from an oligopolistic structure in which a few large firms dominate the market.[4]

The market imperfection can be due to:

* imperfections in the goods markets;
* imperfections in the factors markets;
* internal and external economies of scale;
* governments' interference with production or trade.

Hymer gives two main determinants of direct investment abroad.[5] In both of these the
existence of market imperfections is a key assumption and goes hand in hand with the
desire of the company to further enhance its market power position.

The first determinant is the existence of *specific advantages* that the firm can
profitably exploit abroad, particularly once the domestic investment opportunities
have been exhausted. The advantages are directly linked to market imperfections
because they give the firm, which commands market power, a competitive advantage
over its rivals. Moreover, their exploitation in foreign markets enhances further the
firm's market power and thus it increases the overall level of imperfections in the
market.

Firms can, and sometimes do, sell their advantage via licensing; however, licensing is usually less profitable than direct production and involves the risk of poor
control over the quality of production and the risk of losing their monopoly over
specific knowledge and technological advantages.

The second determinant is the *removal of conflicts* in foreign markets. If rival
firms are already operating in the foreign market or trying to get into it, a conflictual
situation emerges. Our specific firm can collude and share markets with rivals or can
try to get direct control of production abroad. In either case the conflict with other
firms is removed. The strategy of conflict removal, through the acquisition of control
of foreign operations, leads to an increase in market power for our specific firm and
thus, again, to the increase in imperfections for the market as a whole.

A third, 'minor', reason for foreign direct investment on the part of large firms
is given by Hymer as the drive towards *diversification*; a strategy of diversification –
of products or market locations or production locations – helps to spread risks.

Hymer's main message is that, for direct investment to thrive, there must be
market imperfections that create both advantages and conflicts. By investing directly
and by thus reducing competition, the firm aims to reduce or eliminate the conflicts
while exploiting its own advantages.

The two main types of determinants (firm's advantages and removal of conflicts)
are closely linked. The existence of advantages is part and parcel of the market imperfections that lead to conflicts. The competitive advantages of the firm allow the
removal of conflicts via the acquisition of control over the foreign business. Both

determinants (firm's advantages and the removal of conflicts) have their roots in the imperfect market structure. The behaviour of the firm, in its desire to gain control over foreign operations, leads to the enhancement of its market power and thus to increased profits.

3   Later developments by Hymer

Later in his short life, Hymer moved towards a more *Marxist approach* in which he stressed the conflicts and contradictions of the internationalization of produc-tion.[6] The conflicts analysed in these later works are within different parts of the firm itself, between the firm and its labour force, between the firm and govern-ments, and between developed and developing countries. The contradictory and conflictual nature of capitalist production is emphasized in Hymer's later works, which deal with issues such as the effects of MNCs' activities on labour; on poli-tics; on the nation-state and its government; on the effectiveness of economic poli-cies (Hymer, 1966; 1975; Cohen et al., 1979: chs 9 and 11); and on the division of labour (Hymer, 1971; 1972; Cohen et al., 1979: ch. 6) within the firm, the indus-try and the international arena (in particular between developed and developing countries).

His later analysis leads to the conclusion that on the one hand the multinational company is a strong progressive force because it enables the planning and organiz-ation of production on a worldwide scale,[7] and it leads to an increase in productivity and to the spread of new technology and new products. On the other hand, the MNCs, with their large size, power, hierarchical structure and spread of activities into many sectors and countries, contain also the germs of considerable conflicts and contradictions. In particular, the functional and geographical division of labour leads to conflicts within parts of the corporation operating in a single country or in several. This is because development and opportunities spread unevenly, thus creating tensions.

The main contradiction arises out of the formidable planning power of MNCs. The system operates as fully planned at the *micro* level (i.e. within the corporation wherever its network spreads) but unplanned and unstructured at the *macro* level where all is left to the vagaries of the market. The lack of planning and structure at the macro level creates difficulties for the business world itself. This is the more so since economic policies – and demand management policies in particular, which were fashionable when Hymer was writing – are difficult to harmonize internationally.

According to the later Hymer, the gap between micro planning and macro anar-chy may eventually turn against the MNCs themselves, as people will come to re-alize how efficient the system could be if the planning, so far applied within firms only, were to be applied between them, in a comprehensive regional or national framework.

Midway between his early and later phases, Hymer published an article (1968) in French, which seems to sit uneasily with both his radical and Marxist approach to the MNC and its activities. In this article he is clearly influenced by reading Coase whose works are not, however, cited in his dissertation and not much cited in Hymer's later works either.

Hymer (1968) discusses the growth of the firm and its limits, which he attributes to a combination of economies of scale and comparative advantages of coordination of production via internal hierarchical direction versus coordination through the market. In the latter points he follows Coase (1937) in stressing the relevance of transactional market imperfections as a reason for internal growth of the firm.

When expansion takes place directly across national frontiers we have the multinational company. As regards the reasons why the company would want to expand into other countries via direct production and coordination, Hymer concentrates mainly on the advantages of vertical integration. There is also a shorter discussion on the difficulties of trading knowledge on the market.

Hymer (1968) anticipates some of the work of the internalization school. The works of this school and of Coase's – as a precursor to them – are discussed in Chapter 8. The key points of Hymer's theories are shown in Box 4.2.

Box 4.2   *Key points in Hymer's theory of the MNC and FDI*

1 Demarcation between portfolio investment and direct investment based on control

2 Criticism of the neoclassical theory of capital movements as explanation for international production

3 Assumption of *structural market imperfections* at the basis of his theory

4 Existence of firms' advantages, their link to market imperfections and their role as determinants of FDI

5 Removal of conflicts with rivals as a main determinants of direct production abroad

6 Use of the concept of *control* in the following:

  • the demarcation between portfolio and direct of investment; control is the defining characteristic of FDI;

  • the removal of conflicts and the enhancement of market power;[8]

  • control of management over labour and the labour process (in his later works)

7 Stress on conflicts between:

  • rival firms: in his dissertation where conflicts are among the determinants of FDI;

  • various economic actors in his later work, in particular: conflicts between MNCs and labour; various types of labour force; developed and developing countries; MNCs and governments

4 Comments

Hymer's theory was path-breaking in both a backward- and a forward-looking way. In a backward-looking way, because it developed a fully coherent approach and theory in a field where nothing existed, and indeed foreign direct investment was not even considered in the economic literature as an autonomous category in need of explanations. In a forward-looking way because his approach has led – and is still leading – to many theoretical developments.

The issue of *firms' specific advantages* was later taken up and developed further by John Dunning – for the first time in his (1977) article and later in many other publications, of which some are considered in Chapter 9 of this book. Dunning also develops the concept of location advantages, which appears to a lesser extent in Hymer's work.

Hymer and Kindleberger (and later Dunning as well as the internalization school, analysed respectively in Chapters 9 and 8) consider fully the issue of licensing versus directly investing for any particular firm. However, the organization of the firm and the possible efficiency deriving from it were not the key elements behind Hymer's theory.

As mentioned above, Hymer's approach in the 1968 article is not fully consistent with the one in his dissertation. Moreover, it is not much followed up in his later works. It seemed to have been a one-off thought in response to the reading of Coase's work.[9] In this article Hymer appears to anticipate the works of the internalization school though it is unlikely that the writers within this school knew about it. There is, however, one element in Coase's approach which does not figure in the internalization school but is considered in the later Hymer: the emphasis on planning and direction at the level of the firm.

Strategic elements are strongly present in Hymer's work and taken up in different contexts by other writers including Knickerbocker (1973), Graham (1998), Cowling and Sugden (1987) and Ietto-Gillies (2002a; 2002b; 2007; and Ch. 14 in this volume).

One major element of Hymer's theory is his stress on the *removal of conflicts* from the market in which large firms operate. This issue has been taken up by Cowling and Sugden (1987), as will be highlighted in Chapter 13. Ietto-Gillies (2002b) develops Hymer's theory by considering the advantages that firms derive from operating in many nation-states. This development bridges a gap between Hymer's 1960 theory and his later work which emphasizes the relationship between the MNCs and the nation-state as well as the MNCs and labour.

Hymer's theory is developed as a departure from the neoclassical approach and the perfectly competitive market structure. In many ways this puts the theory into the straitjacket of being developed as a comparison with it.[10] Both Hymer and Kindleberger are much preoccupied with the issue of why it is the MNC (usually from the USA) that takes up investment opportunities in the host country rather than the local firm. This emphasis rather underplays the issues of international oligopolists fighting to get into a specific market and production location.

Hymer's main determinants of foreign investment are, to a large extent, determinants of investment in general – at the national and international level – under oligopolistic conditions. This issue could be seen as underplaying the specificity of internationalization. Moreover, there is also an overemphasis on costs of foreign operations. This is a reasonable stance to take in the 1950s and early 1960s. However, the costs and risks of foreign operations have declined considerably since then.

In general, Hymer's conceptual framework in his dissertation – where the theory of determinants of FDI was largely developed – underplays the advantages of internationalization and multinationality per se, including the advantages of spreading production over many countries. This issue will be dealt in more detail in Chapter 14.

SUMMARY BOX 4

Review of Hymer's contribution

Relevant prior theories

Neoclassical analysis (as in Chapter 3), which Hymer criticizes

Key elements of theory

- Demarcation between portfolio and direct investment based on control
- Market imperfections
- Firms' advantages as a determinant
- Removal of conflicts as a determinant
- Concept of control used in a variety of ways
- Stress on conflicts; in his dissertation: between rival firms; in his later – Marxist – works: between MNCs and labour; between developed and developing countries; between MNCs and governments; between various types of labour force
- Different perspectives between the dissertation (1960) and later – Marxist – works (1970s)

Modalities and type of analysis

- Direct production; exports; licensing
- Organization of production

Level of aggregation

Firm; industry and macroeconomy

Other relevant chapters

Chapter 2 (for some of Hymer's Marxist writings)

Chapter 3 (for his critique of neoclassical theory)

Chapter 9 (Hymer's firm's advantages and Dunning's ownership advantages)

Chapter 13 (Cowling and Sugden's analysis of conflicts)

Chapter 14 (on advantages of multinationality)

Indicative further reading

Cantwell, J. (2000), 'A survey of theories of international production', in C.N. Pitelis and R. Sugden (eds), *The Nature of the Transnational Firm*, London: Routledge, ch. 2, pp. 10–56.

Contributions to Political Economy (2002), vol. 21; various articles.

Dunning, J.H and Pitelis, C.N. (2008), 'Stephen Hymer's contribution to international business scholarship: an assessment and extension', *Journal of International Business Studies*, **39** (1), 167–76.

Yamin, M. (2000), 'A critical re-evaluation of Hymer's contribution to the theory of the transnational corporation', in C.N. Pitelis and R. Sugden (eds), *The Nature of the Transnational Firm*, London: Routledge, ch. 3, pp. 57–71.

Notes

1 A brief biography and a critical review of Hymer's work is in Pitelis (2002a). See also Graham (2002). A more extensive work on his research and life is Cohen et al. (1979).

2 Cf., for example, the issue of the Oxford Journal *Contributions to Political Economy* (2002) entirely dedicated to the works of Hymer. *The International Business Review* also dedicated a special issue edited by C. Pitelis in 2005 to developments from Hymer's approach. See also Yamin (2000) and Dunning and Pitelis (2008).

3 On this and many other issues considered in Hymer's dissertation, cf. also the work of his supervisor and mentor, Charles Kindleberger (1969).

4 The imperfection can be also of 'transactional' type. The latter is due to costs of operating on the market and acquiring the relevant information. On the distinction between structural and transactional market imperfections more will be said in Chapter 8.

5 Cf. Yamin (2000) for a detailed analysis of these issues.

6 His later articles were published – a few for the first time – in Cohen et al. (1979).

7 There is here an echo of Lenin's view on the socialization of production as we saw in Chapter 2, section 2.

8 Graham (2002) notes that the removal of conflicts, via increased control, in Hymer might logically lead to monopolistic situations and this has certainly not occurred. Knickerbocker (1973) develops the issue of rivals' countervailing behaviour as we shall see in Chapter 6.

9 Casson (1990) in his introduction to the English translation of the Hymer 1968 article remarks that the paper seems very unpolished and contains quite a few slips and errors.

10 Both Pitelis (2002) and Graham (2002) note that Hymer's analytical thinking is neo-classical in spite of his radical and Marxist approaches.

5 The product life cycle and international production

• •

I   The background

The 1960s saw the development of a new set of theories of international trade around the basic concept of *technological gap* (Box 5.1).[1] Posner (1961) analyses how an initial product innovation in one country leads to cumulative technological advantages and trade advantages. The extent and duration of the trade advantages will depend on the extent of the cumulative advantages for the innovating firm, on the speed with which demand for the new product spreads and on the speed of reaction of other domestic and foreign firms in imitating the new product.

According to Posner, cumulative advantages build up, partly, through the development of *dynamic economies of scale*. It is the experience of past production that gives rise to dynamic economies of scale. He writes: 'Where technical progress occurs, unit costs for a particular firm are lower today than they were yesterday . . . because this particular firm can now draw on its experience of yesterday's production' (Posner, 1961: 329).

Hufbauer (1966) develops further the technological gap theory of trade in the context of an application to synthetic materials. He introduces two main developments compared with Posner's theory. First, he modifies the learning function and the related lag to take account of the length of time the firm has engaged in the new production, and not just of the volume of past production. Second, he takes account of differences in relative wages in the trading countries. Hufbauer highlights the speed and the process with which the manufacture of new products spreads from one nation to another. The desire to crowd out old products quickly acts as an incentive to its rapid spreading. Similarly, the lure of high profits to be made by moving into the new product will increase the speed with which the manufacture of the new product will spread. Hufbauer concludes (ibid.: 32) that: 'The two spreading mechanisms therefore usually ensure that high-wage countries imitate more rapidly than low-wage countries'.

Meanwhile, other researchers – in particular Simon Kutznets (1953) – had been linking the growth of demand for products to the *cycle in the product's life* (Box 5.1) from invention to growth to maturity. The growth of demand tends to be slow in the innovation phase of a product then to accelerate and, finally, to slow down again. Seev Hirsch (1965; 1967) analyses the phases of the product's life in relation to the technology and scale of production, to the type of labour skills needed and to the countries' competitive advantages. He applies his product life cycle hypothesis to the production and trade pattern of the US electronics industry.

The product requires skilled and high-cost labour (engineering, scientific) in the initial phase; capital expenditure tends to be kept relatively low in this introductory phase. The ratio of labour to capital is reduced in the subsequent growth phase, when mass production and mass distribution are introduced. In this phase, the product becomes, in fact, more capital-intensive and the availability of skilled managerial labour becomes essential. In the last, mature, phase the product becomes standardized; both scale and technology are stable, the need for skilled labour is reduced and more unskilled labour is required. The mature phase tends to be very capital-intensive, indeed, more capital-intensive than the previous phases:

> We would expect the 'growth' sectors to employ more skill intensive methods; we would expect the 'mature' sectors to be more capital intensive now than they were when in the growth phase . . . What the product cycle view suggests is that for any particular product the ratio of the capital stock to value added will be higher in the mature than in the growth phase. (Hirsch, 1965: 94)

Hirsch, like Posner and Hufbauer, analyses the trade effects of technological gaps between countries. However, the cumulative effects of technology and dynamic economies of scale we saw in Posner's and Hufbauer's works, are played down in Hirsch's analysis. Instead, we have effects on competition and trade deriving from the various phases of the life of the product. According to Hirsch, in the first phase of the product's life, developed countries have an advantage as they can provide the engineering and scientific skills required. He argues (1967: chs 2 and 5) that this is a phase suited to both small advanced countries (e.g. Britain, Switzerland and Israel) and the USA.

Hirsch concludes also that the US competitive advantage is to be found in the growth phase of the product. This is because in this phase large amounts of capital are needed for mass production, as well as inputs of skilled managerial labour for the organization and management of large-scale production. The USA loses competitiveness in the last phase when the product is standardized and its high requirements of unskilled labour favour locations with relatively low wages. In this last phase, the less developed countries are found to be more competitive.

It follows from this that, according to Hirsch, the product cycle approach to the explanation of international trade throws light on the 'Leontief paradox'. This 'paradox' has its origin in the factor proportions theory of trade, according to which countries relatively abundant in capital will export capital-intensive products while labour-abundant (low-wage) countries will export labour-intensive products. This prediction of the theory was falsified by the findings of Wassily Leontief (1953; 1956). In a study of the structure of US domestic production and foreign trade, Leontief found that, contrary to expectations based on the comparative costs theory, the USA appeared to export products that were less capital-intensive than those imported. A similar paradox, the other way around, was found for Japan whose capital/output ratio was high, though it was, at the time, a labour-abundant country.[2] Hirsch explains the apparent paradoxes by analysing the relationship between trade and the phases of the product. He writes:

> The growth products, in which the United States is likely to be most competitive, are not

necessarily produced in a highly capital-intensive way; indeed their main characteristic – judging from the electronics industry – is their high skill content. The mature products, in which Japan has considerable export success, tend to have high capital–output ratios; but their skill content – in the widest sense – is relatively low. It is in engineering and scientific skill and managerial ability, rather than in capital, that the United States has the greatest competitive advantage. (Hirsch, 1965: 97)

Box 5.1   *Key elements in the technological gap theories and the product life cycle theory*

- Technological advantages lead to competitive advantages.

- Technological advantages are likely to be cumulative for various reasons, including dynamic economies of scale, learning-by-doing and a tendency towards a cumulation of inventions

- Competitive advantages change during the phases of the product: a country which has an advantage at the innovative phase of the product is unlikely to maintain the advantage when the product reaches maturity.

- Imitation effects – in terms of demand and production – are very relevant and likely to be stronger in countries with high incomes.

- The mechanisms and speed of imitation in production are linked to the market structure in which firms operate.

- The product life cycle linked the technological gap approach to the factor proportions theory via the various phases of the products and the different labour skills required during them.

---

2 Vernon's theory

It was against this background that Raymond Vernon used the product life cycle approach to develop a theory of international production. He was working in Cambridge, Massachusetts, at the Harvard Business School up the road from the Massachusetts Institute of Technology where Stephen Hymer had developed his dissertation a few years earlier. The growth of US FDI after WWII led to the growth of research interest in TNCs and their activities. The works of Hymer and Vernon, as well as those of John Dunning in the UK – as we shall see in Chapter 9 – are the expression of such interest.

The origin of Vernon's work is in the technological gap theory as well as in the literature on the life of the product. However, while most previous researchers had been concerned with the effects of technological gaps and/or life of the product on international trade, Vernon (1966) put particular emphasis on international production (see Box 5.2), although many implications for international trade are also present in his article.

Box 5.2   *Questions tackled by Vernon*

- Where new ideas and technology for new products are likely to originate
- Where the production of new products is likely to begin
- What circumstances lead to the location of production abroad
- Where and what are the consequences for the flow of FDI and for international trade

---

He begins 'with the assumptions that the enterprises in any one of the advanced countries of the world are not distinguishably different from those in any other advanced country, in terms of their access to scientific knowledge, and their capacity to comprehend scientific principles' (ibid.: 306). However, equal access to knowledge does not mean an equal probability of application of such knowledge; there is a large gap between the knowledge of a scientific principle and the embodiment of the principle in a marketable product. It is the consciousness of opportunities and the responsiveness to such opportunities that vary from one entrepreneur to another. Such consciousness and responsiveness are associated with the market conditions in which entrepreneurs operate; this makes knowledge inseparable from the decision-making process about its use. Therefore, knowledge is not an exogenous variable.

The US market offers unique opportunities for the exploitation of knowledge and its embodiment in new products, due to the characteristics highlighted in Box 5.3.

Box 5.3   *Characteristics of the US market according to Vernon*

- It is a market in which consumers have high average income per capita.
- It is a very large market; hence even minority tastes are likely to provide a fairly large market.
- It is characterized by high unit labour costs and a large supply of capital; it is, in other words, a market abundant in capital and scarce in labour.

The first two characteristics in Box 5.3 mean that new products, whose demand requires high incomes per capita, are more likely to have a fairly large market in the USA. The third characteristic implies that the USA is also likely to be a fertile ground for products designed to save labour at the consumption or production levels, or both.

An entrepreneur in the USA is more likely to spot opportunities for markets in products designed to save labour and/or requiring high per capita income. Spotting the market is likely to lead to the idea and conception of a new product. Is it, however, likely that the production of the new product will be located in a country where the market has first been spotted (in Vernon's analysis, the USA)? Vernon's answer is affirmative. In his view the new product will be located in the USA, in spite of its high production costs, essentially for the following reason. In the early stages of its introduction the product is unlikely to be standardized, but will instead come in a variety of models. This has many implications, in particular:

*   At the initial stage producers are interested in flexibility and freedom in adapting the product and changing inputs as necessary.
*   It is useful to have not only flexibility in the adaptation of the production process but also, and paramount, flexibility of adaptation to the requirements of consumers and their criticisms. For this second element, proximity of production to the market is essential to ensure swift and effective communication between producers and consumers.
*   The product enjoys, in its early stages, a high degree of differentiation and a monopolistic position. This means that the price elasticity of demand is likely to be comparatively low; thus the producers need not have excessive worries about translating their high costs into prices for the consumers.

The elasticity of demand measures the responsiveness of demand (in terms of percentage change in demand) to percentage changes in one of the variables affecting demand such as price of the product or income of the consumer(s). In the case of the variable 'price of the product', a low elasticity means that the demand for the product does not change much in percentage terms when the price increases. In the case of our theory this is due to two elements: (1) the fact that there is no real competition for the product since it is new and, in the first phase, specific only to our firm; and (2) because the target consumers have high incomes per capita and are therefore prepared to pay high prices.

The income elasticity of demand for the new product, i.e. the responsiveness of demand to changes in incomes, tends to be high and this denotes the relevance of income levels for the success of the new product.

The result of this analysis is that, if the favourable market conditions are in the USA, not only will the product be conceived and developed in the USA, but it will also be produced there in its initial stage. However, as demand for the product grows, and the product reaches maturity, we see the following:

*   The need for flexibility and proximity to customers declines.
*   As competition gathers momentum, concern about production costs is likely to start replacing concern about the characteristics of the product. This is because competition may affect the price that our firm can charge.

While demand spreads at home, there is also likely to be a spreading of demand overseas in advanced European countries. It is the countries with high incomes that are likely to accept the new product. The demand from Western European countries will, at first, be met by exports from the USA. However, a variety of factors may soon support a strategy based on direct foreign production rather than exports. Among such factors are the following:

*   the threat of rivals beginning imitations of the product in European countries;

- lower production costs in European countries;
- the threat of import controls by European governments.

Gruber et al. (1967) explore the issue of international production further. They make two additional points in relation to foreign investment and technological gaps. The authors point out how overseas direct investment usually follows involvement via exports. This means that the 'marginal costs' of setting up production are reduced because the basic information regarding the country and the market are already available to the company. Besides, the research-intensive industries tend to be oligopolistic: 'In the oligopoly industries . . . individual firms are likely to consider foreign investments as important forestalling tactics to cut off market pre-emption by others' (ibid.: 31). The firm may also start sourcing other markets in Europe or elsewhere from production in the particular European country(ies) in which it has invested. It is also possible that, if production costs outside the USA are low enough to outweigh transport costs, the product will be imported into the USA.

Therefore direct production abroad may have wide implications for international trade volume and pattern and, in particular, for the following:

- substitution of international production for exports from the USA to Europe as a market sourcing strategy;
- effects on the pattern of international trade within Europe (for example, if the US firm has invested in the UK, the production facilities in this country can be used to export to Italy or other European countries);
- possible exports from European production location(s) to the US market.

As the product becomes more and more standardized it will require production processes with high capital intensity and unskilled labour. In this phase imitation becomes easier, competition will increase and cost-cutting will become necessary. This may lead to a strategy of location of production in developing countries in search of low labour costs. Imports into the USA will continue to increase. The USA will, therefore, gradually lose its competitive advantage as a production location.

The effects of the product cycle on trade and location of production have been illustrated by Vernon in a clear diagram reproduced in Figure 5.1. The time lag between foreign production and domestic innovation depends on many elements, including: the speed with which demand for the new product spreads; the market position of the innovating firm in European countries; and the comparative costs of production in the USA and Europe. The spread of demand, the spread of production and the spread of technology from the USA to Europe go hand in hand.

The spreading sequence and mechanisms highlighted by Vernon have been supported by the findings of the Organisation for Economic Co-operation and Development (OECD, 1970). This work gives evidence that many innovations originate in the USA and later spread to Western Europe, and that the main mechanism for the spread of technology was – up to 1970 – direct production by US companies through their foreign investment in Europe. The same study finds that the USA tends to show a lead in terms of diffusion of newer innovations (nuclear power, computers);

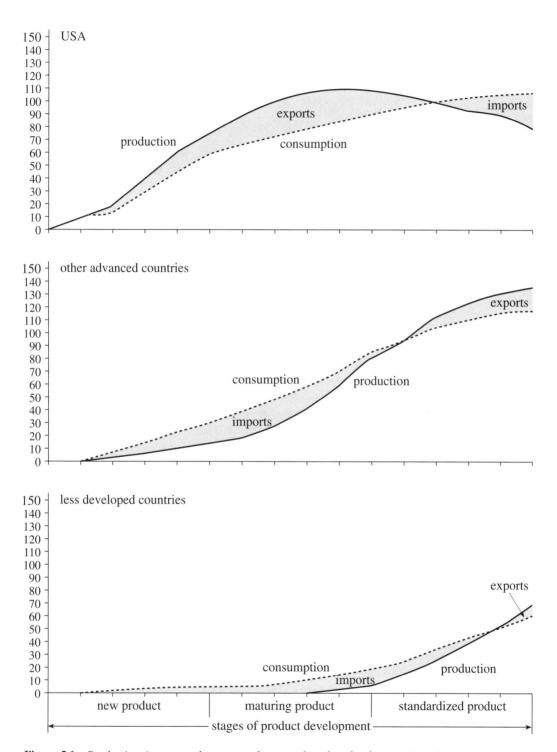

Figure 5.1 *Production, imports and exports and stages of product development in various countries*

Source: Vernon (1966: 200); ©1966 by the President and Fellows of Harvard College. Published by John Wiley and Sons, Inc., *The Quarterly Journal of Economics* **LXXX** (2).

the level of diffusion for more mature products (human-made fibres and plastics) tends to be similar for the USA and European countries.

The general pattern of trade and FDI emerging from the product life cycle was also supported by Gruber et al.'s (1967) findings. In this work the technological gap and the innovative tendencies in various industries are assessed by looking at research and development efforts.

3 Vernon on location of production and oligopolistic structures

In his 1974 paper Vernon develops further the link between location of production, multinationality and oligopolistic structures. Is location of production affected by the fact that decisions are taken by multinational enterprises rather than national firms?

According to Vernon the answer is affirmative for various reasons, including the following. The MNE buys and sells throughout the world, so the factor costs considered are not only those where the subsidiary is located (or to be located) but the costs in other parts of the world as well. Capital can be borrowed anywhere; some labour can be transferred from other countries; components of products can be moved. Multinational enterprises operate in oligopolistic markets to a larger extent than national enterprises, so considerations of oligopolistic equilibrium will play a large role.

In linking MNEs' decisions to oligopolistic structures Vernon identifies three stages of oligopoly characterized by different elements of competitive advantages on the part of the oligopolist(s) vis-à-vis rivals. These advantages may apply also to potential rivals and therefore may act as entry barriers for perspective entrants into the market.

An *innovation-based oligopoly* is one in which the innovator acquires barriers to entry due to the new technologies used, whether in products or in processes. The first location of production of the new products is likely to be in the country where the research takes place and this is likely to be the home country of the company.

In a *mature oligopoly*, 'the basis for the oligopoly is not the advantages of product innovation but the barriers to entry generated by scale in production, transportation or marketing' (Vernon, 1974: 97). The overwhelming concern in such an industry is with stability; this concern is reflected in both pricing and location strategies. On the latter issue, Vernon's conclusion is that 'there is a hint in support of the proposition that the search for stability in the mature oligopolies leads to a geographical concentration of investment which could not be explained on the basis of comparative costs' (ibid.: 102). He reaches similar conclusions regarding location of production by MNEs and writes: 'there is a strong possibility that the existence of multinational enterprises in the mature industries tends to concentrate economic activity on geographical lines, to a degree that is greater than if multinational enterprises did not exist' (ibid.: 104).

There are oligopolistic situations in which economies of scale are not strong enough to act as barriers to entry and thus maintain oligopolistic stability; in these cases enterprises may use other methods to prolong equilibrium, such as cartels or product differentiation. Sometimes these strategies are successful, at other times they are not; in any case the equilibrium is fragile and enterprises may start looking for cost advantages. This is the situation of what Vernon calls '*senescent oligopolies*'.

Many consumer durables markets are characterized by a fragile equilibrium: in spite of 'considerable product differentiation and brand differentiation, cross-elasticities are still uncomfortably high from the producer's viewpoint' (ibid.: 105).[3] In these markets the barriers to entry may not be high enough to maintain oligopolistic stability. Producers will often be seeking cost-cutting as barriers to entry. Cost-reducing locations can be sought at the national or international level. The MNEs are particularly well placed to scan for low-cost locations, particularly in developing countries.

4   The product life cycle in a new macroenvironment

Interestingly enough, Vernon himself has come out with a critical review of his own theory in a paper which analyses 'the product cycle hypothesis in a new international environment' (Vernon, 1979). His self-criticisms are related mainly to the changed environment in European countries. In order to derive conclusions as to the applicability of the product cycle theory in the late 1970s and 1980s, Vernon, in this paper, analyses the following elements:

1   the degree of internationalization and its relation to new products diffusion; and
2   changes in the European macroenvironment

As regards (1) Vernon starts by pointing out that there has been a considerable increase in the spread of the geographical network of MNCs' operations. His analysis of the geographical spread of activities is based on the results of the Harvard Multinational Enterprises Project. It shows that US multinationals would start by locating in familiar countries (Canada, the UK) and only at a later stage would they spread to less familiar locations (such as Asia and Africa). He writes on this point:

> For product lines introduced abroad by the 180 firms before 1946, the probability that a Canadian location would come earlier than an Asian location was 79 per cent; but for product lines that were introduced abroad after 1960, the probability that Canada would take precedence over Asia had dropped to only 59 per cent. (Vernon, 1979: 259)

As MNCs engaged in more and more global planning, not only the spread of their operations increased, but the overall lag between the appearance of a new product in the USA and its introduction and spread in other locations diminished considerably. The two trends reinforced each other as firms with established subsidiaries abroad would tend to spread new products in the locations of their operations more and more quickly.

The findings of the OECD (1970) support Vernon's ideas on this point. The OECD finds that 'there is a tendency for the time lag between the initiation of production in the United States, and production of the same commodity abroad, to diminish' (ibid.: 259).

Vernon then goes on to consider changes in the macroenvironment (2). As we moved from the early 1960s to the late 1970s and 1980s quite a few changes occurred in Europe which gradually closed the gap between Europe and the USA. The differences in per capita income, cost of labour, size of markets and consumer tastes between Europe and the USA have narrowed considerably. This has made the product life cycle theory less applicable than it was in the 1950s and 1960s.

These two elements (1 and 2) led to the conclusion that MNCs have become more and more global scanners and, at the same time, many products have become standardized (computers, pharmaceutical products, etc.). This means that the international environment which generated the product life cycle is disappearing and the theory is less applicable.

There are still some areas in which there is scope for the application of the theory. First, it still applies to innovative activities of smaller firms which are not global scanners and cater for smaller markets and non-standardized tastes. Second, the theory may still be able to explore the spread of innovation between developed countries and developing ones; it might also apply within developing countries. Besides, one must remember that MNCs are not perfect global scanners; to the extent that they are not, there is still scope for cautious behaviour and thus for the trial of some products on the home ground with subsequent spread to other developed countries, in a product life cycle sequence.

5 Comments

The product life cycle theory has been the most quoted, anthologized, used and misused theory in the study of international business. It has also been one of the most criticized theories. The theory is very interesting for a variety of reasons highlighted in Box 5.4.

Similarly to the analysis in Hirsch, Vernon's technological gap theory is linked to the factor proportions theory of trade via the phases of the product's life. As the product matures and becomes standardized, relative costs and wages become more and more relevant. The step from a theory of trade to a theory of both international production and trade is made by Vernon through the incorporation of oligopolistic elements as well as comparative costs in the various locations.

The concentration on the consumers and on demand gives innovation activity a dependent role in relation to demand. It might be possible to see a process of cumulative causation in which innovation affects productivity and growth, and this gives further scope for innovation led by both demand and supply conditions. However, this cumulative process is not in Vernon's analysis.

The excessive concentration on the product and its life constitutes a weakness of the theory; the firm loses proper focus in favour of the product. Considerable elements linked to multi-product firms and diversification strategies – often related to multi-nationality strategies – are therefore lost. Concentration on the product rather than the firm prevents a proper analysis of the spread of innovation and technological (as well as managerial and marketing) advantages from one product to another. In contrast to

---

Box 5.4   *Positive elements in Vernon's theory*

- It is very dynamic: changes in the firm, market and industry and their interactions are intrinsic to the theory.

- It blends elements related to the market with production elements.

- Innovation, technology and knowledge, and their diffusion are considered endogenous and their development is linked to the economic environment of the country considered (the USA) and to market conditions.

- There is a strong interplay between the role and behaviour of consumers, the role of producers and the market structure.

- Conflicts between rival firms for market shares are brought in, although in a role subsidiary to that of consumers and markets.

- Trade and FDI are examined together as part and parcel of the same theory. Their relationship is seen largely as one of substitution though direct production abroad can, at times, be complementary to trade. The geographical pattern of trade is linked to the life cycle of the product and to the technological gap between various countries.

Vernon, Penrose ([1959] 2009), whose theory is expounded in Chapter 15, saw the strength of diversification for explaining growth as well as innovation.

The original technological gap theories emphasized the cumulative aspects of technological advantages deriving from cumulative production and/or the length of time for which the firm has been engaged in the production of the new product(s). Cumulative advantages for the firm, the industry and the country also derive from the tendency for inventions to cumulate and thus for new products and processes to emerge. Some of these cumulative elements are lost in Vernon's analysis. This is partly because the emphasis on the phases of the product's life tends to highlight shifts in advantages between countries rather than cumulation.

Nonetheless, the stress on foreign direct investment linked to the technological gap constitutes a considerable advancement on previous theories. International production becomes a strategy to prevent rivals from imitating the product, but it is also the strongest mechanism for the spread of new technologies to other countries, as highlighted in the OECD (1970) report.

The logic of the product life cycle sequence leads to the conclusion that there is a hierarchy of countries in terms of innovation potential as well as in terms of stages of development and income per capita. It also leads to the related concept of technology transfer from the most to the less developed countries.

Cantwell (1989; 1995)[4] shows that the mechanisms and geographical patterns of innovation activity are different from the ones envisaged by the product life cycle. It emerges that the TNCs are leaders in innovation but this does not necessarily lead to their home country being *the* leader. Transnational corporations' innovative activity has its origin in many countries; they learn from the diversified environment;

moreover, knowledge and innovation spread throughout the company via its wide internal network (Gupta and Govindarajan, 2000; Castellani and Zanfei, 2006; Frenz and Ietto-Gillies, 2007 and 2009). In addition, agglomeration economies attract several companies to the same countries/locations and the innovation activity spreads externally as well as internally. In this approach, innovation and technology development replaces the idea of technology transfer which had such relevance in the 1960s and 1970s literature.

Vernon's (1979) own critique of his theory is not only courageous but also very interesting and valid. However, it raises some problems. First, it seems a pity that, having gone into an analysis of the causes and effects of the geographical spread of operations,[5] he did not see that this element might also affect the location strategies of innovation as highlighted by Cantwell (1995). Second, his excessive concentration on consumers and markets leads to another missed opportunity: the analysis of the effects of global scanning on the production process and labour, on which there is more in Chapters 14 and 18.

Vernon (1979) ends his self-criticism by listing situations in which elements of the product life cycle theory are still applicable. We might add one more case to his list: the possible involvement of advanced western countries and Eastern European ones in a product life cycle sequence.

On the whole, as Cantwell (1995) points out, the theory needs modification to allow for global innovation strategies by TNCs. It also needs updating to allow for the developments in the macroenvironment which have taken place in the last 30 years: specifically those emanating from the diffusion of information and communication technologies and the globalization process. One aspect of such developments is the launch of global products (particularly services such as software) worldwide, contemporaneously in all or most countries of the world.[6] Another aspect is the fact that learning takes place on a global scale and, through it, the TNCs improve their original ownership advantages.[7] The international product life cycle theory is not applicable to such products as it stands.

Indicative further reading

Cantwell, J. (2000), 'A survey of theories of international production', in C.N. Pitelis and R. Sugden (eds), *The Nature of the Transnational Firm*, London: Routledge, ch. 2, pp. 10–56.

Vernon (1966) has been reprinted in P.J. Buckley and P.N. Ghauri (eds) (1999), *The Internationalization of the Firm: A Reader*, London: ITBP, ch. 2, pp. 14–26.

Notes

1 I shall not deal in detail with the technological gap or other theories of international trade, as they are outside the scope of this book. I shall, however, touch on some aspects of the theories that have a bearing on the product life cycle theory of international production.

SUMMARY BOX 5

Review of the IPLC theory

Antecedents

- On technology gap theory of trade: Posner (1961); Hufbauer (1966)
- On the life cycle of the product; Kutznets (1953); Hirsch (1965; 1967)

Key writers and works

Raymond Vernon (1966; 1974; 1979); Gruber (1967); OECD (1970)

Key elements of the theory

- Innovation linked to macroeconomic elements (income per capita; size of market; wage levels).
- The theory is dynamic.
- Stages in the product's life linked to location of production in USA, Europe and developing countries.
- Stages in the product's life and related strategies of location of production linked to the competitive structure of the industry.
- The strategies of international production affect the volume and pattern of international trade.
- There is a hierarchy of countries in terms of development and income per capita as well as innovative capacity. This implies also theories of technology transfer.

Possible criticisms

- Vernon's own (1979): changes in macroenvironment and changes in degree of internationalization
- Theory based on product rather than firm misses effects on other products by the same firm
- Theory too hierarchical in terms of: firms' innovative capacity; countries and their innovative environment

Modalities considered

International trade and international production

Level of aggregation

The firm and the industry; the macroenvironment affects the innovation capability of firms

Other relevant chapters

Chapter 6 (Knickerbocker's theory)

Chapter 11 (Cantwell's theory of technological accumulation and international production)

Chapter 15 (Penrose's theory of the firm)

2 The 'Leontief paradox' raises interesting methodological issues for economists and philosophers of science. Leontief's findings appear to falsify the factor proportions theory of trade. Instead of rejecting the theory, economists have been extremely busy looking for modifications to some of the assumptions in order to accommodate the paradox. This is one instance that shows the difficulty of applying the Popperian falsifiability criteria in science and particularly in economics. The difficulties are highlighted by the so-called 'Duhem-Quine thesis'. This thesis points out how testing is never related to a single hypothesis, but to a cluster of hypotheses and assumptions; thus, scientists can never be sure which hypothesis has been falsified. This leaves the door open for endless modifications to auxiliary assumptions in order to salvage the basic theory. Some of these modifications are no more than ad hoc devices to allow scientists to go on using discredited theories. In economics, where ideological elements are very relevant, the tendency to use ad hoc procedures may be stronger than in other disciplines. Discussions on these points are in Keat and Urry (1975), Lakatos (1978), Gillies (1993: ch. 5). The original theories are in Duhem (1905), Quine (1951) and Popper (1959).
3 Cross-elasticities measure the responsiveness of demand for product 'a' when the price of product 'b' changes. In this case products 'a' and 'b' are seen as substitutes by the consumers, in spite of efforts by the producers to differentiate them. High cross-elasticity means that demand tends to shift to product 'a' when the price of 'b' increases.
4 More on Cantwell's theory and on his critique of the international product life cycle (IPLC) in Chapter 11.
5 For evidence on this cf. also Ietto-Gillies (2002a: chs 4 and 5).
6 This criticism was suggested to me by Joanne Roberts.
7 This point was suggested to me by Antonello Zanfei to whom I owe several improvements as well as avoidance of mistakes in this book.

6 Oligopolistic reactions and the geographical pattern of FDI

I Knickerbocker's theory

In 1973 Frederick T. Knickerbocker published a book on a theory of foreign direct investment, which was the outcome of his doctoral dissertation at the Harvard Business School. His work developed from the theory by Vernon whose research student he was.[1] Knickerbocker's work consists of:

- a theoretical 'informal' model containing the a priori reasons why certain firms' behaviour should lead to FDI and how such behaviour is linked to the market structure;
- the testing of the model; and
- conclusions regarding findings and expectations for the future.

The a priori model should, in theory, be applicable to the behaviour of firms from any advanced western country, although there are some possible restrictions (on which more below). However, the testing is done specifically for the USA. Twelve industries are considered and the source of the data is the 'Harvard Multinational Enterprise Study, a survey of international expansion by major firms', conducted between 1966 and 1971 at the Harvard Business School.[2]

The theory is tested drawing on evidence from the period since the Second World War. The study starts with three preliminary observations, which are confronted by the evidence contained in the data:

- In the post-Second World War period, firms have tended to become more and more international.
- Firms in a number of US industries have tended to locate their outward foreign direct investment in the same countries.
- Firms involved in international expansion belong to industries characterized by oligopolistic structures.

Knickerbocker starts by defining FDI as the capital flow resulting from investment by an enterprise 'in assets outside its home country in order to control, partially or fully, the operation of these assets' (1973: 2). He then defines as '*aggressive* investment' the establishment of the first subsidiary in a given industry and given country, and as '*defensive* investment' the establishment of subsequent subsidiaries on completion of the first.

Knickerbocker's empirical study is concerned mainly with defensive investment and its aims are illustrated in Box 6.1.

Box 6.1 *What Knickerbocker's research aims to discover*

1 Whether the forces that induced aggressive and defensive behaviour were the same or whether defensive behaviour is influenced by forces additional to those that prompted the first move

2 Whether, in fact, defensive behaviour is induced by reaction to aggressive FDI

3 Why and how the pattern of defensive FDI varies according to industries and countries

The author then goes on to develop his informal, a priori model based on oligopolistic structures. The term oligopoly defines – in Knickerbocker's system – a structure characterized by:

- few sellers;
- products that are close substitutes;
- 'substantial market interdependence among the competitive policies of these firms' (ibid.: 4).

The third characteristic means that oligopoly is defined in terms of both the market *structure* and the *behaviour* of firms.

In an oligopolistic structure the interdependence of firms means that their behaviour leads to a pattern of action and reaction, move and counter-move, as in a game of chess. Each oligopolistic firm combines moves to improve its own position with moves to offset aggressive policies by its opponents. An aggressive move may be prompted by special opportunities to seize a market or new technologies or new sources of raw materials. The advantage that the aggressor may gain could, in the long run, be highly detrimental to its rivals, who therefore have to react in order to minimize risks. Such reactions lead to their defensive policies.

Firms are well aware that, in a situation of roughly equal strengths, aggressive moves are likely to lead to defensive ones and thus to the risk of mutually destructive competition. Since they all want to avoid this, the end result is the following: first, price warfare is avoided in favour of the more peaceful, market-enhancing competition via advertising[3]; second, in industries that do not change or grow rapidly, the oligopolistic equilibria tend to be maintained and aggressive policies are unlikely to be used.

The *oligopolistic equilibrium* is defined by Knickerbocker as a state of affairs among sellers such that: 'all rivals having roughly the same competitive capabilities, there is little reason for any one rival to expect that it can, with impunity, improve its market position at the expense of others' (Knickerbocker, 1973: 7). In fast-growing industries, where technologies and markets change rapidly, individual firms may see very profitable opportunities deriving from aggressive behaviour that make it worthwhile running the risk of defensive attacks by rivals; the oligopolistic equilibrium is, therefore, more likely to be disrupted in fast-changing industries.

However, Knickerbocker himself is aware that oligopolistic reactions in themselves cannot explain why the first firm made the move and why the move took a particular form; in our case, why the move took the form of FDI. There is also the need to explain, within the same theoretical framework, divergences between different industries. Knickerbocker sees, therefore, the need to place his theory in a broader context that could allow him to explain why oligopolistic moves and counter-moves take the specific form of FDI.

He sees the need to answer three sets of specific questions and to establish links between them. The questions relate to:

- the reasons why US manufacturing industries have extended their activities abroad;
- why the bulk of such activities have taken place in industries with oligopolistic structures;
- why, under oligopolistic conditions, firms have tended to match each other's moves in FDI.

The fundamental inducement towards FDI is to be found in the analysis of the product cycle model. Vernon's model is at the basis of Knickerbocker's thesis. The product life cycle theory tells us how:

- the US economic environment created opportunities for product development leading to a continuous stream of products that respond to the demands of high-income per capita consumers and/or the need for labour-saving devices for the consumer or producer;
- such products were more likely to be first developed and produced at home rather than abroad.

Knickerbocker emphasizes how this whole process meant that US producers developed special capabilities for:

- developing a stream of new products and managing the organization of the related R&D;
- producing these new products for large markets and managing the organization of production and the necessary continuous adaptation needed in the first stage of the life cycle;
- selling new products by developing sophisticated marketing techniques and using them vigorously.

In a nutshell, the US firms became skilled at 'pioneering' products. The development of special skills in such a variety of areas (production, research and development [R&D] matching laboratory development with marketing skills) is the direct result of the evolution of the economic environment of the USA; the end result is that this process has given US firms an advantage over foreign firms, who could not match such skills and capabilities.

European markets and economies lagged behind those of the USA. However, after a few years, Europe was ready to receive the labour-saving, high-income per capita products. Exports of US products were followed by FDI, which, in some cases, was preceded by licensing.

US firms had disadvantages in producing abroad; in particular, those deriving from the foreign environment, from less preferential treatment by governments compared with domestic firms, from difficulties and costs of gathering information. However, the great advantage they had in the accumulated knowledge of managerial, marketing and organizational skills – which they used also to organize efficiently the lower cost inputs of European countries – meant that US firms had an overall advantage over domestic European enterprises.

'In a few words, U.S. product pioneers stormed foreign markets with competitive weapons forged at home' (Knickerbocker, 1973: 17). Other circumstances may also have pushed US firms towards FDI rather than exporting or licensing. Knickerbocker mentions, in particular, the existence of tariff and non-tariff barriers in European countries as well as the fact that producing near the market allowed firms to offer after-sales services and to adapt the product to the requirements of local customers. However, these circumstances acted only in a subsidiary role; Knickerbocker's conclusion is, in fact, that as regards foreign direct investment: 'the product cycle model suggests that the fundamental consideration underlying such undertaking has been the desire of U.S. businessmen to exploit overseas the novel skills that their firms acquired in the course of satisfying U.S. demand' (ibid.: 18).

There is a link between product pioneering, and thus the product life cycle, and oligopolistic structures. Firms that operate in fast-changing industries and are, therefore, involved in new products and new developments are also likely to experience various advantages. These advantages will, in the long run, lead to few producers and sellers as scale economies eliminate smaller producers and act as entry barriers to new ones.[4] The advantages are due not only to scale economies but also to the special skills accumulated in the course of developing and managing new products, their production and marketing. These skills help in both the domestic and foreign environments. 'The nub of the case being made here is that the special technological and organizational capabilities acquired by these firms first invested them with market power at home and, at a later date, invested them with market power abroad' (ibid.: 20).

So, in a nutshell, the product life cycle can explain why the first firm to pioneer a product will want to expand its activities abroad via FDI; the forces that lead to the development of new products lead to an oligopolistic structure at home and to the search for FDI opportunities. What now remains to be explained is why rivals follow the move of the first firm and engage in defensive foreign investment, thus leading to a 'bandwagon effect' and to an overall pattern of FDI that exhibits 'bunching up' in terms of countries, industries and timing.

Investment in a foreign country involves a considerable amount of *uncertainty*; this is particularly so for the product-pioneering firm that is launching a new product, is using new technologies and is moving into a new country. However, the firm learns with each move and improves its ability to scan the world and reduce uncertainties. A rival firm also faces uncertainties in investing abroad. However, it faces risks if it does not invest: the risk that the first mover would gain considerable advantages from its aggressive move and then use the advantages against its rivals:

> For businessmen, countering was a form of insurance. The premium firms paid to insure the perpetuation of the competitive balance was the cost involved in making a matching move. One reason firms were prepared to pay the premium was that its costs tended to go down since the marginal costs of each additional step into the international market place tended to go down. But the fundamental reason for paying the premium was that its costs were at least partially predictable whereas the costs to a firm, if it did not counter the moves of a rival, were often unpredictable and could, very possibly, far exceed those of countering. (Knickerbocker, 1973: 25–6)

The advantages that the first firm – the one making the aggressive move – could gain are in production or marketing or both. Advantages of large-scale production, of the use of the new productive process, of vertical integration and general access to cheaper inputs, can all result in cost reductions. Similarly, marketing abroad can give advantages to a firm in both the international and the home markets. The further organizational, managerial and marketing skills acquired before and in the course of the first move can then be used for further aggressive policies. All these acquired advantages – whether in the production or marketing or management areas – can then be used to change the competitive equilibrium and gradually eliminate rivals. The other firms want to avoid such a risk and that is why they follow up with their own foreign investment. Ultimately, therefore, Knickerbocker explains the *bunching up* of FDI as the result of firms' *defensive policies*, which are designed to minimize *risks* in an *oligopolistic market structure*.

Knickerbocker claims that his empirical findings support his informal model. Entry into certain foreign markets has tended to be concentrated in peak years. Entry concentration appears to be positively related to industry concentration; this means that firms pursued a more active defensive policy on foreign investment in industries with high sellers' concentration than in industries with low sellers' concentration.[5]

Firms involved in narrow product lines have tended to respond with defensive foreign investments more readily than firms dealing in wide product lines. This is explained by Knickerbocker on the basis that firms involved in many products have wider defensive strategic choices.

Leaders in each industry, i.e. those firms 'that react swiftly to one another's moves, tend to ignore scale considerations when they invest abroad' (ibid.: 195). Followers have tended to give more consideration to scale. 'The profitability of overseas manufacturing industries is positively related to entry concentration' (ibid.).[6] Causation here could, however, go both ways, as Knickerbocker points out: high profitability could lead to high entry concentration or vice versa. On the whole the clustering behaviour varies between industries and markets: in some industries it has occurred more than in others, in some countries more than in others.

More recently Graham (1978; 1985; 1990; 1998), also working at Cambridge, Massachusetts, uses an oligopolistic structure to explain the location strategies of large US and European companies. His model has considerable links with Knickerbocker's. Faced with the task of explaining the so called 'transatlantic reversal' – the shift of the

USA from a position of net outward to one of net inward investor – he develops a model based on 'exchange of threats' between large firms. In oligopolistic situations, companies want to avoid price competition and thus resort to competition for locations. Graham concludes that the defensive behaviour on the part of European firms leads them to invest in the US within the same industry. The resulting pattern is one in which the inter-penetration of markets and production locations goes hand in hand with intra-industry FDI.

Graham (2002) notes that Knickerbocker's work has indirect links with Hymer's. In the latter the firm's aim to gain control over possible rivals might lead to monopolistic situations. However, for Knickerbocker, the countervailing behaviour of rivals means that an oligopolistic market structure in an international setting will prevail.

2 Comments

Knickerbocker's theory is very interesting. It puts right at the centre of analysis a realistic oligopolistic structure and it attempts to deal with uncertainty and risk – indeed risk avoidance is the essential determinant of the clustering of FDI. It is dynamic, as it is all about reactions and counter-reactions, changes in the oligopolistic balance and strategies.

However, a close look at his analysis leaves us with the uneasy feeling that, although the work is a very good start, as the author himself stresses, his theory does not explain the first move: why firms choose FDI as an aggressive policy. Knickerbocker's main concern is with explaining 'bunching up' and he does this with reference to risk avoidance strategies. However, risk is difficult to quantify and risk avoidance strategies difficult or impossible to assess: a point already highlighted by Hymer (1960) in his critique of the neoclassical theory of foreign investment and its emphasis on risk, as mentioned in Chapter 4.

Knickerbocker brings to our attention, and gives systematic quantification to, the tendency towards clustering of FDI and the relationship between entry concentration in foreign countries and sellers' concentration and their industry differences. This in itself is very useful, although there may be doubts about the degree of corroboration his findings offer to the theory.

Knickerbocker's theory takes Vernon's (1966) product life cycle as its starting point. However, Vernon himself has, to a considerable extent, repudiated his first theory in his 1979 article. The product life cycle approach to FDI is linked to bunching up, in that they are both the expression of oligopolistic behaviour; they both aim to explain the first, aggressive move (Vernon's theory) and the following defensive FDI (Knickerbocker's theory). We might be led to conclude that a rejection or reassessment of the product life cycle approach to FDI might bring the same fate to Knickerbocker's theory. However, I am inclined to think that Knickerbocker's theory might still hold because it is a theory of FDI bunching up only. A necessary condition for the theory to hold is the existence of an oligopolistic structure; there is no doubt that such a structure is present both in the real economies and in Knickerbocker's model. It is the behaviour of oligopolistic rivals that leads to the clustering of FDI, independently of whether the oligopolistic structure is or is not linked to the product life cycle. In effect, Knickerbocker explains bunching up in specific locations *independently* of the product life cycle and therefore his theory could, in principle, be accepted even if one rejects Vernon's theory.

There is another advantage in 'decoupling' Knickerbocker's theory from Vernon's. The product life cycle theory is strictly applicable to the USA in a particular historical period; the changed environment in Europe has thrown doubts on its wider applicability to the USA and Europe. Knickerbocker's theory is not linked very closely to the US conditions but only to the existence of oligopolistic structures; this means that the part of Knickerbocker's theory that is independent of the product life cycle (the bunching up) has more general applicability than Vernon's theory, as shown by Graham's applications and developments. However, as already explained, I feel that the risk minimization explanation, though interesting, is not fully satisfactory as an explanation of the clustering pattern of FDI.

A stronger criticism of Knickerbocker's theory may derive from the 'globalization of technology' theory (Cantwell, 1995) considered in Chapter 11. The latter theory rejects – on the basis of evidence from patent filing – the hypothesis of leader country in innovation, in favour of the idea of multiplicity and dispersal of centres of innovation. This, in my view, throws doubts on a location pattern based on first aggressive moves. However, Knickerbocker's theory is compatible with a cluster of FDI by various firms in various countries. Moreover, it could be argued that the globalization of technology pattern refers to innovation activities while Knickerbocker's theory is wider and refers to all types of international production.

There is another point that might be worth raising with regard to Knickerbocker's analysis. He rightly stresses the role of moves and counter-moves in oligopolistic strategies; however, he then confines himself to moves and counter-moves *within* FDI. In reality, firms' strategies can have many dimensions. There can be strategies towards: development and use of technology; diversification by product, by markets or by production location; the sourcing of markets in other countries; vertical or horizontal integration; the labour force; the organization of production of components or business services (via internal production or via outsourcing or via mixed strategies); cooperation with other firms (licensing, joint ventures); towards expansion (via greenfield plants or acquisitions) and so on.

A move towards FDI by one firm could involve a chain of events different from that envisaged by Knickerbocker. *First*, because rivals could react by implementing countervailing strategies, not necessarily in terms of FDI but in terms of other variables and dimensions; for example, in reaction to firm A's investment in country X, firm B could buy up a source of raw materials to acquire a countervailing advantage. This move might make sense because as firm A's resources are engaged in producing its product(s) abroad, it is less likely to be able to invest in raw materials as well. The strategy would also give B a counterbalancing advantage without the risk of excessive competition in the country where A has invested. Knickerbocker briefly touches on these issues when he mentions a possible divergence in strategies between firms involved in narrow or wide product lines. Wide product lines offer firms opportunities for a variety of strategies and hence lead to lower levels of clustering; however, Knickerbocker seems to overlook the fact that other aspects of firms' activities also give scope for a variety of strategies.

Second, in a world of many possible strategies and a fairly continuous sequence of moves and counter-moves, it is difficult to distinguish between aggressive and defensive behaviour; firm A may be the first to invest in country X but this move may have been induced as a defence against other firms' strategies in technology, in subcontracting, towards labour or in terms of moving into new product lines. Essentially what I am saying is that aggressive and defensive moves cannot be seen and assessed in isolation within a single type of strategy, but must be seen in the context of multi-strategic behaviour by oligopolistic firms.

SUMMARY BOX 6

Review of Knickerbocker's theory

Antecedents

Vernon's international product life cycle (1966; 1974 and 1979)

Key writers and works

Frederick Knickerbocker (1973); Edward Graham (1978; 1985; 1990 and 1998)

Key elements of the theory

- Aims to explain the geographical clustering of FDI in post WWII
- Assumes an oligopolistic structure
- Conflicts between rival oligopolists
- Aggressive and defensive strategies by oligopolists
- Relevance of uncertainty and risk
- Theory tested on US data for several industries

Modalities considered

Mainly FDI

Level of aggregation

Firms and industries

Other relevant chapters

Chapter 5 (Vernon's theory)

Chapter 11 (Cantwell's technological accumulation theory)

Chapter 13 (Cowling and Sugden's transnational monopoly capitalism)

The end result is that Knickerbocker's theory cannot be used to predict the behaviour of firms and the pattern of FDI in various countries and industries, essentially for the following reasons:[7]

1   Because, its emphasis on risk makes it difficult to quantify the variables.
2   Because we should allow for the possibility that firms use a variety of strategies and can move into a country via FDI for a variety of reasons. The continuous spread of transnational activities, in terms of countries, industries, sectors, types of activities and contractual arrangements (subcontracting, joint ventures, licensing, etc.), gives wider and wider scope for different strategies and hence for behavioural patterns that move away from the narrow field envisaged by Knickerbocker.

Indicative further reading

Graham, E.M. (1978), 'Transatlantic investment by multinational firms: a rivalristic phenomenon?', *Journal of Post-Keynesian Economics*, **1** (1), 82–99.
Graham, E.M. (1985), 'Intra-industry direct investment, market structure, firm rivalry and technological performance', in E. Erdilek (ed.), *Multinationals as Mutual Invaders: Intra-Industry Direct Foreign Investment*, London: Croom Helm.
Graham, E.M. (1990), 'Exchange of threats between multinational firms as an infinitely repeated non-cooperative game', *International Trade Journal*, **4** (3), 259–77.
Graham, E.M. (1998), 'Market structure and the multinational enterprise: a game-theoretic approach', *Journal of International Business Studies*, **29** (1), 67–83.

Notes

1   This is the reason why this chapter follows directly from the one on Vernon. This decision implies a slight departure from a strict time sequence, in the presentation of the theories, which informs the structure of Parts II and III of this book.
2   The data used by Knickerbocker refer to phase I of the project, covering the history of international expansion between 1900 and 1967 for 187 large US firms; phase II refers to a similar study of 200 non-US-based firms. Details of data sources and methodology are in Knickerbocker (1973, ch. 2). This database is the same used in Vernon (1979), as highlighted in Chapter 5.
3   This point echoes Baran and Sweezy (1966a).
4   This point has similarities with Vernon's (1974) idea of innovation-based oligopoly, as discussed in Chapter 5.
5   Sellers' concentration refers to the share of market commanded by the top few (two, three, four, five) large firms.
6   Entry concentration refers to the concentration of producers – within the same industry – in the same foreign location.
7   The difficulty of making forecasts in a world of industries dominated by a few giants, is mentioned by Knickerbocker himself (1973: 201–2).

7 Currency areas and internationalization

1 The theory and its background

Robert Z. Aliber (1970) develops a theory of direct investment based on currency areas and in which he aims to explain when and why foreign markets are sourced in one of the following methods:

- by domestic production through exports;
- by host country production through licensing agreement involving local firms;
- via direct foreign production by the source country's firms.

His theory is therefore concerned with explaining all the main modalities of internationalization.

He starts by assuming that foreign direct investment involves extra costs and disadvantages related to the management of enterprises at a distance; there is therefore a need to look for compensating advantages.[1] A theory of direct investment must analyse the source of such advantages while explaining the patterns of FDI with particular reference to the characteristics highlighted in Box 7.1.

Box 7.1 *Characteristics of FDI that Aliber aims to explain*

- The fact that a substantial part of FDI worldwide originates in the USA

- The considerable differences in the FDI pattern across industries

- The existence of FDI through takeovers of foreign firms

- The existence of cross-hauling, i.e. the fact that a country engages in outward FDI while also being the recipient of inward FDI.

Aliber rejects explanations of FDI based on superior managerial skills[2] because, in his view, any such type of superiority should be reflected in costs and exchange rates. Similarly, he does not accept explanations based on industrial organization of the Coasian[3] type because such theories, based on advantages of internalization, may explain the growth of firms in general, but not their internationalization. He also rejects the Hymer and Kindleberger explanation based on market power and conflicts.

In approaching the internationalization issue he sees the need to look for explanations that refer to the 'foreignness' of FDI. This means looking at specific elements that define the nation-state and its boundaries. The specific elements of the nation-state considered by Aliber are the existence of currency and customs that characterize a specific area/country with respect to foreign ones. 'The "foreignness" of the investment reflects the movement across the boundaries between customs areas and between currency areas. In the absence of such boundaries, the distinction between foreign investment and domestic investment disappears' (Aliber, 1970: 21). The existence of multiple custom areas affects the prices of products exported from one area to another; the existence of multiple currency areas affects the interest rates on securities issued by borrowers from different areas, reflecting different risks owing to movements in exchange rates.

Aliber assumes that the firm in the source country[4] has a monopolistic advantage which he calls 'the patent'. This can be a general advantage of any type: technological, managerial etc. 'The value of the patent is the capitalized value of the difference between production costs before and after the patent is used' (ibid.: 22). The firm that owns the patent has *three choices* open to it, if it wants to source a foreign market:

1   It can produce domestically and export.
2   It can license its patent to a foreign firm that will produce for the local market.
3   It can produce directly abroad.

Aliber then goes on to develop his argument by first assuming a situation of unified currency areas within separate customs areas, and then assuming the opposite.

The first assumption leads to a situation in which it is advantageous to satisfy demand from local production rather than from foreign production, as foreign production will be subject to tariffs on importation. Economies of scale would favour production in the domestic economy, and the sourcing of foreign markets via exports; however, the existence of tariffs makes it less costly to produce in the country where the market is – the host country – and thus avoid the tariff. There is a trade-off in domestic versus foreign production between reduction in costs due to economies of scale and reduction in prices due to tariff avoidance. The switch-off point on the quantities produced at home or abroad depends on the costs of production (and thus economies of scale) and on the height of the tariff, which affects the price of import in the foreign country. However, foreign production using the monopolistic advantage (the patent) can take place in two different ways: via licensing to a local firm, which will then become the producer, or via direct production by the source country's firm.

The patent produces a stream of incomes whose capitalized value will be different in the three cases: exports of domestic production, licensing and direct investment. The pattern of income streams and capitalized values in the three cases will determine the quantities of production at which the crossover between the three cases occurs.[5] The capitalization ratios, and hence the interest rates, will be crucial in the three choices.

Aliber then develops his model under the second assumption: unified custom areas and separate currencies. The single custom area means that production will tend to be concentrated in a single country to take advantage of economies of scale; this could be the home or host country. In the latter case, a crucial question now becomes whether production will be carried out by the host country firm (through licensing) or by the source country firm: 'the decision whether the source-country firm or the host-country firm exploits the patent abroad depends on the costs of doing business abroad and on national differences in capitalization ratios and not on the height of the tariff' (ibid.: 27).

Income streams of different countries' firms will be capitalized at different rates for various reasons, including the fact that they belong to different currency areas. The theory would therefore predict that: 'Source-country firms are likely to be those in countries where the capitalization rates are high; host-countries firms are those in countries where capitalization rates are low' (ibid.: 28).

The market applies different capitalization rates to assets denominated in different currencies for two reasons. The first is as a premium against exchange risk. The second reason – which is in fact more of a hypothesis – is the following: 'that the market applies a higher capitalization rate to the source income stream generated in the host country when received by a source-country firm than by a host-country firm' (ibid.: 30). This last point would explain why direct investment, rather than licensing, takes place in the exploitation of a certain patent.

According to Aliber different capitalization rates attached to different currencies explain the geographical pattern of FDI. Countries with strong currencies (the USA, the Netherlands, Switzerland) tend to be source countries as their currencies carry high premiums. Countries subject to a low currency premium will, on the contrary, tend to be host countries. The dispersion in capitalization rates is one of the elements that affects the pattern of FDI. Other elements are 'the size of the host-country's market, the value of the patents, the height of tariffs, the costs of doing business abroad in a particular industry' (ibid.: 31). In Aliber's view his theory predicts that FDI will be larger in more capital-intensive industries, 'since the disadvantage of host-country firms is larger, the larger the contribution of capital to production' (ibid.: 32), and similarly for research-intensive industries.

Takeovers across countries can be explained by the difference in capitalization ratios. Cross-flows of investment are explained by Aliber partly by historical reasons; partly because inward investment in the USA comes from a very small number of firms (Shell, Unilever, Phillips, Bayer, etc.). However, he is still left with the problem of why these firms produce in the USA rather than license or export. His answer is that: 'If the price offered for a patent is very low, then the firm may invest in that country rather than license, even though its profit rate will be lower than the profit rates of host-country competitors' (ibid.: 33).

In conclusion, Aliber's theory tells us that the division of the world into different currency areas leads to the market putting a higher premium on certain currencies than on others, depending on its estimate of the risk. This premium affects the capitalization value of the income streams deriving from 'patents' and hence 'determines whether a country is likely to be a source country or a host country for foreign investment' (ibid.: 34).

While his main theory stresses the role of currencies and currency areas (and hence monetary policy affecting them) in MNEs' decisions, in a subsequent article Aliber (1971) focuses on the effect that MNEs' activities may have on exchange rates and monetary policy. In this article Aliber emphasizes the advantageous position in which MNEs find themselves regarding movements of funds into various currencies. Their advantage over 'national' firms derives from the fact that they can have more immediate information on interest rates in various countries in which they have subsidiaries. At the same time the geographical spread of subsidiaries gives them a useful multiplicity of contacts with banks and credit systems. Thus, MNEs tend to react quickly to actual and expected changes in exchange rates and/or interest rates by switching from currency to currency. From this and other related elements, one could draw the 'plausible inference . . . that the volume of funds which are shifted in response to an anticipated change in the exchange is increasing' (ibid.: 56). In Aliber's view this puts pressure on the monetary systems of various countries and 'One possible consequence is a widening of interest rate differentials' (ibid.).

More recently (1993) Aliber has further developed his theory in the direction of giving more relevance to the real economy. The general perspective is again macro, that is, an exploration of what determines the geographical pattern of FDI and why some countries are a source of, and others host to, FDI. The explanations are sought in macro differences between the countries rather than in the basic strategies and decisions of the companies with headquarters in them.

In this later work Aliber notes that nation-states differ in the extent and timing of their development and growth. High growth rates lead to increasing incomes and high levels of demand which generate high investment opportunities with concomitant high profit and interest rates. This situation will attract investments by foreign as well as domestic firms. The injection of extra foreign capital will increase the value of the currency. Conversely, companies based in countries with sluggish growth rates will seek investment opportunities abroad.

2   Some comments

The currency areas explanation of FDI is quite ingenious, but unfortunately it is not very effective in its explanatory and predictive power. It is a classic example of using much to achieve little: the 'much' used is in terms of the complicated presentation and the large number of assumptions that are made. The achievements are the conclusions reported in Box 7.2.

Box 7.2   *Main conclusions from Aliber's analysis*

1 In a world of custom areas there comes a point where firms who want to source a foreign market will find it more advantageous to produce in the country either directly or through a licensee, rather than produce domestically and export.

2 In a world of different currency areas, countries with strong currencies will tend to be source countries and countries with weak currencies will tend to be hosts to FDI.

Point (1) in Box 7.2 is a fairly uncontroversial, obvious and well-known conclusion. Point (2) is not satisfactorily corroborated by Aliber and its conclusions cannot be fully accepted. More will be said on this below. Aliber starts by overemphasizing the difference between his approach and the market imperfections approach of Hymer and Kindleberger. However, in reality, as Dunning (1971) points out, Aliber's theory could be reduced to a special case of market imperfections as, in the last analysis, his explanation is in terms of imperfections in the market for currencies.

Methodologically, the theory seems flawed for the following reason: the conclusion about the relationship between source and host countries and strong and weak currencies (the crux of the matter, in fact) crucially depends on the market applying a higher capitalization rate to the same income stream when received by a source country firm than by a host country firm. If the capitalization rates applied were the same, there would be no incentive for foreign investment. No clear reasons are given for the different valuation, nor any evidence for its existence. Indeed, the whole reasoning may be circular in that, while Aliber's theory implies that differences in capitalization rates are responsible for determining which country is likely to be source and which host, he seems also to argue that we can assess the difference in capitalization rates by considering whether a country is source or host to FDI.

Aliber tries to explain (1971: 52–3) the differences in the capitalization rates due to source countries' firms being more efficient in hedging exchange risk, or to the fact that they provide the investor with a diversified portfolio. However, this cannot be considered as evidence to back his crucial assumption of differences in capitalization rates, but rather as an explanation with reference to the host versus source country situation. Besides, while he argues that superior managerial skills and similar advantages cannot be used to explain the pattern of FDI (Aliber, 1970: 19–20), he does not use the same argument in considering firms' efficiency in terms of exchange risk hedging or portfolio diversification; would this type of efficiency and advantage not be reflected also in costs and exchange rates just like managerial advantages? On the whole, Aliber's (1970) analysis may suffer from its strictly neoclassical approach as evidenced by the efficiency perspective as well as its marginalist methodology.

With regard to the predictive power and the explanation of the pattern of FDI, the theory is in great difficulty, in spite of Aliber's claims, particularly when it comes to explaining cross-hauling or intra-industry FDI. Aliber minimizes the extent of this type of FDI in both his articles (1970 and 1971). The phenomenon is, however, quite a large one. Indeed, most developed countries – with the notable exception of Japan – are both originators and receivers of FDI often in the same industries.

One useful and realistic point made by Aliber (1971) relates to the effect of MNEs' activities on currencies and exchange rates, and hence on monetary policies of national governments and related interest rates. His basic theory implies that interest rates affect the pattern of FDI; his subsequent additions imply that MNEs' activities in general, and particularly those related to short-term investment, affect interest rates. Although I do not accept his main theory as a satisfactory explanation of FDI, I find that this type of interaction between MNEs' activities and the environment in which they operate is very realistic and clearly typical of oligopolistic structures.

The issue of strong versus weak currencies is relevant for the geographical pattern of FDI in a slightly different way from the one envisaged in Aliber (1970) and in a very different way from the one he considered in his 1993 book. Increasingly – and largely after 1970 when Aliber published his article – FDI has been taking the mergers and acquisition (M&As) mode. Companies from high-currency countries are at an advantage in the acquisition of assets in countries with low-valued currencies. This means that the former will be source countries and the latter will be host to FDI. This pattern of cross-border M&As is compatible with Aliber (1970) but not with Aliber (1993). In the latter, high-growth economies tend to have high-valued currencies and yet they attract FDI.

In common with Aliber's earlier work, his later work emphasizes differences between nation-states and their effect on the geographical pattern of FDI. The perspective is, again, the macroeconomy. The background micro theory is one in which firms' choice of investment location reflects a comparison of costs. It is therefore an efficiency-led decision with strategic elements completely overlooked. Moreover, the reference to the real economy is almost entirely to the demand side.

SUMMARY BOX 7

Review of Aliber's theory

Antecedents

There are some elements of neoclassical analysis (Chapter 3); some of Hymer's work (Chapter 4) and some of Knickerbocker's (Chapter 6).

Key elements of the theory

- Aims to explain the geographical pattern of internationalization.
- Aims to explain when the foreign markets are sourced via exports or direct production by the source country firm or via licensing to a local firm.
- Nation-states and their boundaries defined by currency and customs areas.
- Crucial elements of the theory are the markets evaluation of the currencies and the role of interest rates in the capitalization of income streams from the investment.

Modalities considered

Export, licensing and FDI

Level of aggregation

The macroeconomy

Possible linkages with other chapters

On the whole, they are not very strong. However, some linkages with: Chapter 4 (Hymer); Chapter 6 (Knickerbocker); Chapter 9, section 3 (Dunning's development path and Aliber, 1993); and Chapter 14 for the relevance of specific characteristics of the nation-state.

Issues of production, its organization and labour relations are not considered at all. These may, nonetheless, be very relevant for the geographical pattern of FDI.

We must finally note that the globalization process and the new ICTs have increased the flow of information of the financial markets for all agents. This may invalidate Aliber's assertions that MNCs derive special advantages – compared to uninational companies – because their affiliates in host countries give them access to faster and better information on financial and monetary matters.

Indicative further reading

There are not many works dealing with Aliber's theories. Students who want to deepen their knowledge in this field are advised to read the original works cited in the chapter.

Notes

1 This is an issue in common with Hymer as we saw in Chapter 4.
2 As we saw, for example, in Knickerbocker's theory in Chapter 6.
3 More on this in Chapter 8.
4 Aliber refers to 'source' country as the one from where the investment originates. It can be considered to correspond to what we called home country. However, as he is mainly interested in the financial flows for funding FDI, it is possible to have a company whose home country A is funding its investment in B via the transfer of funds from country C where it may already have accumulated profits from past activities.
5 Aliber (1970) illustrates the various cases with two graphs (Figures 1 and 2 on pp. 25 and 26 respectively).

8 Internalization and the transnational corporation

I Introduction

In Part I we noted that theories of international production or of the TNCs or of internationalization in general, may refer to a variety of activities as well as aspects of those activities. One specific focus of analysis has been the organization of production. The traditional neoclassical theory of the firm focused on the type of costs and revenues with little or no concern for how those costs were related to the organization of resources.[1] The focus on the internal organization of resources and thus on opening up the traditionally mysterious 'black box' of the firm started with Coase (1937) and Penrose ([1959] 2009).

The organizational approach to the firm has also brought fruits in terms of advancement in the understanding of the transnational corporation and its activities. The approach that has proved popular and successful with followers of the international business literature is the one based on *internalization*. One of its contributors refers to the theory of internalization as 'the modern theory of the multinational enterprise' (Rugman, 1982: 9).

The internalization approach to the theory of the firm is, in fact, not new. Ronald H. Coase in his seminal paper (1937) brought to the attention of economists the inconsistency between the assumption that, in market economies, resources are allocated via the price mechanism, and the assumption or reality that, within the firm, such allocation is done by planning and direction rather than through arm's-length transactions. He writes: 'Outside the firm, price movements direct production, which is co-ordinated through a series of exchange transactions on the market. Within a firm, these market transactions are eliminated and in place of the complicated market structure with exchange transactions is substituted the entrepreneur-co-ordinator, who directs production' (Coase, 1937: 333). Coase therefore sets for himself: 'The purpose . . . to bridge what appears to be a gap in economic theory between the assumption (made for some purposes) that resources are allocated by means of the price mechanism and the assumption (made for other purposes) that this allocation is dependent on the entrepreneur-co-ordinator' (ibid.: 334–5). The gap is bridged by analysing, from the firm's point of view, the costs of carrying out transactions through the market against the costs of organizing the allocation of resources internally. The latter costs will, among others, set a limit to the size of the firm. In Coase's words: 'a firm will tend to expand until the costs of organising an extra transaction within the firm become equal to the costs of carrying out the same transaction by means of an exchange on the open market or the costs of organising in another firm' (ibid.: 341).[2]

Coase's approach therefore explains the existence and growth of the firm in terms of costs and benefits of internal transactions – and therefore of internal allocation of resources – versus the costs and benefits of external transactions and therefore of allocation of resources through the market. Essentially his task is to explain why and under what circumstances the organization of production takes place via hierarchies rather than through the market. The market, through the price mechanism, is taken to be the best allocator of resources. However, there may be costs associated with this allocation mechanism.

The costs of operating via the markets and, therefore, of using the price mechanism as allocator of resources, derive from *market imperfections* of the transactional type. There are, in general, two types of market imperfections: *structural and transactional*:

- *Structural imperfections* refer to the structure of the market and industry in which the firm operates and thus involve issues of market shares and market power that each firm commands.[3] These are the type of imperfections considered, among others, by Hymer, Vernon and Knickerbocker.
- *Transactional imperfections* refer to imperfection in knowledge and, in particular, to the asymmetry of information between buyer and seller (i.e. to cognitive imperfections). In the course of business transactions these imperfections give rise to specific costs. There are also other types of costs incurred in carrying out the transaction (e.g. legal costs for the stipulation of contracts). All these costs go under the name of *transaction costs*.

It should be noted that there are two important elements in Coase's analysis, both of which contribute to his conclusion on why the firm grows. First, the transaction costs of operating on the market. Second, the fact that the firm and the production process within it are organized via planning and direction rather than via the price mechanism. It is mainly the first of these two elements that has been followed in the massive literature which span off from Coase's work.[4]

2 Williamson's developments

Coase's article has given rise to a very large amount of literature. The most notable contribution is by Oliver Williamson (1975; 1981) and it owes much to Coase's approach as well as to the works of the economic historian Chandler (1962). Williamson starts from the premise that 'the modern corporation is mainly to be understood as the product of a series of organizational innovations that have had the purpose and effect of economizing on transaction costs' (Williamson, 1981: 1537). He uses economies of transaction costs to analyse the organization of production, the growth of the firm, as well as the evolution of the internal structure of modern corporations and the issue of ownership and control within it.[5] He thus interprets the whole of business history, with its internal and external effects, as driven by the firms' aims of achieving economies of transaction costs.

In fact, Williamson takes Coase's analysis a step further by giving a detailed analysis of the reasons why internalization produces advantages. He introduces the concepts of: (1) *bounded rationality*; (2) *opportunistic behaviour* and (3) *assets specificity*, details of which are in Box 8.1.

Box 8.1   *Williamson's bounded rationality, opportunistic behaviour and assets specificity*

Bounded rationality

People and institutions – including firms – operate under conditions of bounded rationality due to imperfect information about the environment in which they operate. They take rational decisions but these are constrained by the limited information they possess. In other words, the system operates under cognitive imperfections. Bounded rationality is – according to Williamson – more problematic the higher the complexity of the environment. The level and quality of information tend to be higher when the operations are carried out within the firm than when they are externalized.

Opportunistic behaviour

The firm may have to guard against opportunistic behaviour on the part of external parties as well as its own employees and managers. The opportunistic behaviour, that is, the pursuit of self-interest, is possible because of an asymmetry of information between the parties. Opportunistic behaviour is likely to generate more problems when the market consists of many small economic agents operating independently. On the whole, internal transactions give better protection against opportunistic behaviour because the level of information, in this case, is higher.

Assets specificity

Within the firm, the skills developed and the assets acquired through time tend to fit each other and therefore they bear higher returns than when they are used separately or for alternative uses. The utilization of assets for uses different from those they were designed for or in conjunction with different resources is less productive. The assets specificity of resources therefore leads to higher productivity when resources are used internally compared to when they are used by other enterprises.

All these elements lead to higher efficiency in internalization compared with operating on the market. Moreover, the approach based on economies of transaction costs sees the growth of the firm as a positive, efficient process, since it leads to private as well as social economies. This is contrary to the more traditional neoclassical approach, which, by focusing on markets and competition, saw growth of the firm and its large size as having some socially harmful effects because of their market power effects.

There are, therefore, important policy implications from Williamson's approach: if internal growth is the result of economizing and if the economies are not only privately but also socially beneficial, then any antitrust regulation ought to assess the various cases not only in the light of market power, but also in the light of benefits deriving from transaction costs economizing. It could be that any negative social effects due to excessive market power are counterbalanced by positive social effects due to economies of transaction costs. He criticizes the view of the firm that stresses power and neglects the complexities of internal organization and the striving towards efficiency of such organizations.[6]

Both Coase (1960; 1991) and Williamson draw implications for the relationship between the legal framework in which the firm operates and its economics. A good legal framework can protect the firm against opportunistic behaviour as well as reduce the uncertainties of operating on the market. The poorer the legal framework and its enforcement, the stronger the incentive to internalize and avoid market transactions.[7] Trust between the parties as well as a robust legal framework become key to the decision between internal and external transactions. Similarly, the information channels and framework play a role in such a decision; the better the information channels, the lower the degree of uncertainty and the higher the incentive to operate on the market.

It is also interesting to trace the development of the transaction costs theory – and the internalization it leads to – to developments in the real economies. The first writings on the subject emerged *as firms grew larger* and industry concentration increased after the Second World War. Economies of transaction costs and economies of scale production combined to lead to the desirability of large units and of growing internalization.

However, the field was further developed and the literature mushroomed in the 1970s and 1980s when the need to analyse the system further in terms of the internalization/externalization dichotomy arose in response to the *opposite trend in the economic system*. What happened was that the internalization process of earlier decades had produced several problems: from the inflexibility of large-scale production systems to high costs of managing such large units, to the increased power of labour who found it easier to organize when working under the same large ownership and managerial umbrella (Ietto-Gillies, 2002a: chs 3 and 6).[8] Therefore the trend in real economies moved in the direction of externalization and the processes and the language of 'outsourcing' and 'downsizing' became increasingly a matter of everyday occurrence and parlance. The trend in the real economy moved from internalization to externalization; however, the analysis in terms of economies of transaction costs was still considered basic to such a trend.

More recently, Casson (1997) developed a theory of the evolution of institutions (such as firms and networks) based on changes in costs and patterns of information. There are similarities between this theory and Williamson's because most transaction costs are information costs. However, Casson points out that the 'converse does not apply. There are important information costs which are not transaction costs' (ibid.: 279).

3   Internalization and the international firm

The extension of the transaction costs theory from the firm in general to the international firm is due to McManus (1972) and Buckley and Casson (1976), with other major contributors including Teece (1977), Rugman (1981), Caves (1982) and Hennart (1982).

McManus aims to develop a theory of the international firm by identifying 'the conditions under which productive activities in different countries will earn a higher total income if their control is internationally centralized' (McManus, 1972: 72). To do so, he uses the costs of operating market transactions as the key to internalization across frontiers. The existence of transaction costs therefore becomes the key to why the TNC establishes foreign subsidiaries which operate directly under centralized control rather than operate at arm's length, via the market. He writes:

> In summary, we have argued that the international firm is one of the methods by which interdependent activities in different countries can be co-ordinated. There are two equivalent statements of the conditions under which the international firm will be chosen by interdependent producers in different countries: the producers will choose to centralize control if the international firm is the least expensive way in which to obtain a given level of efficiency within the joint activity; the producers will choose to centralize control if the international firm yields the highest level of efficiency for a given cost of co-ordinating their joint activity. In other words, resources will be allocated by fiat between two countries if the sum of the values of resources in two or more interdependent, productive activities is greater than it would be if the activities were conducted autonomously. (Ibid.: 84)

McManus's analysis is developed in more detail by Peter Buckley and Mark Casson (1976) in 'A long-run theory of the multinational enterprise'. They start from the following simple postulates:

1   Firms maximize profit in a world of imperfect markets.
2   When markets in intermediate products are imperfect, there is an incentive to bypass them by creating internal markets. This involves bringing under common ownership and control the activities which are linked by the market.
3   Internalization of markets across national boundaries generates MNEs (ibid.: 33).

The imperfections they refer to are transactional ones. The main groups of factors relevant to the internalization decision are the following:

* industry-specific factors related to the nature of the product and markets; they lead to the internalization of markets for intermediate products and thus to vertical integration;
* region-specific factors;
* nation-specific factors;
* firm-specific factors, which reflect the firm's ability to organize and manage internal markets efficiently.

The two most important areas of internalization are *markets for intermediate products* and *markets for knowledge*.

Before the Second World War the major factor that contributed to the emergence of MNEs was demand for primary products, leading to vertical integration across frontiers and to internalization of intermediate markets. Since WWII the major factor has been the growth in demand for knowledge-based products coupled with the difficulties of organizing efficient external markets for intangibles and knowledge. Buckley and Casson stress the specific character of knowledge within the firm. They write, 'Knowledge is a public good within the firm' (ibid.: 35) and therefore its costs of transmission are low and it can be easily internationalized. The growth of MNEs has also, according to Buckley and Casson, been made easier by the 'steady reduction in communication costs, and the increasing scope for tax reduction through transfer pricing' (ibid.: 36).

Why do firms internalize? What are the limits to internalization? There are benefits of internalization and there are also costs; the balance between the two will determine the limit to internalization. The benefits of internalization stem from *transactional market imperfections* and relate to one or more of the situations illustrated in Box 8.2.

Box 8.2   *Situations leading to benefits of internalization according to Buckley and Casson (1976)*

- When there are long time lags between initiation and completion of the production process and, at the same time, futures markets are non-existent or unsatisfactory

- When the efficient exploitation of market power over an intermediate product requires discriminatory pricing of a kind difficult or impossible to implement in an external market, though possible to implement internally[9]

- When imperfections would lead to bilateral concentration of market power and thus to an unstable situation under external markets

- When there is inequality in the position of the buyer and seller regarding knowledge on the value, nature and quality of the product; the resultant buyer uncertainty may encourage forward integration[10]

- When there are imperfections deriving from government intervention in international markets such as the existence of ad valorem tariffs, restrictions on capital movements, discrepancies in rates of taxation

---

In certain markets the incentive to internalize is particularly strong; this is the case in markets for knowledge. Specifically, the R&D (and the knowledge deriving from it) shows all the above types of imperfections because of its characteristics, as listed in Box 8.3.

Buckley and Casson (ibid.: 51) stress that their R&D concept (and its linkage to knowledge) is very broad and includes marketing-orientated R&D as well as technical R&D.

The costs of internalization may derive from problems related to internal communication and organization. In the case of internalization across national boundaries there may also be costs due to discrimination against foreign producers by the governments of the host countries.

So much for internalization; how does this lead to a theory of the multinational

---

Box 8.3   *Characteristics of R&D and of markets for knowledge*

- Long implementation lags

- Monopoly power over results of R&D

- The likelihood of the prospective purchaser being a monopsonist and thus a sole buyer for the fruits of the R&D

- Difficulty on the part of the buyer in assessing the true value and quality of the 'knowledge' to be acquired

- An ideal situation for transfer prices manipulation since the price of the knowledge being transferred is difficult to assess.

---

enterprise? An MNE implies internalization across national boundaries. Buckley and Casson (ibid.: 45) write on this issue: 'There is a special reason for believing that internalization of the knowledge market will generate a high degree of multinationality among firms. Because knowledge is a public good which is easily transmitted across national boundaries, its exploitation is logically an international operation'. So the conclusions seem to be that imperfect markets generate incentives to internalize; the market for knowledge is highly imperfect, so there are strong benefits in internalizing it. *Knowledge is a public good within the firm*: this means that it can be used in various branches of the firm at little or no extra cost. Knowledge is easily transmittable across national boundaries, so transmission of knowledge will tend to generate internal markets across frontiers and therefore to generate MNEs. Another relevant conclusion of Buckley and Casson's analysis is that the characteristics of MNEs are not attributable to costs and benefits of multinationality per se, but rather to their internalization drive and to the fact that they operate in industries and markets where there are strong incentives to internalize (such as markets for knowledge and for intermediate products).

Buckley and Casson explain the post-WWII pattern of FDI, in particular large cross-investment between developed countries, with reference to the market for knowledge and its internalization. Firms would tend to invest in countries where they can use and exploit their knowledge by adapting it to the countries where there is availability of those labour skills which are necessary for the processing of their knowledge-based products. Essentially, the internalization theory of the MNE is based on the assumption that transaction costs are high in transborder activities. This increases the incentive to internalize such activities by direct production abroad rather than via market transactions or licensing.

Recent works by Buckley and Casson (1998a; 1998b) try to develop a more dynamic agenda in the attempt to explain a variety of internationalization modes and their time sequence. They link the increase in uncertainty in the economic and business environment in the last two decades with the search for flexibility on the part of companies. The latter can be organizational or locational flexibility and may refer to contractual arrangements with other businesses or with labour.

4   Horizontal and vertical integration across borders: Caves' analysis

Richard E. Caves' focus is the analysis of the internationalization of firms according to whether their operations are of the horizontal, vertical or diversified variety. An early article (Caves, 1971) has a strong strategic focus played by two elements:

- the oligopolistic structure of the market;
- the firm's desire to erect entry barriers as a shield against potential rivals.

His later works (Caves, 1982; 1996) deal with the same subject matter, but use transaction costs theory to arrive at conclusions. Thus, his later works rely more on efficiency than on strategic elements in the choice of internationalization mode and they generally fall within the internalization tradition.

He uses a model of multiplant production to explain the MNE and its presence in more than one country,[11] which he categorizes into three groups:

> (1) One type of multiplant firm turns out broadly the same line of goods from its plants in each geographic market. (2) Another type of multiplant enterprise produces outputs in some of its plants that serve as inputs to its other activities . . . (3) The third type of multiplant firm is the diversified company whose plants' output are neither vertically nor horizontally related to one another. (Caves, 1996: 2)

Correspondingly, Caves identifies three types of MNEs: the *horizontally and vertically integrated MNE and the diversified MNE.*

As regards the *horizontally integrated* MNE he writes: 'The transaction-cost approach asserts, quite simply, that horizontal MNEs will exist only if the plants they control and operate attain lower costs or higher revenue productivity than the same plants under separate managements' (ibid.).What are the conditions leading to the lower costs of internal production? Caves looks at the non-production activities within the firm and the complementary characteristics of such activities. These activities have their origin in *proprietary assets*, that is, assets with the following characteristics: they are owned by the firm; they are fairly mobile across space; they are fairly long-lived; and they differ in productivity from similar assets owned by competing firms. The complementarity of the assets and their specificity to the firm mean that, when used within the firm, they are more productive than in an outside environment and thus give a higher return. These are the reasons for internal retention of these assets and their output.[12] The proprietary assets can be tangible or intangible. The latter can be research and knowledge or brand names.

The *vertically integrated* MNE internalizes the market for intermediate products across countries. The trade-off between internal production and contractual arrangements with external firms depends on the transaction costs and on the costs of switching contracts once they are established.

Diversification of production across frontiers is guided by the usual principle of risk aversion. Diversification can take the form of product or location diversification.

In the latter case, production in several countries can reduce risks. The risks can derive from the markets as well as from the behaviour of the macroeconomy and their different trade cycles, or from the behaviour of governments in the host countries. Multinational enterprises operating in many countries attain diversification and cut risks. However, according to Caves, it is not clear that risk aversion is the main reason for their location strategies.

5   Comments

The internalization theory of the multinational enterprise has proved very successful and, indeed, has led to the spread of the 'internalization–externalization' vocabulary. It is, in fact, a very interesting approach developed on the back of the transaction costs bandwagon. Its strongest point is, in my view, the detailed analysis of the organization of the firm and its possible links to the internationalization process.

There are, nonetheless, many drawbacks. Auerbach (1988) criticizes it because the theory assumes that a market always exists and that the managers have a choice between expanding via the market or internally. He argues that in reality some products may not have markets outside the firm.

The basic theory is a theory of the existence and growth of the firm and as such the whole approach can be tautological: internalization is another way of expressing the fact that firms exist and grow, and hence it cannot be taken as an explanation for the growth of the firm. Many of the authors who have either originated or embraced the internalization theory seem aware of the dangers of slipping into tautology. For example, Casson (1982: 24) writes: 'Internalization is in fact a general theory of why firms exist, and without additional assumptions it is almost tautological'. Buckley (1983: 42) expresses similar doubts when he writes: 'At its most general, the concept of internalisation is tautological; firms internalise imperfect markets until the cost of further internalism outweighs the benefits'. Teece (1983: 51) thinks that 'the tautological nature of transaction costs or "internalisation" reasoning can be avoided, and a contingency theory of the MNE developed' by distinguishing between those transactions that can be dealt with at lowest cost by the market and those transactions that can be dealt with at the lowest cost by the MNE. There have been some attempts to operationalize the concept, but problems still remain.

It should be stressed that the internalization theory is not a theory of internationalization in general, but rather a theory of the firm and why and in what circumstances its growth pattern follows the multinational route. However, one problem with it is that the purely multinational elements in this approach seem rather weak (transfer pricing advantages and government regulations of transactions across frontiers). Firms could, after all, internalize and grow at home and source foreign markets by exports: why do they choose to internalize by spreading activities in many countries?

Considerable relevance in the theory is given to R&D and to the fact that MNEs tend to operate in knowledge-based industries. The link between knowledge and multinationality is identified by Buckley and Casson in the fact that knowledge is easily, cheaply and risklessly transmittable internally but not externally. This makes it easy to transmit across frontiers internally but not externally to the firm. However, while this may explain why big firms prefer direct production to licensing in their foreign operations, it does not explain why they do not choose to service foreign markets through exports which would involve them in internalization but within the domestic arena, rather than through direct internal production. The lack of analysis of the full range of options open to large firms (domestic production and exports, international production, licensing) is one of the drawbacks of the theory. It is a problem addressed by John Dunning as we shall see in the next chapter. Buckley and Casson (1998a; 1998b) try also to address it within their own framework.

An alternative approach to the issue of boundaries of the firm with emphasis on the social nature of knowledge, is provided by Kogut and Zander (1993) and we discuss it in Chapter 11 alongside a critique developed by John Cantwell.

Another serious drawback is the authors' failure to analyse multinationality per se; indeed, they seem to deny that there are advantages of multinationality per se or that they play a role in shaping the characteristics of TNCs. This lack of a multi-nationality perspective stems from their strong concentration on internalization, from which it follows that internationalization is seen as a by-product of internalization. This outlook constrains their analysis and prevents them from realizing that the two issues of internalization and internationalization are not always part of the same package. In particular, internationalization cannot be simply viewed as an extension of the internalization process; in some cases it may be a reaction to problems created by internalization (such as enhanced power of labour and trade unions) as we shall discuss in Chapter 14.

The last serious drawback is the lack of analysis of labour and of the relationship between labour and capital. Coase's approach in terms of costs and benefits of internal transactions makes no specific reference to labour other than indirectly through a brief reference to 'variations in the supply price of factors of production to firms of different sizes' (Coase, 1937: 342). Since he was writing in 1937, his oversight may have been justified. However, in considering nowadays the costs and benefits of internalizing, it is not justified to overlook the effects that the firm's expansion has on labour.

The overall internalization approach might be seen close to the neoclassical paradigm in that it is efficiency led[13] and particularly led by the aim of minimizing costs of operating on the market versus costs of operating internally to the firm. Moreover, Cantwell (1989: ch. 9; 2000) points out how the internalization approach is based on exchange rather than production[14] and this, in my view, is another point in common with the standard neoclassical approach.

Both transactional and structural market imperfections are taken as exogenous[15] and there is little effort to consider how the two types are related. The reality of the economic system is different. Structural imperfections are linked to the transactional ones through the following mechanisms: the firm's growth in response to its efforts in economizing transaction costs leads to larger and more powerful firms, and thus to structural market imperfections. At the same time, a large and powerful firm has advantages and achieves economies because it can access and process higher levels of information (Cowling and Sugden, 1987) and it operates with high levels of assets specificity.[16] These elements will increase its tendency towards internalization and thus towards more structural imperfections in a vicious circle.

Nonetheless, this approach is much more realistic than the standard neoclassical analysis often used to evaluate the effects of international production on its own or as an alternative to international trade (Mundell, 1957; Miller, 1968; Bhagwati, 1973; Brecher and Diaz Alejandro, 1977). The standard approach is not only based on efficiency criteria and static profit maximization objectives, but it is often based on unrealistic assumptions[17] of perfect competition and varying degrees of factors or product immobility. The internalization approach has introduced a good deal of realism into the analysis of firms because of its emphasis on the organization of production.

However, the main criticism that can be levelled at the internalization theory – whether applied to the domestic or international arena – emerges from the empirical reality of the last three decades. The theory predicts trends towards further internal-

---

SUMMARY BOX 8

● ●

Review of the internalization theory

Antecedents

Coase (1937); Williamson (1975)

Key writers and works

McManus (1972); Buckley and Casson (1976); Teece (1977); Rugman (1981); Hennart (1982); Caves (1982)

Main elements of the theory

- Transactional market failure lead to growth of the firm
- Analysis of internalization advantages applied to the international context
- Emphasis on the organization of production
- Internalization of intermediate products (pre-WWII) and of knowledge-based products (post-WWII)

Modalities considered

Direct foreign production versus licensing

Level of aggregation

The firm

Linkages with other chapters

Chapters 9 and 11

ization unless the costs of transactions decline (Auerbach, 1988). However, while there is evidence of such a trend in the 1950s to 1970s, the 1980s and early 1990s have seen a considerable amount of growth in externalization (outsourcing, downsizing) at both the domestic and international levels. The internalization theory cannot explain this trend as there does not appear to have been changes in the level of transaction costs.

It should be noted that from the mid-1990s we have been witnessing some reversal of the trend in the mode of organization of production. A growing number of firms are reverting to internal production and vertical integration, thus reducing their outsourcing commitments. These changes through time may be difficult to explain by the internalization theory. In Chapter 14 a different approach will be used to explain these dynamic elements in the real world; an approach which is strategic and based mainly on possible strategies towards labour on the part of TNCs.

In conclusion I feel that the internalization theory is not fully successful in explaining international production, partly because the 'efficiency' approach has put it in a straitjacket. This comment applies also to Kogut and Zander's approach to the boundaries of the firm (Chapter 11). Decisions about international production, whether related to the location or to the type of involvement, are strategic decisions; although efficiency elements may play a role, the strategic ones are likely to be the more relevant ones. However, the internalization approach has proved useful in giving a theoretical framework for highlighting the strong role that organizational issues play in firms' decisions, including decisions on their international activities.

Indicative further reading

Buckley, P.J. and Casson, M.C. (1999), 'A theory of international operation', in P.J. Buckley and P.N. Ghauri (eds), *The Internationalization of the Firm: A Reader*, London: ITBP, ch. 5, pp. 55–60.

Buckley, P. and Casson M.C. (2001), 'Strategic complexity in international business', in A.M. Rugman and T.L. Brewer (eds), *The Oxford Handbook of International Business*, ch. 4, pp. 88–126.

Cantwell, J. (2000), 'A survey of theories of international production', in C.N. Pitelis and R. Sugden (eds), *The Nature of the Transnational Firm*, London: Routledge, ch. 2, pp. 10–56.

Hennart, J.-F. (2000), 'Transaction costs theory and the multinational enterprise', in C.N. Pitelis and R. Sugden (eds), *The Nature of the Transnational Firm*, London: Routledge, ch. 4, pp. 72–118.

Hennart, J.-F. (2001), 'Theories of the multinational enterprise', in A.M. Rugman and T.L. Brewer (eds), *The Oxford Handbook of International Business*, Oxford: Oxford University Press, ch. 5, pp. 127–49.

Notes

1 The organization of industry had, of course, been the subject of much analysis by Marshall (1920).
2 There is a large literature on Coase and transaction costs; see in particular Pitelis (1993).
3 Essentially, economists consider markets to be structurally imperfect when they do not conform to the model of perfect competition.
4 Cowling and Sugden (1998a) take up the second element, as we shall see in Chapter 13, section 2.
5 Williamson's evolutionary approach has proved useful in applications to business history cases such as the one in Cox (2000).
6 See also Pitelis (1993).
7 See also Hennart (2000).
8 More on this in Chapter 14.
9 The authors write on this point: 'For example, in the absence of discrimination a monopoly of a factor input may be exploited only by charging a uniformly high price which encourages substitution against the input. A discriminatory tariff based on the derived demand curve for the factor would more or less maintain the average price of the factor while removing entirely the incentive to substitute against it. It would therefore increase the monopolist's profit without reducing that of his customers. It follows that when discriminatory pricing in an external market is impracticable, internalization of the market through merger of the firms concerned will potentially increase their combined profits by facilitating discriminatory pricing' (Buckley and Casson, 1976: 37–8).
10 The issue of buyer uncertainty over quality – as an incentive for backward integration – is further explained in Casson (1982: 34–5). On the risks for the sellers of the debasement of quality for a branded good or service by the distributor see also Williamson (1981: 1549–50).
11 A similar assumption is made in the 'new trade theories' models (see Chapter 12).
12 This analysis of proprietary assets is very close to similar concepts introduced by McManus and also by Williamson.
13 Acocella (1992) also criticizes the internalization theory because it is efficiency led; he calls for a more strategic approach.
14 Further criticisms by Cantwell are in Chapter 11.
15 The relationship between efficiency of internalization and endogenous or exogenous market imperfections is explained in more detail by Yamin and Nixson (1988). It should be noted that Buckley (1983: 45) accepts that: 'It is a valid criticism of the internalization rubric that market imperfections are taken as exogenous to the (internalizing) firm'.
16 Casson (1997) does consider the information economies of large firms.
17 On the methodological controversy regarding the realism of assumptions, see note 3 in Chapter 3.

9 Dunning's eclectic framework

I The theory

John Dunning worked on international production issues since the 1950s and until his death in 2009. His early research was on the factors leading to the high productivity of US investments in British manufacturing. In 1977 he published a paper on a 'systemic' theory – whose origin he traces to his earlier work (Dunning, 2000b) – designed to explain internationalization modes and processes. In his paper he begins by analysing the nature of a country's economic involvement with other countries and considers *two types of involvement*:

- The first is related to those economic activities that take place within the national boundaries – and thus use national resources – but concern goods and services directed towards foreign markets.
- The second type of involvement is related to the activities of national economic agents that use resources located in a variety of foreign countries to produce, locally, goods and services, in order to supply directly foreign markets.

The first type of involvement falls within the domain of conventional international trade theory; the second within the domain of international production and foreign direct investment.

Therefore, while the internalization theory (cf. Chapter 8) deals with the firm and why it becomes multinational, Dunning's preoccupation is with international production and trade and their determinants at both the micro and macro levels.

Dunning's first perceptive insight is in realizing that these two activities must be seen as part of the same process and that any realistic theory of international economic involvement must attempt to explain them both. In terms of a company's strategy one has to explain *why* and *when* it decides to produce abroad directly – rather than to export domestically produced output or to license – and *where* the FDI is likely to be directed.

Dunning's approach to internationalization consists of an attempt to analyse the *why*, *where* and *when/how*[1] decisions in terms of *ownership, locational* and *internalization* (OLI) advantages. The meanings of these three sets of advantages are presented in Box 9.1.

In some cases a country will have a locational advantage, which will favour domestic production by firms based in the same country or by foreign firms. In other cases, its own enterprises will have special ownership advantages, which will favour them in producing in other countries: 'Foreign production then, implies that location-specific endowments favour a foreign country, but ownership endowments favour the

---

Box 9.1   *Dunning's OLI advantages*

- *Ownership advantages* are those that are *specific to a particular enterprise*. They constitute competitive advantages towards rivals and enable the company to take advantage of investment opportunities wherever they arise.

- *Locational advantages* are those advantages *specific to a country* which are likely to make it attractive for foreign investors.

- *Internalization advantages* are all those benefits that derive from producing internally to the firm; they allow it to bypass external markets and the transaction costs associated with them. They are, essentially, benefits of operating within *hierarchies rather than markets* (as we saw in Chapter 8).

---

home country's firms; these latter being sufficient to overcome the costs of producing in a foreign environment' (Dunning, 1977: 399). Dunning (1980) identifies three types/groups of *ownership advantages* as highlighted in Box 9.2.

One question related to the third type is the following: 'given the ownership endowments, is the location of production by multinational enterprises (MNEs) likely to be different from that of non MNEs?' (Dunning, 1977: 409). The answer is affirmative because the MNE is in a better position to exploit fully the advantages of internalization in many countries. The same question is asked by Vernon (1974), who arrives at similar conclusions as was highlighted in Chapter 5.

Transactional market failure of the type we saw in Chapter 8 generates *internalization incentives advantages*. Public intervention may increase market imperfections and is therefore likely to lead to further internalization. Lack of common policies among countries and, generally, lack of harmonization creates incentives for internalization across frontiers (to take advantage of differential tax rates or expected movements in exchange rates). Dunning points out the interrelationship between ownership and internalization advantages by noting that internalization helps enterprises to acquire or increase those assets that give them an ownership advantage.

Location-specific advantages are all those advantages linked to the geographical and political space such as: quality of transportation and communication; legal and commercial infrastructure; government policies; quality and price of inputs (Dunning, 1980: 276, Table 2).

Dunning (1980) develops a detailed dynamic analysis of the effects of a country's *characteristics* on the ownership advantages of firms, on the tendency towards (and benefits deriving from) internalization and on the development of locational advantages.

A country's overall competitive situation depends not only on its locational advantages and on the ownership advantages of its enterprises, but also on 'the desire and ability of these enterprises to internalise the advantages resulting from this possession' (Dunning, 1977: 402). Moreover, countries' characteristics affect the ownership advantages of firms originating in them.

Box 9.2   *Dunning's three types of ownership advantages*

1 The first type comprises standard advantages which any firm can have over another producing in the same location; they are independent of whether the firm is multinational or not. They include benefits related to the following:

- special access to inputs or/and markets;

- established market position;

- superior technical and/or organizational knowledge;

- size;

- monopoly position.

2 The second type of ownership advantages, which a branch of a national enterprise may have over a *new* enterprise, relates to all those economies and benefits deriving from belonging to a larger pre-existing organization. They include benefits of:

- access to cheaper inputs;

- knowledge of markets and local production conditions;

- access to innovation and technology available at zero or low marginal costs (if they have already been developed by other branches of the company).

3 The third type of ownership advantages is that deriving from the *multinationality* of the enterprise; this means that a company with a history of international operations is in a better position than a firm with experience at the national level only, to take advantage of different factors endowment and market situations.

In his 1980 article, Dunning identifies three conditions for FDI to take place, as illustrated in Box 9.3.

The essence of Dunning's approach is the contemporaneous analysis of advantages of ownership, location and internalization and its application to both inter-

---

Box 9.3   *Conditions under which FDI takes place*

1 The enterprise concerned must possess 'net ownership advantages *vis-à-vis* firms of other nationalities in serving particular markets' (Dunning, 1980: 275).

2 The enterprise must have benefits from internalizing the use of resources in which it has an advantage rather than selling them on external markets, e.g. via licensing.

3 The country where the FDI takes place must offer special locational advantages to be used in conjunction with those deriving from *ownership* and *internalization*.

national trade and production as well as to the organization of production. This means that he is able to analyse the three main internationalization modes (trade, international production and licensing) within the same framework.

In his original paper Dunning calls his theory *systemic* because 'it relates to the way in which the enterprise coordinates its activities' (Dunning, 1977: 406). The approach is also seen by himself and others as *eclectic* because it combines various strands and features of internationalization theory.

2   Dunning's later developments

It is impossible to review – and do justice to – all or most of the published work of such a prolific writer and thinker as John Dunning. Nonetheless, this section will attempt to touch on some of the major developments in his own writing which relate to the original eclectic approach of 1977. Most of these developments can be seen as refinements of the original approach in response to either changes in the economic and business world or/and criticisms by other researchers.

There are four major directions of such developments:

*   operationalization;
*   dynamization of the original framework;
*   international production and countries' development patterns;
*   incorporations into the framework of new and growing organizational forms such as mergers and acquisitions and inter-firm collaborative agreements.

Operationalization

The original eclectic approach (Dunning, 1977; 1980) is far too wide to be useful in practice. In his 1980 article Dunning lists at least 20 possible ownership advantages, at least 11 internalization incentives advantages and at least 16 location-specific advantages; in each case the list can increase when subcategories are considered. There is a danger of slipping into a 'shopping list of variables' (Dunning, 2000b) for each of the three sets of advantages (OLI). Dunning himself is aware of this problem and of the difficulties it poses for the explanatory and predictive power of his approach. In fact, in later works, he prefers to abandon the term 'theory' with regard to his approach and uses instead expressions such as 'paradigm' or 'systemic framework'. The latter term implies that his approach is a broad framework on which various theories can be fitted and tested. This begs the question of how to make the framework operational and derive testable theories from it.

He suggests that *the key to operationalization* is *contextualization of the variables* linked to the three sets of advantages (Dunning, 2000a). The contextualization of the ownership advantages can be done by reference to the kind of MNE activity and FDI that economists are confronted with in the specific context of their research. Dunning (1993a; 2000a) distinguishes FDI according to whether it is:

- resource seeking;
- market seeking;
- efficiency seeking;
- assets seeking.

A preliminary analysis of the specific type of FDI will help to select appropriate variables within the ownership variables group. The choice of location-specific variables should be done via a preliminary analysis of the prevailing conditions in the host country. Similarly the choice of internalization variables should emerge from the specific conditions of the industry and the company, including the type of technology used.

Dynamization

The second development is in terms of dynamics of the framework. This requires the consideration of time and change within the framework. Moreover, it requires an analysis of the relationship between exogenous and endogenous variables, and how their character may change through time; specifically, how the three sets of variables (OLI) affect each other through time and whether they should be treated as endogenous or exogenous. Variables that are considered exogenous in the short run, may become endogenous in the long run. Quite a task, which Dunning (1993b: ch. 3) begins to tackle.

Countries' development path

The injection of dynamics into the framework leads also to the analysis of how FDI induces changes in the overall economic system and how, in turn, the FDI levels and patterns are affected by such changes. Thus, the obvious step for Dunning is to consider the relationship between the *development path* of countries and their position in terms of inward and outward FDI. The pattern of FDI is affected by the stage of development of the country. Conversely, the country's pattern and speed of development is partly related to the inward FDI it can attract and partly to the strength of its multinational companies as witnessed by the amount and pattern of its outward FDI (Dunning, 1981: ch. 5; Dunning and Narula, 1996).[2]

Alliances and M&As

Dunning's desire to keep his framework in touch with the real world, naturally, led him to take on board major changes in the pattern of MNEs' activities that have taken place in the last 30 years of his life. Among these there are two very striking changes: the increase in the penetration mode via *mergers and acquisitions* and the growth in the number and range of *inter-firm partnerships* (Ietto-Gillies, 2002a: ch. 2). How can these two major changes in the penetration modes of MNEs be fitted into the eclectic framework? Dunning seems to see no problems with either.

Acquisitions should be seen – according to Dunning – as just a way to quick internalization of assets held by other companies. As regards inter-firm collaborative agreements, Dunning prefers to concentrate mainly on a specific type: alliances between more or less equal partners. His conclusion is that alliances are alternative ways of internalization or of bypassing the market in order to reduce transaction costs. They are another mode of internalization complementary to, rather than a substitute for, hierarchies. 'The choice between a hierarchical and alliance modality as a means of lessening arm's length market failure clearly depends on their respective costs and benefits' (Dunning, 1997: 74). He sees the advent of *alliance capitalism* as a development from *hierarchical capitalism* and one which offers a plurality of modes along the same internalization route. 'In other words, interfirm agreements may provide additional avenues for circumventing or lessening market failure where the FDI route is an impractical option' (ibid.: 85). He also considers the effects that alliances have on both ownership and location advantages (ibid.: ch. 3).

3   Comments

Dunning's approach to the study of international activities undoubtedly has many strong points which have made it very successful indeed. Any conference on international business is likely to have a number of papers using Dunning's framework. It has certainly been very successful in introducing the taxonomy of OLI advantages.

The strongest point, in my view, is the fact that his approach highlights how internationalization issues and modes are all interlinked. This means that issues specific to companies and their competitive advantages must be seen in conjunction with issues related to local conditions and to issues of markets and industrial organization.

The problem with standard trade theory is that it is developed only from a macro point of view as if there were no firms/organizations producing and exchanging behind the products being exported and imported. Similarly, theories that concentrate only on the firm – such as the internalization theory – cannot capture the richness and interlocking of internationalization activities.

However, the development of such a comprehensive framework comes with a high cost for Dunning's approach. This cost is in terms of the explanatory and predictive power of the framework. The main problems are caused by the fact that the number of elements and variables emerging from the three OLI classes of advantages are very large and susceptible to endless additions. The framework is not a theory and can, at worst, be seen as no more than a taxonomic system. Dunning himself acknowledges the problem when he writes: 'In presenting the systemic theory, we accept we are in danger of being accused of eclectic taxonomy' (Dunning, 1977: 406). The danger is certainly there: in a nutshell, the approach is helpful as a descriptive and classificatory device but much less so as an explanatory theory.

Any ex-post study of FDI is bound to find that it fits with at least some of the above characteristics; this means that the eclectic approach can always be applied without fear of falsification. However, in terms of scientific methodology, this point, rather than constituting a strength, may be a major weakness.[3] Popper (1963) writes with reference to theories that 'appeared to be able to explain practically everything that happened within the field to which they referred' (ibid.: 34): 'It was precisely this fact – that they always fitted, that they were always confirmed – which in the eyes of their admirers constituted the strongest argument in favour of these theories. It began to dawn on me that this apparent strength was in fact their weakness' (ibid.: 35).[4]

Dunning faces this criticism head on (2000a), and accepts it to some degree. He claims that his is a systemic framework or a paradigm from which specific testable theories can be developed to make it operational. He writes: 'The eclectic paradigm is more to be regarded as a framework for analyzing the determinants of international production than as a predictive theory of the multinational firm' (Dunning, 2000b: 126). The way to arrive at specific theories from the framework is on the basis of contextualization as we saw in section 2.

However, doubts remain in this writer's mind, because the contextualization is never likely to be clear-cut. There is a danger that the framework can be used as an umbrella to justify any ad hoc theory. In a nutshell, we are in danger of ending up with a list of theories in order to overcome the problems of a 'shopping list of variables'. Moreover, if the framework is not a theory and theories have to be developed and stuck onto the approach, one wonders what the ultimate use of the framework is.

There are other problems. One would have expected Dunning's analysis of ownership advantages – which can be self-reinforcing as the company acquires increasing multinational power – to have led to analysis and behaviour linked to market power. We would have expected this element to play a bigger role in Dunning's approach, as indeed it did in Hymer's dissertation. Yet it does not. For all his analysis of ownership advantages and in spite of his criticisms of the internaliz- ation theory (Dunning, 2000b), Dunning's framework gives the main weight, in the choice of internationalization mode, to internalization and to the efficiency of hier- archies versus markets. The stress is on transactional rather than structural market fail- ure. Dunning, as much as the advocates of the internalization theory, falls into the trap of over-reliance on exchange rather than production issues and relations; this means that the criticism raised by Cantwell (1989; 2000), and mentioned in Chapter 8, applies to his approach as well.

The partial neglect of structural market failure and the overemphasis on inter- nalization advantages lead Dunning to see the choices in terms of cost economizing and efficiency rather than of strategic elements, and this is very clear in his analysis of 'alliance capitalism'. This becomes the weakest point in his thinking on this specific issue.

Though some lip-service is paid to the possible impact of acquisitions or alliances on market power, in the last analysis these modalities are seen as the result of the firm's desire to economize on market transaction costs. Indeed, Dunning does not see any big break or change with the pattern of firms' organization and inter- nationalization of the previous decades. This is the more surprising as he seems keen to introduce dynamism into his paradigm.

Dunning's analysis implies that hierarchies have continued to grow in the last few decades and that, moreover, the last two decades have seen further internalization of a specific type via alliances. The two internalization modes (FDI and alliances) are seen as complementary rather than substitutes and Dunning talks of a plurality of internalization modes.

However, in the real world we have seen a different pattern with a variety of forms of inter-firm collaborative agreements, from alliances to subcontracting to licensing and franchising, as we discussed in Chapter 1.[5] This pattern can be better understood if we look at the emergence and growth of inter-firm collaborative agreements in terms of a break in the forms of organization of production rather than a continuum of more or less the same form through the last 60 years. After the Second World War we had three decades of internalization and of growth of hierarchies, but the late 1970s witnessed the beginning of a break and the reversal of this pattern.

From the 1980s onwards we saw a trend towards disintegration of hierarchies and organizational fragmentation: firms downsized, outsourced and generally relied on more external – sometimes long-lasting – collaborative agreements. These are not just alliances between equal partners linked to research and technology activities. Mostly they are in the field of production and relate to a variety of contractual arrangements (including subcontracting) for the production and supply of components. It is not just that alliances are being formed where market relations previously existed, i.e. alliances replacing markets. In many cases we have seen the emergency of looser and more externalized organizational structures replacing hierarchies. The parlance and reality of the 1980s and – to a lesser extent – since has been of 'downsizing' and 'outsourcing', not of more and more internalization. Though some alliances are being formed where market relations existed, on the whole it is hierarchies that are being replaced by a variety of inter-firm contractual agreements. Why? These patterns cannot be explained via efficiency elements. We must look into strategic elements, where strategies can be directed towards rivals or labour or governments. This will be done in Chapter 14.

Indicative further reading

Cantwell, J. (2000), 'A survey of theories of international production', in C.N. Pitelis and R. Sugden (eds), *The Nature of the Transnational Firm*, London: Routledge, ch. 2, pp. 10–56.

Cantwell, J. and Narula, R. (2001), 'The eclectic paradigm in the global economy', *International Journal of the Economics of Business*, **8** (2), 155–72.

Dunning, J.H. (1999), 'Trade, location of economic activity and the multinational enterprise: a search for an eclectic approach', in P.J. Buckley and P.N. Ghauri (eds), *The Internationalization of the Firm: A Reader*, London: ITBP, ch. 6, pp. 61–79.

Dunning, J.H. (2000b), 'The eclectic paradigm of international production: a personal perspective', in C.N. Pitelis and R. Sugden (eds), *The Nature of the Transnational Firm*, London: Routledge, ch. 5, pp. 119–39.

SUMMARY BOX 9

Review of the eclectic paradigm

Antecedents

Hymer (1960, publ. 1976) for 'ownership advantages'

Coase (1937) and Buckley and Casson (1976) for 'internalization advantages'

Trade theory for 'locational advantages' [for an introductory summary see Grimwade (2000: 29–69)]

Key writer and works

John Dunning (1977; 1980; 1997 and 2000a)

Main elements of the approach

* *Ownership advantages* explain which firms are in the best position to take up investment opportunities.
* *Locational advantages* explain which country is in the favourite position for attracting investment.
* *Internalization advantages* explain why and when direct production is preferred to other modalities such as franchising or licensing.

The approach was later reconsidered to take account of the following:

* operationalization, via contextualization of the variables linked to the three sets of advantages;
* dynamic elements;
* interaction between international production and countries' development path;
* growth in mergers and acquisitions and in alliances.

Modalities considered

All modalities: exports; FDI and licensing/franchising as well as alliances

Level of aggregation

Firms, macro and – to a lesser extent – industries

Other relevant chapters

Chapter 4 (Hymer's theory)

Chapter 8 (internalization)

Chapter 11

Chapter 14

Notes

1 The 'when' refers to the situation in which direct production would be the preferred modality. This point is sometimes referred to as '*how*', meaning which internationalization mode might be used.
2 As noted in Chapter 7, there are analogies between this work and Aliber's (1993) approach.
3 Bukharin (1917) makes a similar methodological point in discussing a rival theory of imperialism. He writes that the theory 'is untrue because it "explains" everything, i.e. it explains absolutely nothing' (ibid.: 112).
4 A discussion of methodological issues in the special case of theories that have a large number of adjustable parameters is in Gillies (1989). The case discussed has many similarities with the eclectic theory.
5 For an analysis of the issues around inter-firm collaborative agreements cf. Dicken (2003: 238–73) and Ietto-Gillies (2002a: 39–62).

10 Stages in the internationalization process: the Scandinavian School

I Introduction

Many of the theories we considered in the previous chapters deal to a greater or lesser degree with the issues of alternative internationalization modes. Hymer touches on licensing as well as dealing extensively with FDI; Vernon considers the sequence exports and direct production; Aliber considers choices between all three modalities; the internalization theory is about the alternative between direct international production versus outsourcing through licensing. Dunning's eclectic approach incorporates the possibilities of all the three main modes: exports, direct production abroad and licensing.

However, these approaches consider the alternatives in a *static* framework in which the choice is either one or the other mode. The only exception is Vernon who analyses the penetration of foreign markets in terms of a *dynamic* sequence in which the producer who wants to meet demand abroad, first exports the new products and later starts direct production in the foreign country.[1]

A group of Swedish economics and management academics probed further into the dynamics of internationalization in their analysis of the process leading from domestic-only production and sales to foreign sales (Johanson and Wiedersheim-Paul, 1975; Johanson and Vahlne, 1977; 1990). Their approach draws on Penrose ([1959] 2009); Cyert and March (1963) and Aharoni (1966), and it looks into the black box of the firm in order to analyse its decision-making process in a specific field: sales in foreign markets.

The authors study the organization of sales and marketing in one or more foreign countries and come up with the idea of *stages in the internationalization process*. What emerges is a dynamic model involving a time sequence that develops in a logical and linear pattern, and in which elements in one stage form the input for the next stage.

2 The model and its background

The work of the Scandinavian School starts with empirical research into the internationalization process of Swedish manufacturing firms (Johanson and Wiedersheim-Paul, 1975). The authors study in detail the following four firms: Sandwik AB, a steel and steel products manufacturer; Atlas Copco, a producer of railway materials and components; Facit, originally a producer of calculating and typing machines who later, in 1972, merged with Electrolux; and Volvo, the car manufacturer.

The authors aim to analyse the stages through which internationalization takes place in any one country as well as the sequence of penetration into different countries.

In a later work, Johanson and Vahlne (1990) specify that the model they developed in 1977 – partly on the basis of the empirical work in Johanson and Wiedersheim-Paul (1975) – can explain *two patterns in the internationalization* of the firm:

* the firm's engagement in a specific foreign market/country, which develops according to an *establishment chain*; and
* the involvement into several foreign countries, which proceeds in a time sequence related linearly to the psychic distance from the home country.

The psychic distance is defined in Johanson and Vahlne as 'the sum of factors preventing the flow of information from and to the market. Examples are differences in language, education, business practices, culture and industrial development'[2] (1977: 24). The countries psychically closer to the domestic market see international involvement earlier than the more distant countries. Psychic and spatial distance tend to be very closely related. In the case of the Swedish firms, the countries which are spatially close tend also to be countries which are culturally and linguistically close to Sweden; they are the ones in which the firm looks for foreign markets first. International involvement into countries which are more distant – psychically and, usually, also spatially – comes later (Johanson and Wiedersheim-Paul, 1975).

Johanson and Vahlne (1977) concentrate on the *first pattern: increasing involvement in the same foreign country*. On the basis of previous empirical work, they see that the establishment of various modes of market involvement into a foreign country follows a specific linear chain (*'the establishment chain'*) along the following sequence: exports via independent representatives (agents); sales subsidiary; and, finally, production subsidiary.

The task the authors set themselves is to explain why and how this sequence evolves. To this end they develop a model of internationalization in which the various steps are explained. Theirs is a dynamic model in which 'the outcome of one decision – or more generally one cycle of events – constitutes the input of the next' (ibid.: 26).

In their model they distinguish between variables related to *state* and those related to *change aspects* of internationalization: the present state of internationalization affects the change in internationalization and therefore the future state aspects. They identify and analyse two *state aspects* and two *change aspects* as in Box 10.1.

Essentially the *state* aspects refer to elements of the situation *as it is* at the time of the analysis and as the result of investment made and resources committed in the past in that foreign market. It could, for example, also include the resources committed to the training of local labour force or for the deployment of managers and technical staff from other units of the company.

Aspects related to *change* have to do with results and decisions that extend through time such as the current performance of past investment or the decisions already taken to commit resources in the near future.

As regards the *state aspects*, the amount of resources committed is close to the size of the investment widely interpreted to also include 'investment in marketing, organization, personnel and other areas' (ibid.: 27).

The *degree of commitment* is influenced by the amount of resources already

---

Box 10.1   *State aspects and change aspects*

State aspects

1   *Resource commitment* to the foreign market

2   *Knowledge* about foreign markets and operations

Change aspects

1   *Performance* of current/present business activities

2   *Decisions to commit resources*

The first state aspect – *resource commitment to market* **– is composed of two elements:**

*   *amount of resources* already committed in the foreign market;

*   *degree of commitment.*

---

committed. However, it also depends on other factors such as: the degree of integration of the resources to other parts of the firm, thus, for example, vertical integration leads to a higher degree of commitment; and the level of specialization of the resources to a specific market. The ease with which resources can be deployed to other markets affects the degree of commitment: the more difficult the redeployment of resources, the higher the degree of commitment.

The second state aspect refers to *market knowledge*. The authors here follow Penrose ([1959] 2009)[3] in her distinction between 'objective knowledge' and 'experiential knowledge'. The former can be taught and thus can be easily transmittable. The latter can only be learned through experience in a particular environment and therefore cannot be taught. This makes its transmission from person to person and organization to organization difficult. Moreover, the authors believe 'that the less structured and well defined the activities and the required knowledge are, the more important is experiential knowledge' (Johanson and Vahlne, 1977: 28). Knowledge related to social activities such as those involving management and marketing is one such type of knowledge.

An important corollary of this distinction is the fact that experiential knowledge is at the basis of perception and formulation of opportunities. The authors write: 'On the basis of objective market knowledge it is possible to formulate only theoretical opportunities; experiential knowledge makes it possible to perceive "concrete" opportunities – to have a "feeling" about how they fit into the present and future activities' (ibid.).[4] In terms of marketing type of knowledge, they distinguish between *general knowledge* and *market-specific knowledge*. The former refers to any marketing methods and customers' characteristics, irrespective of their geographical location. The latter is 'knowledge about characteristics of the specific national market – its business climate, cultural patterns, structure of the market system, and, most importantly, characteristics of the individual customer firms and their personnel' (ibid.). Both general and market-specific knowledge are necessary for the establishment and performance of business activities in foreign countries.

Knowledge is seen as a resource and, therefore, the better the knowledge about a market, the higher the value of the overall resources committed, therefore the stronger is the commitment to that market. 'This is especially true of experiential knowledge, which is usually associated with particular conditions on the market in question and thus cannot be transferred to other individuals or other markets' (ibid.).

As regards the *change aspects*, the following points emerge from the analysis. The consequences of current activities are felt with a time lag: the longer the lag the stronger the degree of commitment.[5] Moreover, current activities are the prime source of experience and thus of knowledge about the firm and its market.

Both firm and market experience are needed for foreign operations and this restricts the range of people or organizations that can be used to engage in foreign operations. This is why someone who has acted as an agent for the firm may be a preferred manager for leading a subsidiary. Similarly, the acquisition of a whole or part of a local sales firm may be seen as a good strategy for enhancing marketing activities in a foreign country.

Commitment decisions are made in response to perceived problems and opportunities. Problems are usually discovered by those people who are part of the organization and are working in the market. Opportunities are perceived mainly by those working on the market. In either case – whether led by problems or opportunities – the commitment decision is related to operations currently performed on the market. However, it is recognized that opportunities can also be spotted by people in organizations that the firm is collaborating with. The same people may also be in a position to propose alternatives.[6]

The authors distinguish between *economic and uncertainty effects of additional commitment*. The economic effect is associated with the scale of operations on the market. The uncertainty effect relates to market uncertainty which tends to be high in very dynamic markets and also whenever there is a threat from new or potential new entrants into the market.[7] The level of uncertainty can be reduced by developing greater interaction and integration with the market such as better communications with customers. Reduced uncertainty or increase in the level of acceptable risk is likely to lead to an increase in the scale of commitment.

The authors conclude the discussion on 'commitment decisions' 'by observing that additional commitments will be made in small steps unless the firm has very large resources and/or market conditions are stable and homogeneous, or the firm has much experience from other markets with similar conditions' (Johanson and Vahlne, 1977: 30–31). Therefore the conclusion is that involvement in any single foreign country will proceed cautiously and in accordance with the following stages in the establishment chain:

- exports via agents;
- setting up of sales subsidiaries;
- setting up of production subsidiaries.

The above sequence is the result of state and change aspects in which the nature of knowledge and uncertainty play a large role. The dynamic sequence is linear in two ways: because each stage leads to the next one and because each new stage involves a larger commitment of resources than the previous stage.

The *second internationalization pattern* refers to the spread of internationalization *from one foreign country to others*. Here the sequence is also dynamic and linear proceeding by stages from the foreign country(ies) psychically closer to those more distant. Psychic and spatial distances tend to be strongly related.

In both types of patterns – within a single foreign country and across many – we see internationalization as a result of a *series of incremental decisions*. It proceeds dynamically and linearly: from one stage to the next; from small to large resource commitment; from a single foreign country to several (Box 10.2).

Box 10.2   *Stages in the internationalization approach*

First pattern of internationalization: increasing involvement into the same country

Second pattern: spread of internationalization from one foreign country to others

Elements common to the two patterns

• Incremental decisions

• Dynamic and linear sequences: from small to large commitment of resources; from one stage to the next; from one foreign country to several

Variables related to *state* and *change aspects* of internationalization

State aspects

1 Commitment of resources to foreign markets; two elements:

  • amount of resources already committed

  • degree of commitment

2 Knowledge about the foreign markets; relevance of experiential knowledge:

  • general knowledge related to marketing

  • market-specific knowledge

Change aspects

1 Performance of current business activities

2 Decisions to commit resources in response to problems and opportunities; economic and uncertainty effects of additional commitments

3   Comments

The Scandinavian School starts with the observation of empirical regularities and then goes on to develop a general model to explain internationalization patterns and their regularities. The authors put forward the idea that internationalization develops in stages, which are of the following two types:

1   Stages in the *establishment chain*: a dynamic and linear sequence leads from exports via agents to sales subsidiaries and later to production subsidiaries. A related linear pattern can also be detected in terms of amount of resources committed at each stage in the establishment chain with more advanced stages in the internationalization process requiring larger commitment of resources.
2   Stages in the geographical spread of internationalization from one country to many: this follows a linear pattern related to psychic distance between the home and foreign countries.

The model explains various stages in the internationalization process via an analysis of *states* and *change aspects* of internationalization. The nature of knowledge and in particular experiential knowledge and its environment-specific character, play a strong role in the development of the various stages. So does uncertainty.

The strength of the model is the realization that internationalization is not an either/or situation with regard to mode of operations or number of foreign countries of involvement. Rather it is a *dynamic sequence* with each stage affecting the change and thus the next stage: the performance variables in each stage become inputs for the next. It is also a cautious *incremental approach* to internationalization in which the firm tests the internationalization water before walking in and later dipping in. The commitment is gradual and the sequences are linear. This gradual stages approach is strongly linked to uncertainty and to the relevance of non-transmittable experiential knowledge.

The model leads the authors to probe into the organization/institution and its decision-making process. In this respect it follows other organizational types of studies though the authors confine themselves to the study of the organization's marketing and sales functions. There is very little on production, its organization, its problems and how opportunities might arise or strategies be formulated in relation to the production elements such as costs or innovation and technology, or availability of labour skills.

The stress on marketing and on linear stages of foreign involvement brings the model close to Vernon's international product life cycle. However, there the analogies end. Unlike Vernon's model, the present one has nothing on innovation or interaction with rival firms or interaction between developed and developing countries. It has a strong realistic role for uncertainty, as in Knickerbocker's model (as highlighted in Chapter 6). However, the latter author's role of oligopolistic rivalries in defining the nature of uncertainty and the direction of strategies is absent.

There is a rather deterministic feel about the Scandinavian School model; the various stages follow a linear, almost predetermined, pattern. Though the model is not driven by efficiency considerations, the scope for strategic decisions seems limited in its well-defined linear patterns.

Johanson and Vahlne (1990) mention some of the main criticisms levelled at their model. They range from: the applicability of the model only to early stages of internationalization or only to firms originating in small industrialized countries such as Sweden; or only applicable to the manufacturing sector. They claim that various studies conclude that the model has more general validity in terms of the type of country from which internationalizing companies can originate.

A more challenging criticism derives from the so-called 'born global' companies: those that do not go through stages of internationalization but operate in many countries from the very beginning (Oviatt and McDougall, 1994; Knight and Cavusgil, 1996). This is partly due to the new technological and knowledge environments. The wider use of new technologies and the wider and deeper knowledge of foreign locations enable the 'born global' phenomenon.

Vernon (1979) also criticizes his own earlier model – as we saw in Chapter 5 – on the basis of changes in the environment identified in terms of changes towards a higher degree of internationalization as well as a new macroenvironment. The degree of internationalization may also be a crucial one in the applicability of the Scandinavian model. Deeper knowledge of the international environment may lead to some 'born global' firms. Moreover, in terms of the individual firm, learning from the international environment may affect the sequence and speed in the establishment chain as well as the pattern of internationalization into many countries. There may, in fact, be external benefits of internationalization.[8]

The authors do not seem to pay much attention to these elements or, in general, to the relationship between the firm and its external environment other than the part constituted by the market and the customers. There is not much on rivals or the industry, and how they learn from each other, or on the role of government agencies in the learning process. Essentially, there is not much on the meso and macro environments.

Moreover, the fact that the model is entirely driven by market and marketing considerations constitutes a major problem. Much international production seems to be driven by constraints and opportunities on the production side, be those related to costs or technological innovation. It is also driven by strategic behaviour towards rivals or labour or other actors in the economic system. Would the Scandinavian School model and its stages be different if we, realistically, include elements on the production side? And if so how? These are questions worth exploring.

Meanwhile we should stress the relevance of the theory for the emphasis on dynamic sequences and on how the present state affects commitment of resources and decisions about changes and thus future states. The lack of dynamism is a major problem for most theories of international production. The Scandinavian School model may be a good starting point for ideas on the injection of dynamism in more realistic and complex theories.

SUMMARY BOX 10

Review of the Scandinavian School's approach

Antecedents

Penrose ([1959] 2009); Cyert and March (1963); Aharoni (1966) and Vernon (1966)

Main writers and works

Johanson and Wiedersheim-Paul (1975); Johanson and Vahlne (1977 and 1990)

Main elements of the theory

See Boxes 10.1 and 10.2

Modalities considered

Exports; sales through agents and direct sales and production

Levels of aggregation

The firm

Other relevant chapters

Chapters 5 (Vernon)

Chapter 6 (Knickerbocker)

Chapter 15 (Penrose; networks)

Indicative further reading

The papers by Johanson and Wiedersheim-Paul (1975) and Johanson and Vahlne (1977) as well as Aharoni (1966) have been reprinted in P.J. Buckley and P.N. Ghauri (eds) (1999), *The Internationalization of the Firm: A Reader*, London: ITBP. They are, respectively, ch. 3, 27–42; ch. 4, 43–54 and ch. 1, 3–13.

Notes

1 Kogut (1983) also moves away from the view of 'FDI as a decision made at a discrete point in time' in favour of a view that stresses 'the series of sequential decisions which determine the volume and direction of these transferred resources' (ibid.: 42). However, the sequences refer to an aspect of the internationalization decision – the funding mode – different from that analysed by the Scandinavian School.

2 The authors' concept of psychic distance and its use implies that 'foreignness' is a constraint:

investing abroad involves additional costs and disadvantages which can be overcome by additional perceived advantages. In Chapter 14 a different view is put forward, one in which multinationalization per se can bring advantages.

3 More on Penrose in Chapter 15.

4 Here there is an echo of Vernon's idea that there is a considerable gap between knowledge of the scientific principles and the embodiment of scientific principles into marketable products, though applied in different areas (see Chapter 5).

5 Aharoni (1966) highlights also the time lag needed to reach a decision and considers how this lag affects the type of decision arrived at.

6 Aharoni (1966) talks of a social system within which decisions are taken. The system consists of people working within the organization as well as with other organizations which interact with our chosen one.

7 These issues are well developed in Knickerbocker (1973) as we saw in Chapter 6.

8 More on this in Chapters 11 and 14.

11 Evolutionary theories of the TNC

I Introduction

In the last three decades the international business literature has become increasingly interested in – and indeed contributed to the development of – the competence-based and evolutionary theories of the firm. These two conceptions of the firm are not alternatives: the latter can be seen as emerging from the former with an added emphasis on evolutionary concepts taken from biology.

In the conventional neoclassical view, the firm's resources are taken as given and the subject matter of economics is their allocation within and outside the firm. This assumption is at variance with the reality of firms growing and developing their resources and capabilities. Competences, skills, learning have been considered in the economics of the firm by many authors starting from Adam Smith.[1] However, the first comprehensive treatment of the subject is in Penrose ([1959] 2009), on which more in Chapter 15. She characterizes the firm as a bundle of resources and competencies evolving qualitatively and quantitatively in response to purposeful activities and leading to the growth of the firm.

The 1982 book by Richard Nelson and Sidney Winter, *An Evolutionary Theory of Economic Change*, also focuses on competencies within the firm: how they evolve and how the social nature of their utilization and development makes them firm- and context-specific. Nelson and Winter drew on biology for their analysis, thus giving the competence-based theory an evolutionary twist.

Penrose's work went unnoticed for several decades and is, at last, being given the success it deserves. Nelson and Winter's work was successful very early on and it proved influential in shaping later analyses of the firm, growth and innovation as well as related policy recommendation.

In both Penrose's and Nelson and Winter's books the emphasis is on learning, team work and on change and dynamic elements: on how firms and their competencies evolve while searching for solutions to problems; how history matters. It matters because it affects the building up of capabilities within the firm and the economy.[2]

Both Penrose's and Nelson and Winter's theories are about the firm, not the TNC.[3] However, the competence-based theory has proved very influential in the development of theories of TNCs and their activities, particularly those of John Cantwell (1989) and of Bruce Kogut and Udo Zander (1993).

Cantwell starts by criticizing the first attempt to link technological innovation and international production: Vernon's international product life cycle (IPLC). Cantwell then goes on to criticize the internalization theory of international production as the approach that has come to be accepted as the main theory of the multinational enterprise (Chapter 8).

Kogut and Zander's point of departure is their analysis of the firm as a social community from which a specific type of knowledge emerges. They also start by criticizing the internalization theory and then go on to develop their own.

2   Cantwell's theory

Cantwell's main problem is to explain why – within a given industry – some firms become more successful at international activities compared with rival firms. In looking for solutions to this problem, he develops a highly dynamic theory. In most existing theories the firm is seen as a *passive* reactor to demand, costs or government intervention and research has tended to focus on the *modalities* of internationalization as an either or alternative. Modalities are therefore, too often, seen as static alternatives.[4] This approach neglects the question of why some firms may be engaged, simultaneously, in more than one modality and, indeed, become successful in all of them.

Cantwell considers innovation and technology to be the area in which firms can best forge their competitive advantages. Companies that are innovation and technology leaders get ahead of competitors at home and in the international arena. He writes: 'MNCs in manufacturing emerged historically and became successful through the generation and cultivation of innovative ownership advantages'. The accumulation of technology and innovation gives cumulative competitive advantage, whether the innovation is in products or processes and whether it cumulates in the same products/processes or is diversified (Cantwell and Piscitello, 2000). 'International production is . . . explained as the developmental outcome of the competitive process between firms belonging to common industrial groups' (Cantwell, 1989: 207). Moreover, a strong competitive advantage in the technology field supports not only international production but also a variety of international activities and modalities.

In Cantwell's view, the firm can be an *active* generator of its own competitive advantages. Here lies one of Cantwell's dynamic points: ownership advantages can be created by the strategic behaviour of the firms themselves rather than being a static characteristic of them. The MNCs are in a particularly strong position to develop their ownership advantages in innovation. By operating in many countries – often characterized by diverse knowledge and innovation contexts – they can acquire knowledge from the localities and use it to further their innovative activities. In this process the MNC is aided by its involvement in two types of networks: (1) its internal network between the various units of the firm spread in a variety of geographies; and (2) external networks between units of the firm and suppliers/distributors, consumers and partners in collaborative ventures.

The external networks enable units of the MNC to acquire knowledge from their external environment. This knowledge is incorporated within the unit and also transferred to other units of the TNC via its internal network. The MNC with its geographically diversified structure, its variety of organizational interactions with the external environments and its internal network is in the best position to accumulate innovation and technology across countries and through time. The internal networks raise issues of control of the subsidiaries by the headquarters of the company. The external networks raise issues of the degree of embeddedness of the subsidiary into the local economy, on which more in Chapter 15.

In Cantwell's analysis knowledge and innovation spill over from the localities to the MNC. But the spillover process also operates in the opposite direction: knowledge and innovation spill over from units of the MNC to the localities in which they operate. The latter units embed self-generated knowledge as well as knowledge acquired by other units of the MNC via its internal network. Here we have another strong dynamic element in Cantwell's theory: the analysis of *interaction between ownership and location advantages*. Successful innovators tend to invest in innovation activities in several centres/countries. As they do so, their investment generates spillover effects to the locality and the industry, thus encouraging more investment and innovative activities by other firms. The centres then become the location of several innovative companies and this generates external economies of agglomeration. Each innovating firm brings external benefits to the locality in which it invests. Conversely, the investors benefit from the favourable technological environment that develops in the locality. Agglomeration economies are generated and they further strengthen the centres and the position of the firms operating in them. This means that firms located in the same centres benefit from each other's innovative activities and that the locality as a whole also benefits: there are positive externalities in the innovation field and the overall positive effects are higher than the sum of the individual effects on each firm.[5]

In this perspective, location advantages are not seen as exogenous but *endogenously* created by the innovation and location strategies of firms combined with the spillover effects of their activities. What emerges is a complex 'dynamic interaction between the ownership advantage of groups of firms and the locational advantages of the sites in which they produce' (Cantwell, 1989: 207).[6]

Companies learn from each other partly directly and partly through the external environment. The agglomeration economies of each centre as well as the diversity of the environments in which they operate become sources of learning, innovation and, thus, competitive advantage for the firms. For the individual MNC, locational diversification of technology and production in many centres pays off.

Cumulative causation processes can be seen to develop in two related fields: at the meso and the macro levels. At the industry (meso) level, the spillover effects from each firm affect the industry as a whole as well as the locality. In each industry there are likely to be several innovation centres/countries rather than a single main one. Industries that are dominated by technology leaders have a different pattern of international trade, production and licensing compared to industries where no leaders can be clearly identified. Moreover, there are cumulative effects at the macro level. The accumulation of technology leads to high productivity and therefore high growth and incomes per capita. The latter generates high levels of demand, thus attracting high levels of investment and new waves of innovation.

Cantwell's model therefore sees the MNC as innovation leader. However, its creation of innovation and technology is geographically dispersed in many centres. Therefore, though we can talk of companies as technology leaders, we cannot extend the concept to countries. No single industrialized country can be designated as leader in the way Vernon did with the USA in his original article (1966). In other words, *in innovation there is a hierarchy of companies but not a simple hierarchy of countries.*

Cantwell tests his theory through empirical research on the location of innovation activities using patents data for manufacturing firms from seven industrialized countries. (See Box 11.1 for a summary of the main points in Cantwell's theory.)

Box 11.1   *Main points in Cantwell's theory*

- Ownership advantages are endogenous and developed via firms' strategies.

- Innovation and technology give the firms competitive advantage in a variety of international activities and modalities.

- Exports, international production and licensing tend to be complementary modalities rather than substitutes and firms that are leaders in technology are likely to engage in all of them simultaneously.

- Innovation activities generate spillover effects to the locality and the industry as a whole.

- As several firms locate their innovation activities in the same locations, we see the emergence and development of positive agglomeration effects.

- Location advantages are therefore also endogenously created by the innovation and internationalization behaviour of firms.

- While we have leader firms in innovation, we cannot equally talk of leader countries.

---

3   Cantwell's critique of the international product life cycle

Cantwell's theory has many points in common with Vernon's ILPC. Both put innovation and technology at the centre of analysis; both are quite dynamic in their approach; both see innovation and internationalization as closely linked. However, there are also major differences between the two. Cantwell's own critique of the IPLC is in his 1989 (ch. 3) work and in his 1995 work. He sees the IPLC theory based on two main hypotheses: (a) 'innovations are almost always located in the home country of the parent company, and usually close to the site of the corporate technological headquarters'; (b) 'international investment is led by technology leaders, as a means by which they increase their share of world markets and world production' (Cantwell, 1995: 155).

On the basis of his empirical results on the geographical location of patents, Cantwell rejects the first hypothesis and accepts the second one. This means that while we can have firms that are leaders, we do not have single leader countries. Thus, the

IPLC model as a model of technology *transfer* cannot be accepted. Instead, Cantwell's own model of technology *creation* and spread into various countries seems to be more corroborated by the empirics.

Two further elements seem to differentiate Vernon's and Cantwell's theories:

- Vernon's innovations are demand and consumer led and, in fact, a macro-environment characterized by high income per capita is an essential ingredient of his theory on the generation and adoption of new technologies. In contrast, Cantwell[7] links innovation to production rather than consumption, thus following a more classical route. Nonetheless, his view is that firm-specific learning processes interact with the growth of demand as well as with supply conditions within the firm and the industry. Innovation leads to high productivity and growth, thus to high incomes per capita and high demand for new products in a cumulative causation process.[8] This means that a high level of demand by consumers is as much a consequence as a cause of innovation and not just the latter as in the IPLC.
- Cantwell sees innovation spilling in a variety of ways including spillage from product to product in a multi-product firm and industry. This approach mirrors what happens in the real world. However, no such spillover possibility can be seen in Vernon or could be attached to his approach. This is because the IPLC is a model based on the product and not on the firm, as discussed in Chapter 5. Innovation refers to a new product, not to a general activity involving a variety of products and or processes within the firm.

4   Cantwell's critique of the internalization theory

Cantwell's research was done while he was at Reading University. It was therefore bound to be affected by the work of other academics based at the same university, namely, Dunning (see Chapter 9) as well as Buckley and Casson (see Chapter 8).

Cantwell – like Dunning himself – considers Dunning's eclectic approach as a framework rather than a theory. It is a framework which he partly uses; in particular, it is the one that is likely to have led to his emphasis on ownership advantages and location advantages. Nonetheless, Cantwell further developed the analysis of these two sets of advantages by making them both endogenous rather than exogenous.

Cantwell's main criticisms are reserved for the internalization theory. Some of these criticisms will, of course, also apply to Dunning's framework in as far as it uses internalization advantages.[9] His criticisms can thus be summarized:

- The internalization theory is based on exchange and not production elements.
- The firm's managers have a purely passive role: they react to market conditions and to their imperfections rather than having an active strategic role.
- The theory considers ownership advantages as unnecessary for the explanation of international activities.
- The theory considers location advantages as exogenous. The modalities of

internationalization are seen as alternatives to each other in a static framework. This goes against the findings of Cantwell's empirical work. He writes, on this point: 'Theories that simply counterpose domestic exports, international production and non-affiliate licensing as alternatives are not very helpful to an understanding of the current evolution of international industries' (Cantwell, 1989: 135–6).

5   The TNC as social community

Cantwell's analysis focuses on why some firms are more successful than others and therefore on the ownership advantages of firms, on their interaction with locational advantages and on the role of innovation activities in them.

Kogut and Zander's analysis focuses on the role played by knowledge in the boundaries of the firm, i.e. the extent to which the firm decides to expand via internalization or through external, contractual relationships. The authors test their theory empirically via a questionnaire to Swedish project engineers who know about the history of major manufacturing technological innovations. The engineers were asked questions on the transfer mode to foreign units. The results point towards the choice of owned subsidiaries for the transfer of knowledge with a high degree of tacitness.

Kogut and Zander start by criticizing the standard view on the boundaries of the firm: the internalization theory. In the latter the boundaries are set by the failure of the market to protect knowledge and by market transaction costs. Moreover, in the internalization view the boundaries of the firm are independent of its ownership advantages.

Kogut and Zander's (1993) key insights are the view of the firm as a social community and the development of knowledge as a product of the social group.[10] They write: 'firms are social communities that serve the efficient mechanisms for the creation and transformation of knowledge into economically rewarded products and services'. In Kogut and Zander (2003: 511) we read on this point: 'knowledge exists in networks and in institutionalized contexts'.

It is not made very clear whether the whole firm or groups within it form the social community.[11] Whatever the interpretation of social community we give to Kogut and Zander's analysis, the social nature of the firm and the social nature of knowledge creation within it mean that units within the firm share common identities, values and procedures.

Whenever knowledge is embedded in – and dependent on – social structures, it is more context-specific and, largely, tacit. This makes it less likely to be codifiable, teachable and transferable to other social settings. The social community setting of knowledge development means that: (a) knowledge is more likely to be tacit because it is emerging from shared experiences and procedures; and (b) further knowledge development is likely to emerge from the shared experiences. Here we have clear pointers towards the fact that the social nature of the firm and of groups within it lead to a specific type of knowledge and to ownership advantages and value creation. Thus, the tacit nature of knowledge is linked to the social nature of the firm. The authors write: 'Cooperation within an organization leads to a set of capabilities that are easier to transfer within the firm than across organizations and constitute the ownership advantages of the firm' (Kogut and Zander, 1993: 627). The social community setting of the firm also applies to the MNC because its subsidiaries tend to share identities and values or, at least, they share them to a higher degree than each subsidiary would share with independent external firms.

The social setting enhances knowledge creation and internal transfer though not transfers to other social settings and, hence, outside the firm. Therefore the characteristics of knowledge emerging from specific social contexts lead to decisions on the modality of knowledge utilization, i.e. via internalization: the boundaries of the firm are set by the nature of the knowledge it develops. In Kogut and Zander's theory the decisions to externalize are sequential to the decision to internalize. Internal versus market-based operations is not a one-off static decision as in the internalization theory.

For Kogut and Zander, the limits to the firm are, therefore, set not by market failure but by the firm's efficiency in acquiring knowledge. They write: 'In our view, firms are efficient means by which knowledge is created and transferred . . . Through repeated interactions, individuals and groups in a firm develop a common understanding by which to transfer knowledge from ideas into production and markets. In this very critical sense, what determines what a firm does is not the failure of the market, but the firm's efficiency in this process of transformation relative to other firms' (ibid.: 631).

Moreover, the authors see knowledge as the main source of ownership advantages and there is, therefore, interaction between ownership advantages and internalization. The ownership advantage characteristic of knowledge is enhanced by the fact that tacit, uncodifiable knowledge is also more difficult to imitate: knowledge is therefore an advantage on which the firm can further build up without fears from rivals' imitations. 'Firms compete on the basis of the superiority of their information and know-how, and their abilities to develop new knowledge by experiential learning' (ibid.: 540).

Knowledge is cumulative. Older knowledge is more easily codifiable and therefore more easily transferable outside the boundaries of the firm. The costs of technology transfer vary with the degree of tacitness of the related knowledge.

Thus, established technology is not a public good; it is transferable at a cost and the cost varies with the accumulation of experience and learning about codification procedures.[12] As knowledge becomes more codifiable with the passage of time, the company is likely to move from internalization to externalization, from FDI to licensing in international operations. The sequence and its timing depend on the degree of tacitness and codifiability of the knowledge specific to the firm. (See Box 11.2 for a summary of Kogut and Zander's theory.)

Box 11.2   *Key elements in Kogut and Zander's theory*

- The firm is seen as a social community and knowledge as the product of social groups within the firm.

- Knowledge is largely tacit, uncodifiable and unteachable. This leads the firm to expand internally – and the MNC to expand via FDI – rather than externally via licensing.

- The boundaries of the firm are set not by transaction costs and risks of opportunistic behaviour but by the firm's efficiency in creating knowledge and transferring it internally.

- Knowledge creation binds together internalization and ownership advantages.

---

6   Comments

There are many common elements between the two theories we have presented. They both: (a) have roots in Nelson and Winter's (1982) evolutionary theory of the firm; (b) deal with issues of knowledge and innovation; (c) are critical of the internalization theory; (d) are tested for the manufacturing sector.

However, there are many differences between the two approaches. For a start, they are involved in explaining different aspects of internationalization: Cantwell aims to explain the competitive advantages of MNCs and their interaction with the localities. Kogut and Zander aim to explain the boundaries of the firm, i.e. the extent to which the MNC will develop via international activities or via external, contractual arrangements.

Cantwell's theory is much more dynamic and with a more strategic focus in the development of ownership advantages. Kogut and Zander's approach is more efficientist: the firm as social community is efficient in developing and utilizing knowledge within a specific modality. Its dynamic elements are mainly in terms of the development of knowledge by the social group and the role of past, shared experiences within such development.

Kogut and Zander's theory is very strong and perceptive in its emphasis on the social nature of the firm and of the development of knowledge within it. They have made a major and welcome contribution by developing these elements in the context of the MNC and by bringing them to the attention of international business scholars. They did so by starting with a critique of one of its most successful theories: the internalization theory.

It is, however, an irony that Kogut and Zander's theory is, in fact, about the boundaries of the firm and thus about internalization versus externalization: their distance from the internalization theory may have been overstated. In Kogut and Zander (2003) the authors state that one of their ambitions in their original 1993 articles was to '*balance* the at the time overwhelming emphasis on transaction cost economics as an explanation for direct investment and as a theory of the firm with a perspective that allowed for a wider, more humanistic understanding of human motivation in the context of social communities' (ibid.: 505). They reject the 'opportunism' elements in the original internalization theory and they inject elements of: the firm as social community; the firm as efficient user of knowledge; knowledge as determinant of both the boundary of the firm and of ownership advantages.

The interaction between ownership and location advantages enables Cantwell to extend his theorizing to the role of the MNC in the industry, locality or macroeconomy. As Kogut and Zander's focus is the boundaries of the firm, no such extension has been possible for them. However, extensions are possible and maybe other researchers have already or will take the challenge. In fact, both theories have the

---

SUMMARY BOX 11

Review of Cantwell's and of Kogut and Zander's theories

Cantwell	**Kogut and Zander**
	Antecedents
Vernon (1966); Dunning (1977); Nelson and Winter (1982)	Nelson and Winter (1982); internalization theory (Ch. 8)
	Key writers and works
John Cantwell (1989; 1991 and 1995)	Kogut and Zander (1993; 2003)
	Main elements of the theories
See Box 11.1	See Box 11.2
	Modalities considered
All modalities: exports, direct production, licensing/franchising	FDI; licensing
	Level of aggregation
Firms and industries; to a lesser extent the macroeconomy	The firm
	Other relevant chapters
Chapter 5 (Vernon's IPLC)	Chapter 8 (internalization)
Chapter 8 (internalization)	Chapter 9 (Dunning)
Chapter 9 (Dunning)	Chapter 15 (Penrose and network theory)
Chapter 15 (Penrose)	Chapter 14

great advantages of opening avenues for further research in international business. For example, the strategic role could be further developed in Cantwell's theory.

Cantwell considers the MNC's active role in developing direct competitive strategies towards rivals. However, direct strategies towards other players in the economic system – and their possible indirect impact on competitive strategies towards rivals – could also be developed. Geographical diversification gives the TNC not only advantages in the acquisition of innovation, it may also give a variety of advantages towards players other than rivals, as will be argued in Chapter 14.

Kogut and Zander's view of the firm as a 'harmonious' social community may be at variance with the reality of conflicts between management and workforce (see Chapter 14) and between managers of different units (see Chapter 15).

Kogut and Zander's approach is not strategic; however, their theory could be further developed in that direction. A more strategic focus towards the development, transfer and utilization of knowledge could open up new avenues for research. There are already several contributions to the role of knowledge and innovation in firms' strategies apart from Penrose, Nelson and Winter and Cantwell's works discussed here, for example Teece (1988). Nonetheless the field is still largely underdeveloped.

Indicative further reading

Cantwell, J. (2000), 'A survey of theories of international production', in C.N. Pitelis and R. Sugden (eds), *The Nature of the Transnational Firm*, London: Routledge, ch. 2, pp. 10–56.

Cantwell, J. (2003), 'Innovation and information technology in the MNE', in A.M. Rugman and T.L. Brewer (eds), *The Oxford Handbook of International Business*, Oxford: Oxford University Press, ch. 16, pp. 431–56.

Hodgson, G.M. (1998), Evolutionary and competence-based theories of the firm, *Journal of Economic Studies*, **25** (1), 25–56.

Kogut, B. and Zander, U. (1993), 'Knowledge of the firm and the evolutionary theory of the multinational corporation', *Journal of International Business Studies*, **24** (4), 625–45.

Kogut, B. and Zander, U. (2003), 'A memoir and reflection: knowledge and an evolutionary theory of the multinational firm 10 years later', *Journal of International Business Studies*, **34** (6), 505–15.

Verbeke, A. (2003), 'The evolutionary view of the MNE and the future of internalization theory', *Journal of International Business Studies*, **34** (6), 498–504.

Notes

1 See Hodgson (1998: 36–42) on the 'genesis of competence-based theory of the firm'.

2 An excellent contrast between the contractarian approach to the firm – as emerging from Coase and Williamson (see Ch. 8) – and the competence-based approach, is in Hodgson (1998).

3 Penrose made several comments on the MNC later in life and we shall deal with those in Chapter 15.

4 Though not in the Scandinavian School approach (Chapter 10) where different modalities are seen as stages in a dynamic internationalization process.

5 These aspects of the theory have been applied to the analysis of regional systems of innovation (Cantwell and Iammarino, 1998; 2003). Agglomeration effects are also present in the new trade theories (see Chapter 12).

6 More recent work by Dunning (1998) and by Cantwell (2009) further stresses the interaction between the TNC's organization and the location of its activities.

7 See also Cantwell and Fai (1999).

8 The original technology gap theory of international trade (Posner, 1961) did indeed have elements of cumulative causation and interaction (see Chapter 5).

9 Analyses of the eclectic paradigm can be found in Cantwell (2000) and Cantwell and Narula (2001). In private correspondence Cantwell expressed to me the view that more attention should be given to the relationship between ownership advantages and transactional costs.

10 Apart from Penrose and Nelson and Winter, the social nature of knowledge, innovation and learning processes are emphasized by several authors including Lazonick (1994) and Teece and Pisano (1994).

11 See also Forsgren (2008: ch. 4) on this point.

12 The difficulties of international technology transfer are clearly highlighted in Teece (1977).

12 New trade theories and the activities of TNCs*

I Introduction

Since the 1980s successful attempts have been made at incorporating the TNC[1] within the equilibrium framework and thus within the body of mainstream economics. This is the result of major developments in the theory of international trade which have led to the so-called 'new trade theories'. Concomitantly, and linked to the new trade theories, we have seen a surge of interest in the theory of location of economic activity and in particular in theories of the geographical concentration of activities.

Both the classical and neoclassical trade theories – briefly mentioned in Chapter 3 – are based on the assumption of constant returns to scale, the only one compatible with the assumption of perfect competition. The new theoretical approach – new trade theories – originated with developments in the mathematical modelling of imperfect competition and increasing returns (Dixit and Stiglitz, 1977).[2] This modelling has allowed economists to move away from the traditional assumption of perfect competition and constant returns to scale to one of imperfect competition and increasing returns to scale. Up to that point, economists knew that constant returns to scale was neither a realistic assumption nor one compatible with imperfect competition. However, they only moved away from this overall assumption when the mathematical techniques for dealing with increasing returns, and thus imperfect competition, were developed.

These developments, in turn, have affected the way we analyse international trade and location of economic activity as well as patterns of economic development and growth. Krugman, (1991a: 10) writes that: 'increasing returns are in fact a pervasive influence on the economy, and . . . these increasing returns give a decisive role to history in determining the geography of real economies'. It can be added that their introduction into economic theory is having a pervasive influence on economics. Indeed, the new approach may be considered to be a new paradigm in that it is affecting a very large part of economics, it is widely accepted by the economics profession and it is giving scope for the rethinking, reformulation and remodelling of a large body of economic theory.

The assumption of increasing returns injects a large dose of realism into economic modelling in general. It also affects the results of various models in terms of firms' specialization and of patterns of industrial location. This means that, suddenly, the geography of real economies has become relevant in economics circles.

As the theory of industrial location came to the forefront of economic analysis, economists were bound to start asking questions about the role of multinational companies in their theories: after all, the study of MNCs' activities is largely about the location of production into various countries. Thus, some economists have attempted to incorporate MNCs' activities in the new trade and location theories.

This chapter aims to explain – and comment on – the new trade theories of TNCs' activities developed in the context – and as a by-product – of the new approaches to the theory of international trade.

2   The new trade and location theories and their implications

The new trade theories (Krugman, 1985; 1991a; 1998) stress that trade and specialization are due to: (1) advantages of economies of scale, as well as (2) traditional comparative advantages due to differences in factor endowments (as in Ricardo and Heckscher-Ohlin). Thus, trade and specialization are driven by some static and exogenous elements due to factor endowments and by more dynamic and endogenous elements linked to increasing returns. The latter can be of two types, going back to their two major contributors in this area: Edward Chamberlin (1899–1967) and Alfred Marshall (1842–1924).

The first type of economies of scale – associated with Chamberlin's theory of monopolistic competition – is *internal to the firm* and the relevant scale is that of the plant/firm. As already mentioned, it is normally considered that increasing economies of scale are not compatible with perfect competition because, as unit costs decrease, the firm grows bigger than other firms in the industry and thus the economies give advantages to the specific firm which experiences economies of scale. These Chamberlinian types of scale economies require, therefore, a departure from the perfect competition model and a move towards monopolistic competition. In the latter model, products are seen as differentiated and the firm has a monopoly in relation to its own differentiated product. However, the existence of a large number of firms in the industry tends to wipe out any monopoly profits. When this general framework is applied to new trade theories, the firm is usually assumed to operate with a single plant and thus firm economies and plant economies coincide.

In the second type of economies – external economies of the Marshallian type – increasing returns are achieved through *spillover effects* from firm to firm and thus the economies refer to the industry as a whole rather than the single firm.[3] In this approach scale economies remain compatible with perfect competition because the scale of the industry is the source of the increasing returns and not the scale of the firm/plant (Krugman, 1985; 1991a).

The internal and external types of scale economies are not exclusive and, indeed, they can combine with each other to accelerate the process of specialization and the concentration of industry in specific locations. Internal economies are likely to push the firm towards specialization. The existence of external economies leads firms within the same industry to locate in the same area in order to reap the benefits of spillover effects. This leads to spatial agglomeration effects within the same industry.

This locational concentration of industry can take place horizontally and/or vertically. The vertical concentration and clustering can be enhanced by the non-tradability of some intermediate products, i.e. because some intermediate products (including services) are specific to the firm and its final products and may not have a market outside the firm or not a market our firm wants to utilize. This non-tradability characteristic combined with increasing returns at the industry level, can 'induce the formation of "industrial complexes", groups of industries tied together by the need to concentrate all users of a non-tradable intermediate in the same country' (Krugman, 1985: 30). The assumptions behind the various theories and models are summarized in Box. 12.1.

Box 12.1   *Main assumptions behind the 'new trade theories'*

- Existence of transportation costs and other spatial transaction costs

- Immobility of labour and capital

- The existence or gradual formation of scale economies of internal (Chamberlinian) and/or external (Marshallian) type

- A large market due to the size of the population combined with high incomes per capita (Krugman, 1985 and 1998)

Thus, increasing returns, whether linked to the firm or the industry, are used to explain trade, location of economic activity, clustering and agglomeration. They are also used to explore the effects of regional integration and of the changing pattern of activity in the North–South divide.

New trade theories and regional integration

Krugman and Venables (1996) explore the links between integration, clustering and adjustment problems deriving from integration. The authors see the probability of clustering of activities to be higher at the interregional level than at the international level because barriers are stronger at the international than regional level. In the context of their analysis, international integration is defined in terms of reduction in such barriers; in fact 'as a reduction of cost of doing business across space' (ibid.: 961).

An integrated international economy becomes more like the interregional economy. The increased integration leads to the removal or reduction of barriers to agglomeration; more intermediate and/or final products will be located in areas where industry already thrives. Thus, the final result will be further polarization and uneven development within the integrated region. One of the conclusions, relevant for policy, is that integration is best achieved between countries at similar stages of development. Whenever the countries are at different stages of development, the outcome of integration will be further polarization, leading to an increase in the economic gap between rich and poor areas.

The new paradigm allows economists to give a role to history, historical accidents and historical developments. As scale economies are achieved dynamically (i.e. through operations in time) as well as statically, *history matters* (Krugman, 1991a; 1991b). This can be interpreted in two ways:

- The first is in the sense that companies grow gradually and achieve internal economies in a pattern of a cumulative virtuous circle.
- It also means that regions and countries are affected by historical accidents that lead to the location of some industries within them and thus to a possible virtuous circle of further clustering and agglomeration. Conversely, a historical negative accident may put in motion a cumulative vicious circle of decline.

Does this mean that locations/countries are destined to be part of a polarized irreversible system? That once the virtuous or vicious circle starts there is no turning back? Krugman and Venables (1995) give a negative answer to these questions in explaining the apparent reversal in the pattern of industrial location between North and South.

The 1960s and 1970s were characterized by concerns about uneven development worldwide, with industrialized core countries of the Northern Hemisphere gaining at the expense of the peripheral underdeveloped countries. The 1980s and 1990s saw the expression of opposite concerns: the alleged de-industrialization and immiseration of the North because of relocation of production to the developing countries.

Krugman and Venables explain both these concerns and indeed the trends behind them with the aid of the new trade theories and increasing returns. The key element in their explanation is the gradual reduction, over time, of transportation costs combined with immobility of labour across nations. When the reduction in costs reaches a first critical level we have concentration of industries in the core countries – where the high levels of incomes per capita secure the bulk of demand – because costs are low enough for the products to be exported. Further reductions in transportation costs may lead to another critical level at which the low wages in developing countries combined with low transport costs may make it cost-effective to locate industries in developing countries and export the products to the developed ones.[4] Thus, both elements in the core–periphery relationship are explained by the dynamics of changes in transportation costs over time. Moreover, the expectation of changes and shifts in itself can initiate and accelerate the changes, as it happens in many aspects of economic life: 'expectations may be self-fulfilling' (Krugman, 1991a: 27). In conclusion, the pattern of agglomeration and uneven development need not be permanent and cumulative. As the technology and costs of transportation change, the pattern of location of activity also changes.

3   Multinationals within the 'new' trade and location theories

In the approach just sketched, increasing returns – whether linked to the firm or the industry – are used to explain trade as well as the geography of economic activity (Krugman, 1991b), clustering and agglomeration, industrial districts (Krugman, 1991a; 1998; Venables, 1998). They are also used to explore many policy issues stemming from agglomeration and cumulative processes (Krugman, 1987; Krugman and Venables, 1996). This framework, however, cannot explain direct production in other countries by TNCs. Essentially, if there are external economies of agglomeration and the internal economies are plant economies, then it can only make sense to produce in one location/country and supply other markets through exports. There is a basic conflict and tension between a theory that predicts clustering of production activities and a reality of companies that spread their activities in space sometimes horizontally, sometimes vertically, sometimes both ways.

At the theoretical level it is possible to solve the conundrum by adjusting some of the assumptions, and this is what economists have done.[5] The assumption of capital immobility – underlying much trade theory – obviously has to be removed when dealing with theories of direct foreign production and FDI, which by their nature imply capital mobility. Moreover, constraints to the movements of products are sometimes introduced, such as barriers to trade.

However, the main adjustment is in the treatment of *internal economies of scale*. They are split into two types:

- internal economies at the level of plants;
- internal economies at the level of the firm.

These economies separately or together are of the Chamberlinian, internal type and they are therefore analysed in the context of imperfect competition. The first type of economies – those at the plant level – are linked to more traditional fixed inputs, those deriving from traditional physical assets such as machinery; they give rise to fixed costs. The second type of economies derives from inputs and assets such as organizational, technological, managerial/marketing; the services deriving from them – whether material or, more often, immaterial – are of benefit to, and can be used by, the company as a whole and therefore by its head office as well as by its affiliates. These are *joint inputs within the firm* because they can be used by different parts of the firm for the same product and/or for different products. No matter how many plants (and affiliates) are going to use these inputs, the marginal cost of using the inputs in additional plants – at home or abroad – is low or negligible. In addition to this, the industry as a whole may also achieve scale economies of the external, Marshallian type.

Within the general framework of these assumptions there are two main routes to the introduction of international production by MNCs: they deal with international production directed towards: (1) developing and (2) developed countries. The split between economies at the level of the plant or the level of the firm is used in both these routes. Common to both of them is also the – realistic – assumption that MNCs' home countries are the developed countries and therefore that outward FDI originates from developed countries.[6]

Explaining FDI in developing countries

The first route is designed to explain why MNCs – originating in developed countries – locate in developing countries. This is done by assuming different factor endowments in the two countries (developed and developing) and by also assuming the production of both intermediate and final products (Helpman, 1985; Helpman and Krugman, 1985) .

At this point the above assumption of plant and firm economies becomes relevant. It is, in fact, assumed that the company as a whole achieves internal economies of scale due to joint inputs. Moreover, some outputs from these inputs are assumed to be *specific* to the company. These outputs are usually services linked to research or to brands and advertising. Their specificity means that they cannot be traded on the market without loss of quality or loss of monopolistic position over, for example, the results of research. Thus, the services of the joint inputs must be internalized, that is, produced and used within the firm. They are likely to be transferred between different parts of the firm and this creates scope for intra-firm trade in invisibles. This is part of the debate in the industrial organization literature between internalization versus externalization decisions, as we saw in Chapter 8. The model leads to a pattern of vertical integration of production across countries and to intra-firm and intra-industry trade. The different factor endowments lead to specialization between countries; joint inputs favour production under common ownership, i.e. within the same company; the specificity of outputs favours internalization within the firm in a single country as well as across countries.

Within this overall framework, Helpman (1984) assumes that:

- at the plant level we can have either fixed and variable costs, or only variable ones;
- there exist fixed costs that are company-specific but not plant-specific.

The latter fixed costs relate to joint inputs, i.e. to inputs that are common to many parts of the company such as marketing services, brand names and managerial expertise. This means that the services that derive from these inputs can be enjoyed by various parts of the company at no extra cost. The inputs – and the related services derived from them – are also assumed to be specific to the company; this means that they cannot be traded on the market without loss of quality. Thus, the services of the joint inputs must be internalized to avoid such losses of quality. The company cannot sell at arm's length or under licence: it must produce directly in various countries if it wants to exploit the differences in factor prices. The services of the joint inputs will be traded internally between subsidiaries or subsidiaries and parent, thus giving rise to intra-firm trade. Helpman, however, does not deal with transfer prices and their cause/effects link with intra-firm trade.[7] This is an issue analysed by the internalization theorists (Chapter 8).

Krugman (1985) also approaches the issue of MNCs' activities in the context of the new trade theories. He lays stress on technology as a fixed cost/joint input that gives rise to a product that could theoretically be sold on the market or licensed. The reason why the external market solution is not used has to do with the fact that there are transaction costs of operating on the market. Therefore, production across countries is internalized within the company, and this is what MNCs are about. Krugman writes: 'multinational enterprise occurs whenever there exist related activities for which the following is true: there are simultaneously transaction cost incentives to integrate these activities within a single firm and factor costs or other incentives to separate the activities geographically' (ibid.: 33–4). In a passage that has echoes of Hymer's dissertation, Krugman sees the main defining characteristic of MNCs as the control of activities across borders: 'What the new models make clear, above all, is that multinational enterprise is *not* a type of factor mobility. It represents an extension of control, not necessarily a movement of capital. The key lesson is that direct foreign investment isn't investment' (ibid.: 34). (See Box 12.2 for a summary of assumptions and outcomes.)

Box 12.2   *New trade theories and FDI in developing countries: assumptions and outcomes*

Assumptions

- Countries at different levels of development and thus with different factor endowments.

- Internal scale economies at the plant and at the firm level.

- Outputs from joint inputs are specific to the company.

Outcomes

- FDI from developed to developing countries.

- International vertical integration.

- Internalization rather than licensing is favoured because of joint inputs and of the specificity of the related assets and outputs.

- Intra-firm trade.

New trade theories and FDI in developed countries

The *second route* deals with the location of FDI into developed countries. The approach starts with Markusen (1984) who stresses the relevance of intangible assets for multinational enterprises and links intangibles to economies of multi-plant operations. His formalization of the notion of joint inputs is further developed in his later works. Markusen (1995) probes into the circumstances that lead a company to produce directly abroad or to license or use other entry modes. He starts by giving some stylized facts at the macro and micro levels as highlighted in Box 12.3. They refer, mostly, to MNEs' activities worldwide in the previous decade or so.

Box 12.3   *Markusen's stylized facts*

At the macro level

- Considerable growth in FDI.

- Two-way FDI in most advanced countries.

- A large amount of FDI takes place on an intra-industry basis and is horizontal rather than vertical.

- A large share of international trade takes place on an intra-firm basis.

At the micro and meso levels

- The degree to which production is accounted for by MNCs varies considerably across industries.

- MNEs tend to be prominent in industries characterized by high R&D intensity, they tend to have high value in intangible assets, to employ a large technical and professional workforce, and to engage in product differentiation.

- Corporate age and multinationality tend to be correlated.

- Size seems unimportant above a certain threshold.

- There is some evidence that plant-level scale economies are negatively correlated with multinationality.

Markusen goes on to expound and use Dunning's eclectic framework – presented in Chapter 9 of this volume – based on ownership, location and internalization advantages, and then to consider more specifically the last set of advantages in the context of the internalization theory of the MNC.

He then develops his own model of MNCs' activities and location. His model is based on two countries at similar levels of development; in fact, he deals with *two developed countries*.

In conclusion, MNCs' activities and direct production of an intra-industry type are to be found in industries in which, at the firm level, there are large fixed costs combined with intangible assets – 'knowledge capital' – and intangible outputs. However, plant-level fixed costs and economies are not very significant. There are large costs of spatial transactions such as transport costs and there may be barriers to trade though not to FDI. The large markets – due to the size of the country and the high level of incomes per capita – secure the viability of production in both countries. The similar stage of development of the countries means that they have similar factor endowments and thus similar costs of production.

In the context of this framework, Markusen explains the pattern of FDI, bilateral cross-country FDI in developed countries and intra-industry FDI. He identifies the conditions for home-only production with the existence of uninational companies

(UNCs), which are responsible for producing at home and for meeting foreign demand through exports. In contrast to this pattern of sourcing, MNCs meet foreign demand via FDI and direct production in the country. He writes on this issue: 'multi-nationals displace national firms and trade as countries become more similar in size, technology, and relative factor endowment' (Markusen, 1995: 180) and later he talks of: 'a process of multinationals displacing trade' (ibid.: 181).

The end result is that international production is – according to Markusen – of the horizontal type and FDI exhibits an intra-industry pattern. Direct production abroad is preferred to export due to assumptions (2) and (4) (in Box 12.4). As in Helpman (1984), the intangibility of the assets poses constraints on the degree to which the company can license and generally externalize its activities without risk of losing quality control or its monopoly over innovation and technology. This leads to a process of internalization across countries similar to what we saw in Chapter 8.

Box 12.4   *New trade theories and FDI in developed countries*

Assumptions

1 International production is of the horizontal type only, thus the MNCs produce the same/similar type of products in both countries.

2 Both countries are at the same stage of development, they both have large markets and similar size of markets, thus plant economies of scale can be achieved in both.

3 The two countries have similar factor endowments and thus the same costs of production.

4 There are large transport costs and/or barriers to trade but not to FDI.

5 There are large fixed costs of production at the level of the firm related to joint inputs such as R&D or costs linked to the development of brand names such advertising. These joint inputs derive mainly from intangible assets (such as brands). The latter type of assets are becoming very relevant for firms. The intangibility of these assets poses constraints on the degree to which the company can license and, generally, externalize its activities without risk of losing quality control or its monopoly over technology.[8] Thus, direct production is preferred to licensing. This assumption is similar to the one used to explain FDI in developing countries.

Outcomes

• FDI takes place between countries at similar levels of development and specifically developed countries.

• Direct production rather than exports.

• Intra-industry trade.

• Intra-industry FDI.

4   Tensions and contradictions in the new paradigm

As we saw in the last section, multinationality of production is introduced in the new trade and location theories by postulating a series of assumptions related to the following points:

1   Fixed costs at the firm level over and above any fixed costs that may (or may not) exist at the plant level; this means that there are economies of organizing production under the same company umbrella though not necessarily under the same plant.
2   This, together with an assumption of high transport costs, leads to the efficiency of production near the market and therefore to multi-plant production and to different plants in different countries.
3   The company specificity of the services deriving from the joint inputs (particularly in terms of R&D) leads to advantages of internalization and thus to a preference for direct production over licensing.

Within this general framework some authors concentrate on horizontal FDI (Markusen) and some on vertical FDI, according to what facts they are trying to explain: for example, intra-industry FDI (as in Markusen, 1995) or industrial districts (as in Krugman, 1985). Moreover, the assumptions about factor endowments in the host and home countries are the basis for dealing with outward FDI in developed or developing countries.

There are various basic elements of contradictions and tensions in the paradigm. Dunning (1995) points out how neither old nor new trade theories take account of the following two major issues which have been and are extensively researched in other branches of economics and business studies. The first is the organization of production and its impact on the volume and pattern of trade.[9] The second one is the growing relevance of created firm-specific assets which are more mobile than the traditional country-specific natural assets. The different specificity of the assets combined with firms' multinationality of operations may lead to a divergence between comparative advantages of countries and the competitive advantages of firms. This, according to Dunning, affects the pattern of international transactions, including the volume and structure of trade.

I identify a major element of tension in the contradiction between theories that predict clusters and agglomeration and the reality of TNCs that spread their activities wide[10] (Ietto-Gillies, 2002a: chs 4 and 5). Some new trade theorists solve the contradictions by postulating production conditions that avoid discrimination against multi-plant production and, specifically, conditions of internal economies of scale at the firm level. Basically, they assume the existence of joint inputs at the firm level due largely to specific and often immaterial assets and outputs that can be used at low marginal costs in various plants within the firm. Moreover, the specificity of assets and outputs leads to a preference for direct production over licensing.

The solution offered to the basic contradiction is a *theoretical* one, involving a set of theoretical assumptions. However, at the level of real economies, the contradictions remain and new trade theorists find that the empirical reality does not quite fit the conclusions of their models. The issue is highlighted in the following explicit passage by Krugman (1998: 15): 'preliminary efforts . . . have found that such models are not at all easy to calibrate to actual data; in general, the tendency toward agglomeration is stronger in the models than in the real economy!' Another type of contradiction relates to the compatibility of the Chamberlinian framework with the nature and characteristics of TNCs, including their size and power. The framework is one of small firms producing differentiated products, while typical TNCs are large and operate in oligopolistic markets.

A further problem of the enlarged (to include TNCs) paradigm is the fact that, in the real world, we have coexistence and complementarity of trade and FDI in contrast with the conclusions of the new trade theory models. The latter approach is also inconsistent with a more detailed theoretical analysis of the relationship between international production and trade, as we shall see in Chapter 19 and as is also considered in Cantwell (1994) and Ietto-Gillies (2002a: ch. 2).[11] This issue is particularly prominent in Markusen's model, where he concludes that multinationals' direct production displaces production by national firms and their sourcing of foreign markets via exports.

In fact, Markusen's model leads to the identification of UNCs with trade and of MNCs with FDI only. This is a problem, because MNCs are responsible not only for all FDI worldwide but also for most of world trade.

The involvement of TNCs in international trade – on which more in Chapter 19 – is due to a variety of elements in their international production pattern.[12] First, when international production is vertically integrated across countries, this automatically leads to the movements of components from country to country for further processing, and thus to trade in components, which often takes the form of intra-firm trade. Second, the location of horizontal plants/subsidiaries across countries may be motivated by the desire to penetrate markets in third countries. The case of US and Japanese investment in the UK in the run up to its membership of the European Community (EC) was partly motivated by the opportunity it offered of jumping trade barriers in other European countries from the UK location. Moreover, horizontal and/or vertical production in other countries may lead to the exports of investment goods by other companies from the home to the host country (Reddaway et al., 1967; 1968). Markusen's concentration on horizontal-only FDI leads to his neglect of the first type of exports, those generated by international vertical integration, which can be very substantial (Casson and associates, 1986).[13]

The last problem derives from the treatment of interregional and international issues in the new theories and it is connected to the main contradiction mentioned towards the beginning of this section: the contradiction between the prediction of agglomeration in the theory and the reality of TNCs spreading their activities widely across the world. This I consider to be the main point of tension and to it we now turn.

The new paradigm deals with TNCs' activities in the context of a theory of location in which appropriate theoretical assumptions lead naturally to a multi-plant organization of production.[14] This approach is specific to spatial location; it is one that geographers have been concerned with for a long time and one that economists – in their newly found enthusiasm for location and agglomeration – are now embracing. In fact, Krugman (1991a: 33–4) argues 'for the acceptance of economic geography as a major field within economics, on a par with, or even in some sense encompassing, the field of international trade'. This approach roots the theory in geography and space; however, this is not the same as fitting the theory into a framework related to nation-states and their characteristics.

As we saw from the works reviewed in the previous sections of this chapter, the basic assumption common to the two strands of MNC-enlarged theories of location is the following. There are large, fixed costs at the firm level mostly related to large and intangible knowledge-based assets; there are, therefore, economies of organizing production under the same company umbrella though not necessarily under the same plant. The specificity of services and/or assets deriving from the joint assets, leads to advantages of internalization and thus to a preference for direct production over licensing.

In the approach to the explanation of TNCs' activities summarized in the previous sections, the main assumptions leading to so-called multinational production are not specific to *international* activities; they relate to the structure of inputs and costs at the firm and plant levels and they apply just as well to *interregional* (intra-national) locations of activity. The models are multi-plant models in which the various plants could be located in different regions of the same nation-state (Ohio, Texas, Michigan) or in different nation-states (Italy, Germany, Switzerland, the UK). The difference between the two situations is one of degree: the spatial transaction costs per unit of distance may be higher between than within nations; the constraints to factors mobility may be higher; there may be restrictions to trade at the international level which would not exist at the interregional level.

In the TNCs-enlarged new trade theories, nations are defined in terms of the extra costs and barriers to factors and products mobility they pose over and above the costs of operating at the interregional level. Krugman (1991a) is quite explicit on this point. He writes, 'Nations matter – they exist in a modelling sense – because they have governments whose policies affect the movements of goods and factors. In particular, national boundaries often act as barriers to trade and factor mobility' (ibid.: 71–2) and later: 'countries should be defined by their restrictions' (ibid.: 72). The emphasis here is on spatial and other transaction costs and on barriers to the mobility of factors and products. In the approach taken by the new trade theorists the differences between regional and national economies is a matter of degree: greater distances; greater differences in cultures; more difficult and costly operations. However, as regards the main assumption which is supposed to explain MNCs' main activities (joint inputs and economies of scale at the firm level) this is *not* an element specific to nation-states.

In Chapter 14 a different approach will be considered in which *national frontiers pose qualitatively different situations*. Within that approach transnationality gives the firm specific advantages and opportunities for developing a range of strategies not open to firms operating within the frontiers of a single country. Such advantages and opportunities help to make sense of high levels of geographical spread (by nation-states) of TNCs' activities.

SUMMARY BOX 12

Review of the 'new trade theories' approach to TNCs

Antecedents

Classical (Ricardo) and neoclassical (Heckscher-Ohlin) theory of trade; Dixit and Stiglitz (1977) on imperfect competition and increasing returns

Main writers and works

Helpman (1984); Markusen (1984 and 1995); Krugman (1985, 1987; 1991a and b; 1998); Krugman and Venables (1996); Venables (1998)

Main elements of the theory

- The applications to activities of TNCs are based on the models of 'new trade theories' and incorporate the assumption of increasing returns.
- Increasing returns can be of internal (Chamberlinian) type and external, spillover type (Marshallian). The former relate to the plant/firm; the latter relate to the industry.
- The internal (Chamberlinian) economies may relate to the plant level or the firm as a whole. The latter case is used to explain location in many plants/sites.
- The specificity of assets (and services derived from them) which give rise to joint inputs, is used to explain the preference for direct production over licensing.
- Other assumptions relate to transportation costs, as well as possible barriers to trade.
- Different assumptions on factor endowments in the home and host countries lead to attempts to explain location of FDI either in developed or developing countries.

Modalities considered

Mainly direct production and FDI; licensing; to some extent exports; some analysis of intra-firm and intra-industry trade

Level of aggregation

Firms, industries and the macroeconomy

Other relevant chapters

Chapter 8 (internalization)

Chapter 9 (Dunning's paradigm)

Chapter 14

Chapters 19 and 20

A more realistic modelling of TNCs' activities within the new trade and location paradigm should contrast the costs and benefits of operating interregionally versus internationally and not just those of operating within a single or multi-plant framework. In other words, the transnationality of operations with its strategic elements, its advantages and disadvantages should be at the forefront of analysis and not come out as a by-product of spatial analysis. There are some spatial issues in transnational production, but there are also some very relevant non-spatial ones, which fall within the institutional, political and distributional spheres. We shall revisit some of these issues in Chapter 14

Indicative further reading

Mainly the works discussed in the chapter and in particular the following:

Dunning, J.H. (1995), 'What is wrong – and right – with trade theory?', *International Trade Journal*, **9** (2), 163–202.

Helpman, E. (1985), 'Multinational corporations and trade structure', *Review of Economic Studies*, **52** (3), 443–58.

Krugman, P. (1985), 'Increasing returns and the theory of international trade', *National Bureau of Economic Research Working Papers*, No. 1752, November.

Krugman, P. (1991a), *Geography and Trade*, Cambridge, MA: MIT Press.

Krugman, P. (1991b), 'Increasing returns and economic geography', *Journal of Political Economy*, **99** (3), 483–99.

Krugman, P. (1998), 'What's new about the new economic geography?', *Oxford Review of Economic Policy*, **14** (2), 7–17.

Markusen, J.R. (1984), 'Multinationals, multi-plant economies and the gains from trade', *Journal of International Economics*, **16** (3/4), 205–24.

Markusen, J.R. (1995), 'The boundaries of multinational enterprises, and the theory of international trade', *Journal of Economic Perspectives*, **9** (2), 169–89.

Barba Navaretti, G. and Venables, A.J. (2004), *Multinational Firms in the World Economy*, Princeton and Oxford: Princeton University Press, chs 2 to 5.

Notes

* Different versions of this chapter can be found in Ietto-Gillies (2000a; 2002a: ch. 8).

1 In this chapter the expressions MNE and MNC are also used in accordance with the use of the various authors whose theories are discussed.

2 Prior to the new trade theories there was a considerable body of economic literature dealing with increasing returns (Young, 1928; Kaldor, 1967), as well as a body of economic geography dealing with agglomeration issues (cf. Krugman, 1998). What was lacking at the time was the ability to model them mathematically.

3 This is one type of spillover and agglomeration effect also considered by Cantwell (1989; 1995) with respect to innovation and technology activities, as we saw in Chapter 11.

4 This conclusion is similar to the one reached by Vernon (1966) within a different theoretical framework, as we saw in Chapter 5.

5 For a detailed presentation of the new trade theory applied to the MNCs see Barba Navaretti and Venables (2004).

6 As we mentioned in Chapter 1, over 82 per cent of outward FDI stock in 2010 originated from developed countries.

7 More on intra-firm trade and transfer prices in Chapters 19 and 20 of this book.

8 These assumptions are also made in Helpman (1984) and in Krugman (1985) as noted above.

9 Helpman (1985) and Helpman and Krugman (1985) do consider some advantages of internalization leading to intra-firm trade, as noted in section 3.

10 This is a point also made in Dunning (1998).

11 Indeed, Cantwell (1989: ch. 6) argues that it is misleading to consider international production without considering trade, and vice versa.

12 Within the 'new trade' theories complementarity elements are explored in Helpman (1984; 1985), Helpman and Krugman (1985) and Markusen (1997).

13 However, Markusen (1998) considers both horizontal and vertical integration within the same model. The vertical integration part leaves scope for intra-firm trade.

14 Caves (1996) also uses a multi-plant framework for dealing with TNCs' activities as we saw in Chapter 8, section 4.

13 Transnational monopoly capitalism

I Background: the under-consumptionist thesis revisited

In 1982 Keith Cowling published a book, *Monopoly Capitalism*, which followed on the trail of the under-consumptionist Marxist approach to the analysis of capitalism and its crises. The approach originated with Hobson and Luxemburg (as we saw in Chapter 2) and was later developed in works by Kalecki (1939; 1954; 1971), Hansen (1938), Steindl (1952), Sylos Labini (1964) and Baran and Sweezy (1966a).

The work by Baran and Sweezy had a tremendous impact on a whole generation of economists approaching the issue of the possible stagnationist tendencies in the advanced economies in the 1960s and 1970s. From the 1980s onwards economic analysis based on the demand side and on the Keynesian paradigm went out of fashion and was replaced by supply-side analysis under the neoclassical paradigm. The financial crisis of 2008 is raising doubts about the latter paradigm and its policy prescriptions. While this chapter is being revised it is too early to say whether Keynesianism and demand-side analysis will regain power within the academic and political communities.[1]

In defiance of the dominance of the neoclassical paradigm, Keith Cowling was greatly influenced by the works of Steindl as well as Baran and Sweezy. Cowling (1982) is the result of such influence. Moreover, this work forms the main building block of Cowling's later work with Roger Sugden, *Transnational Monopoly Capitalism* (Cowling and Sugden, 1987).

Paul A. Baran and Paul M. Sweezy's most famous work (1966a) deals specifically with the inner workings of giant corporations and their effects on the macro-economy.[2] They consider lack of effective demand and a stagnationist tendency to be a permanent feature of modern capitalism in its monopolistic phase. They trace the reason for such a tendency to the price formation under oligopolistic conditions. Big firms are price-makers and leader firms tend to fix prices that will be followed by the whole industry. In an oligopolistic market structure, rivals avoid price wars[3] and competition among giants tends to take other forms, leading to sales efforts – through various marketing strategies – and cost-cutting.

The end result of all this is a tendency for the economic surplus to rise; Baran and Sweezy conclude that the law of the rising surplus has replaced the law of the falling rate of profit.[4] They define the economic surplus as the 'difference between total output and the socially necessary costs of producing total output' (ibid.: 84). The economic surplus includes profits, rents and interests; however, the rising surplus can manifest in a variety of ways, including under-utilized capacity.

One problem with this approach at the operational level is that, theoretically, the surplus is an ex ante concept and hence its full manifestation cannot be estimated via *actual* levels of the various variables but should be estimated via their *potential* levels. Nonetheless, the theory predicts that, unless the monopolistic system can find ways of utilizing the surplus, the economy will be plunged into a deeper and deeper depression. Like previous Marxist authors (Lenin and Bukharin) Baran and Sweezy rule out that, under capitalism, the increase in effective demand needed to absorb the potential surplus can be found via an increase in consumption deriving from income redistribution.[5]

An increase in sales efforts via advertising as well as an increase in the output of other sectors which are not (or not fully) socially necessary (such as banking and insurance) will help to absorb the surplus and utilize capacity. However, any such strategy itself would lead to an increase in surplus as the advertising and financial industries generate large profits, for which it may be difficult to find further investment opportunities. Baran and Sweezy's most controversial conclusion is that modern monopolistic systems have found a way out of permanent stagnation via arms expenditure. Defence expenditure and wars are therefore seen as a way of bailing the capitalist system out of the tendency to permanent depression. Here there is an echo of Luxemburg's point on the useful role of the arms industry for the absorption of surplus, as we saw in Chapter 2. However, this particular outlet for the economic surplus plays a much bigger role in Baran and Sweezy than in Luxemburg.

Baran and Sweezy discuss foreign investments and their role in increasing effective demand as part of 'exogenous' investment; other 'exogenous' types of investment are those linked to population growth or new products, processes and technologies. The authors see little scope for exogenous investment as an overall surplus absorber. With regard to foreign investment in particular, they acknowledge its ability to raise the level of effective demand exogenously. However, foreign investment gives rise to high profits and, indeed, countries like the USA or the UK tend to have very large inflows of profits and dividends from cumulative past outward investment.[6] All in all, therefore, foreign investment generates a large surplus in its own right and hence compounds the long-term problems of absorption: 'foreign investment aggravates rather than helps to solve the surplus absorption problem' (Baran and Sweezy, 1966a: 113).

Cowling (1982) develops the under-consumptionist thesis along similar lines to Baran and Sweezy: prominent roles are again given to the oligopolistic structure of industries, price-setting under oligopoly, barriers to entry, and to stagnationist tendencies in the macroeconomy. He spells out in detail the links between the degree of monopoly, under-utilization of capacity, lack of effective demand and the gap between potential and actual profits, all leading to long-term stagnation.

As in Baran and Sweezy's work, the international side is not fully developed. In a chapter devoted to international competition Cowling (ibid.: ch. 6) argues that imports are not a powerful competitive force for monopoly capitalists because most large firms are themselves in control of international trade. The international side of his theory is developed in Cowling and Sugden's (1987) theory of *transnational monopoly capitalism*. To this work we now turn.

2   Cowling and Sugden's approach to the TNCs

Keith Cowling and Roger Sugden (1987) start their analysis with a definition of firms and TNCs based on *control* rather than legal ownership of assets. Control is not an easy concept to formulate. The authors follow Zetlin (1974) for whom 'control refers to the capacity to determine the broad policies of a corporation . . . to a social relationship, not an attribute' (ibid.: 1090). For Zetlin, having control means that the controlling group are 'able to realize their corporate objectives over time, despite resistance' on the part of other groups (ibid.: 1091).

The concept of control is closely associated with the concept of strategic decisions, which, according to Cowling and Sugden (1998a: 64) are 'the pinnacle of a hierarchical system of decision-making'. Moreover, they write that: 'the power to make strategic decisions can be equated with the power to control a firm, where control implies the ability to determine broad corporate objectives . . . This includes the power broadly to determine a firm's geographical orientation, its relationship with rivals, with governments and with its labour force' (ibid.: 64).

Cowling and Sugden (1987) demarcate between firms and transnationals and thus define the two: '*A firm is the means of coordinating production from one center of strategic decision-making. A transnational is the means of coordinating production from one center of strategic decision-making when this coordination takes a firm across national boundaries*' (ibid.: 12). This early work is further developed in Cowling and Sugden (1998a), where the authors consider the Coasian view of the firm[7] and play down/reject the efficiency aspect usually emphasized in the more orthodox literature, i.e. the fact that the organization of business within the firm allows savings on transaction cost.

Instead, they emphasize a neglected aspect of Coase's theory (as noted in Chapter 8, section 1): the fact that within the firm we have organization of business via direction and planning, which imply strategic decisions. They write: 'the firm is not primarily about a set of transactions. Rather, *it is primarily about strategic decision-making*' (Cowling and Sugden, 1998a: 67). This wider view of the firm allows the authors to take account of a variety of businesses working with/for the main large company. This means that, for example, subcontractors are seen as part of this wider concept of the firm because they fall within the strategic control of the principal, large firm.

In their 1987 work, the authors then go on to argue that the profit maximization objective of firms rules out a perfectly competitive environment; the contradiction between this objective and the assumption of perfect competition is, for the authors, obvious because:

> firms in perfectly competitive markets merely achieve normal profits, which they will undoubtedly find unsatisfactory. Clearly, then, they will attempt to avoid such competition; i.e. they will try to dominate product markets and, in the extreme, obtain pure monopoly profits. Moreover if they succeed the competition view is misplaced. (Cowling and Sugden, 1987: 17)

Cowling and Sugden (1987) therefore place TNCs firmly in a realistic *oligo-polistic framework in which collusion and rivalry coexist*. 'Rivalry means that firms must be in a position to both *defend* against rivals (i.e. prevent others gaining profits at their expense) . . . and *attack* (i.e. improve their profits to the detriment of rivals' (ibid.: 18); in this game the existence of retaliatory power becomes crucial. Firms will seek strategies that give them high retaliatory power; in fact they can use their world-wide production and resources to retaliate against a given rival. The end result is that 'firms will become transnationals to pursue profits in a rivalry and collusion environment which follows from the profit maximising assumption' (ibid.: 21).

Transnational companies have great *detection power* owing to their ability to collect, process and use information to their advantage; this helps them to secure high price–cost margins and high market power. The desire to control markets leads to more and more monopolization; here Cowling and Sugden point out how the presence of both foreign and domestic TNCs in a particular country increases monopolization.

Firms become transnational 'either because of the risks which lead them to defend against rivals, or because of the advantages which cause them to attack' (ibid.: 61). Defence and attack strategies against rivals are also the subject of Knickerbocker (1973) and Graham (1978; 1992), who use them to explain the geographical pattern of FDI, as we saw in Chapter 6. According to Cowling and Sugden, a specific strategy used by oligopolists to defend themselves against attacks from rivals is to secure lower labour costs. Hence transnationalism is linked to the search for cheaper labour and for a divided labour force – therefore for a labour force with less bargaining power. This view is further developed in Sugden (1991) and in Peoples and Sugden (2000).

Cowling and Sugden's (1987) analysis mainly stresses strategies towards rivals and sees the 'divide and rule' strategy towards labour as a by-product of the search for advantages over rivals. By focusing primarily on cost-cutting, the authors are led to emphasize the location of TNCs' activities in developing countries. They write: 'In short, then, our analysis leads to the so-called "new international division of labour"' (ibid.: 69). However, as already pointed out in Chapter 1 of this book, by far the largest share of the world FDI (over 65 per cent) is directed towards developed countries. The authors dismiss the claim that the 'divide and rule' hypothesis is untenable – as claimed by many economists – because, after all, 'transnationals appear to pay wages at least as high as their rivals and they therefore cannot be founded on a division of the workforce to lower labour costs' (ibid.: 70). They point out various fallacies in this argument, including the fact that wages are only one element in labour costs.

Cowling and Sugden see an *increase in monopolization* owing to the presence and the overall activities of TNCs. Moreover, the authors claim that the increase in the number of small and medium-size firms cannot be seen as a move towards a more competitive environment as many such firms are controlled by large TNCs. The following reasons are given for the increased monopolization of economic systems:

- International trade does not act as a competitive element in a particular country (e.g. the UK) because trade itself is controlled by TNCs;[8] a view first put forward in Cowling (1982).

- The power structure is moving more in favour of capital and away from labour.
- Transnationalism is spreading throughout the world in both advanced and developing countries.

Cowling and Sugden see many effects deriving from these trends, as set out in Box 13.1.

Box 13.1   *Effects of transnational monopoly capitalism*

- A tendency towards stagnation as a high degree of monopoly leads to a lack of effective demand. This argument follows Cowling's previous work (1982).

- This lack of effective demand may also lead to low actual profits in spite of the high potential profits that monopolization could generate.

- De-industrialization in some advanced countries is not necessarily followed by industrialization and growth in the developing ones. Relocation strategies by TNCs result in a negative-sum game; this is because 'the allocation of production and investment is not guided primarily by questions of efficiency' (Cowling and Sugden, 1987: 98) but is motivated by issues of control over production, over the labour process and over the distribution of incomes between wages and profits.

- Distribution away from labour and the related curtailment of the power of unions will further strengthen the stagnationist tendencies.

- At the same time, nationally-based policies of demand management aimed at full employment will become less effective, given the presence of corporations operating transnationally.

The last point – a theme present in Hymer's later works (1970; 1971; 1972) – is a manifestation of Cowling and Sugden's strong interest in policy issues in the development of their analysis of TNCs' activities and their effects. Their overall approach leads also to relevant insights into industrial policies, an area further developed in some of their later works (Cowling and Sugden, 1990; 1993; 1994).

While recognizing that TNCs are innovative institutions, Cowling and Sugden express doubts about the directions and use of innovation. If the innovation is in products, TNCs will use the advantage to achieve further monopolization, leading to further stagnationist tendencies. If the innovation is in processes, it is used to control the work process and to push down wages, again leading to curtailment in aggregate demand and hence to stagnation.

Cowling and Sugden see the solution in a higher level of democracy and participation as well as in state intervention designed to achieve coordination between various industries and sectors. These views are further developed by the authors in Cowling and Sugden (1998a) and in Cowling and Tomlinson (2000).[9] In both these works the authors take the view that transnationalism is not necessarily to be associated with large size and market power. They put forward a possible and desirable scenario of networks of small and medium-size enterprises which operate transnationally as networks rather than as individual enterprises.[10] The positive outcomes from this scenario are the following: a higher level of control by society as a whole, over TNCs, their strategies and effects; avoidance of the problems connected with transnational capitalism, including the stagnationist tendency; and a higher level of efficiency, partly enhanced by a higher level of democratic participation to economic and social decisions.

3   Comments

Cowling and Sugden (1987; 1998a) develop a very interesting approach to transnationalism within the Marxist tradition while utilizing and developing concepts from more conventional post-WWII literature on the TNCs. In particular, they revisit Hymer's role of market power in the internationalization of production (Chapter 4); Vernon's concept of 'global scanning' (Chapter 5) in their concept of 'detection power'; and Knickerbocker's concept of strategies of 'defence and attack' by oligopolists (Chapter 6). Cowling and Sugden also utilize and develop, very effectively, literature which is less well known to economists, such as that on the concepts of control and strategic decisions (Zetlin, 1974). (For a summary of Cowling and Sugden's main insights see Box 13.2.)

Nonetheless, Cowling and Sugden's work is not without problems. The all-embracing approach, though interesting in many parts, leads to lack of depth in some chapters, particularly those dealing with de-industrialization, democratic processes and policy recommendations. However, the latter two issues have been developed further in later works by the two authors together (Cowling and Sugden,

---

Box 13.2   *Main insights in Cowling and Sugden's analysis*

- A novel view of the firm based on 'control'.

- The development of a theory of transnational capital based on strategic decisions and thus a move away from the restricting framework of efficient markets and efficiency objectives.

- As regards Coase's theory of the firm, emphasis on 'planning and coordination within the firm' rather than on the efficiency of 'transaction costs savings'.

- Incorporation of labour issues within the overall framework of strategies towards rivals and market power.

- Attempt at merging together macro and micro elements through the links between monopoly power, degree of monopoly and macro analysis. This is an area developed on the basis of Cowling (1982).[11]

1993; 1998a) or with others (Cowling and Tomlinson, 2000; Peoples and Sugden, 2000 and Branston et al., 2003).

That further monopolization in the system may lead to stagnationist tendencies is a thesis already worked out in previous literature, including Cowling's own (1982). However, the case for claiming a growing degree of monopolization owing to TNCs is not corroborated.[12] Transnationalism has certainly increased but does this lead automatically to increased monopoly power? Cowling and Sugden's case rests mainly on the high 'detection' power possessed by TNCs and their use in defence and attack toward rivals. A stronger case can be made as to why transnationalism gives specific advantages as argued in Kogut (1983) and in the next chapter of this book.

SUMMARY BOX 13

Review of Cowling and Sugden's approach

Antecedents

Kalecki (1939; 1954 and 1971); Steindl (1952); Baran and Sweezy (1966a); Hymer (1960, published 1976); Knickerbocker (1973); Zeitlin (1974)

Main writers and works

Cowling (1982); Cowling and Sugden (1987; 1998a); Peoples and Sugden (2000)

Main elements of the theory

See Box 13.2

Modalities considered

Mainly international direct production and FDI; international trade is considered as effect of FDI.

Level of aggregation

The firm and industry; the macroeconomy is considered mainly in relation to effects of TNCs' activities and to policies.

Other relevant chapters

Chapter 2 (pre-WWII Marxist writers)

Chapter 4 (Hymer)

Chapter 6 (Knickerbocker)

Chapter 14

In the real world, there are major contradictions and conflicts between institutions that are truly transnational such as the TNCs in their planning, strategies and operations, and institutions or groups that, by their own nature and for historical and other reasons, cannot rely on a transnational infrastructure, such as trade unions, consumers and governments. It is in relation to these institutions that TNCs have particular advantages, and they can use their global scanning, detection power and all other sources of power to further their advantage. It is not maintained here that issues of market power and strategies towards rivals are not relevant, but that it is in the contrast between the power of transnationalism and the power of non-transnational institutions that we are likely to see main contradictions and conflicts; a major reason why TNCs use strategic planning is to turn this contrast to their maximum advantage.

Some of these points are, to a degree, met in Cowling and Sugden's later works where they consider or develop the following: (1) the need to encourage transnational networks of SMEs in order to give the advantages of transnationalism to smaller firms (Cowling and Sugden, 1998a; Cowling and Tomlinson, 2000); and (2) the 'divide and rule' strategy of large TNCs towards labour (Sugden, 1991; Peoples and Sugden, 2000).

Indicative further reading

Cantwell, J. (2000), 'A survey of theories of international production', in C.N. Pitelis and R. Sugden (eds), *The Nature of the Transnational Firm*, London: Routledge, ch. 2, pp. 10–56.
Various works by Cowling and Sugden, as discussed in this chapter.

Notes

1 A link between the financial crisis and under-consumption theories is in Ietto-Gillies (2010).
2 Baran and Sweezy (1966b) deals specifically with imperialism, its origins and effects.
3 Sweezy (1939) had, in fact, previously presented a theory of prices under oligopolistic conditions, which gave theoretical backing to the empirical observation of price stability. His approach and other similar ones were further developed by Stigler (1947). Both Sweezy's and Stigler's articles have been reprinted in the American Economic Association Series, *Readings in Price Theory* (1953), London: George Allen and Unwin, chs 20 and 21, 404–9 and 410–39 respectively.
4 For a discussion on the falling tendency of the rate of profit, see Sweezy (1942: ch. 6).
5 Since Baran and Sweezy's writings the distribution of income and wealth has become more concentrated at the top with negative effects on the overall propensity to consume.
6 Ietto-Gillies (2000b) analyses some empirical and theoretical issues deriving from the inflow and outflow of profits and dividends. The potential problems of large inflows of profits and dividends are analysed by Rowthorn and Wells (1987: app. 7) under their concept of 'wealth trap'.
7 Cf. Chapter 8 in this book.
8 See also Cowling and Sugden (1998b) and Branston et al. (2003).

9 Branston et al. (2003) stress in particular the need for governance of companies based on democratic participation of all the relevant stakeholders such as workers and consumers as well as managers and shareholders.

10 Cf. also Cowling (1999).

11 For further comments on this part of Cowling's work see Ietto-Gillies (1983).

12 Different results and arguments on this issue are provided by Fine and Harris (1985: 93–4) and Cowling et al. (2000). See also Auerbach's (1989) review of Cowling and Sugden (1987).

14 Nation-states and TNCs' strategic behaviour

I Introduction

The theory presented in this chapter[1] is built on the assumptions that: (a) the transnational companies operate in industries characterized by oligopolistic structures. They therefore have various degrees of market power which they strive to increase or maintain. (b) To this end they act proactively and strategically in order to increase their competitive advantages. (c) Moreover, companies develop strategies not only with respect to rivals but also with respect to other players in the economic system. These are players with which the companies interact in the course of their activities and towards which they have various degrees of power, specifically bargaining power.

Alongside the idea of strategically 'created' advantages, the theory stresses the advantages of operating transnationally; they can also be created or enhanced by the firm's strategic behaviour.

The stress on advantages of transnationality draws attention to the role of nation-states and national frontiers as relevant elements in the explanation of the companies' behaviour and strategies. In the introduction to the book I considered the issue of TNC-specific theories and asked whether we actually need such theories as against theories of the firm in general. In that context I argue that the existence of nation-states creates scope for specific strategies by TNCs and thus generates the need for TNC-specific theories.

The current chapter develops a theory that links international production to advantages of transnationality deriving from the characteristics of nation-states. The pattern of activities of TNCs is therefore seen as being, partly, determined by the opportunities for specific strategies offered by the existence of national frontiers.

2 Liability of foreignness or advantages of multinationality?

The traditional approach to the study of international production is based on the assumption that there is 'liability of foreignness',[2] i.e. that producing abroad is more costly and disadvantageous compared with producing in domestic locations, and that we must therefore look for compensating advantages in explaining international production. This is, in fact, an issue that goes back to Hymer's famous dissertation (1960)[3] and Kindleberger's (1969) follow-up. In the 1960s, at the time the pioneer analyses by Hymer and others were developed, it was very reasonable to emphasize the disadvantages of producing in foreign countries. But is it now? International production has been increasing at a very fast pace; it is involving more and more countries, more and more companies. Large TNCs with a tradition of foreign investment are spreading their internal geographical networks wider and wider (Ietto-Gillies, 2002a: chs 4 and 5). Moreover, the international involvement of smaller companies is now considerable and growing. Given these developments it seems appropriate to move away from the emphasis on disadvantages of foreign investment and start stressing the advantages of transnationalization as such.[4] However, the stress on the advantages of transnationalization does not mean denying that foreign production may involve some additional costs; it just means that conditions are ripe for emphasizing the advantages of operating abroad and of spreading activities in host countries.

The following developments point to the 'ripeness' of conditions. The growing internationalization has meant that companies have learned more about their international environment. They can use the experience of investing abroad in developing strategies for future investment in the same country as well as in others. The acquisition of information on the conditions in different countries gives companies added advantages. Already in the 1970s, Vernon (1979) considered large TNCs to be 'global scanners' capable of scanning the world for investment opportunities and locations. Cowling and Sugden (1987) – Chapter 13 – emphasize TNCs' 'detection power', that is, power to obtain, process and use information to their own advantage; for example, to get a stronger market position. Thus, TNCs learn to become more involved in international production partly through their own experience: because they have done it in the past, the process becomes easier. International involvement, in whatever mode (exports or direct production or licensing), may lower the cost of further involvement in the same or different mode(s) (Petri, 1994).[5]

There are also spillover effects and external economies including those generated by labour mobility which facilitates the inter-company and inter-industry transfer of international skills. In countries with a long tradition of outward foreign investment we are likely to witness the generation of external effects and benefits, some of which are specific to the home country and are linked to learning from the experience of past FDI; others may be linked to learning from operating in the different environments of host countries. Thus, the marginal cost of investing abroad may diminish for the company with a long tradition of FDI but also for newcomers into the foreign investment field. This may help to explain the growing number of smaller companies which are investing abroad.

In both home and host countries a whole cultural and institutional infrastructure is developed around internationalization, and this leads to cumulative effects. The economic and historical relevance of FDI for the country(ies) is likely to lead to the establishment of powerful governmental and/or private agencies which help the foreign investment process both at home and in the host countries. At the same time, foreign policy and trade missions smooth the path towards operations in more foreign countries or towards making further inroads into the ones where domestic TNCs have already invested. Moreover, private consultancy agencies spring up ready to train, advise and prepare for international operations. Business schools train the new white-collar workforce to embrace an appropriately outward-looking culture. With the increase in international mobility the condition of expatriation is made more widely acceptable and, indeed, fashionable. Difficulties are smoothed as boarding schools for one's children are available at home and – even more important – international schools develop in host countries. Financial advice on taxation and housing also becomes available with the growing numbers of expatriate employees. Therefore the overall process becomes cumulative and the resistance to operate abroad on the part of capital, managers and employees diminishes.

For all these reasons, it seems that times are ripe to stress the relevance of the firm's advantages of multinationality rather than – or not just – its costs. This will be the stance taken in the rest of this chapter.

3   The nation-state and regulatory regimes

The nation-state can be a very significant player in the establishment of firm's advantages. In order to understand how this comes about let us start with an analysis of different dimensions of operating across national frontiers. We can identify three such dimensions, listed in Box 14.1.

Box 14.1   *Three dimensions of operations across nation-states*

1   **Spatial/geographical dimension.** The distance between locations in different nation-states is often greater than the distance between locations within the same nation-state. But this is not always the case. For example, the distance between Milan and Reggio Calabria is greater than the one between Milan and Geneva. Similarly, the spatial distance between Boston and Montreal is less than the one between Boston and Los Angeles.

2   **Cultural and linguistic dimension.** The cultural distance – including business culture – is usually greater between nation-states than between regions of the same nation-state. But again, this is not always the case. The cultural distance between Milan and Geneva is not necessarily higher than the one between Milan and Reggio Calabria.

3   **Regulatory regimes dimension.** By regulatory regime I mean the sets of all laws, regulations and customs governing the economic, social and political life of a country. It therefore includes the sets of institutions and regulations governing production, markets and the movement of resources across countries. Each country has a specific regulatory regime and thus a specific set of rules and regulations which often have historical as well as institutional origins and connotations. Countries differ – sometimes substantially – in terms of their specific regulatory regime. However, the regulatory regime tends to be fairly – though not completely – homogeneous and consistent within each nation-state.

Business across national frontiers may involve additional costs compared to business within the boundaries of the nation-state. The costs are associated mainly with the first two dimensions: spatial and cultural dimensions. The third dimension may also involve extra costs because, for the TNCs, the mastering of – and managing in the context of – different laws, regulations and customs by their managers, may also be costly.

In the context of the third dimension, the nation-state is here seen as the locus of a set of *regulatory regimes*, that is, of a set of specific rules and regulations which apply to people, firms and institutions within the borders of the nation-state. Some of these rules and regulations stem from the legal or institutional system, some from government policies. Most of them embrace several or all aspects of both institutional and policy frameworks[6] as highlighted in Box 14.2.

Box 14.2   *Elements of nation-states' regulatory regimes*

- Rules and regulations regarding the social security system and in particular different regimes regarding labour and its organization

- Fiscal regime

- Currency regimes

- Regime of industrial policy with regard to incentives to businesses

- Rules and regulations regarding environmental and safety standards[7]

The elements in Box 14.2 create opportunities for the TNCs to enhance their advantages via strategic behaviour. The relevant strategies have two specific characteristics: (1) they are directly linked to operations across nation-states; and (2) they can have different objectives and be developed with respect to different players in the economic system. Box 14.3 lists five specific types of advantages that can arise from the existence of national frontiers. They will be considered in detail in the next section.

Box 14.3   *Specific advantages of transnationality*

1 Towards labour

2 In negotiations with governments

3 Arising from different currency and tax regimes

4 Risk spreading

5 Acquisition of knowledge and innovation

---

4 Why multinationality can generate advantages

The existence of different regulatory regimes across nation-states allows companies that can truly plan, organize and control across frontiers to develop strategies to take advantage of differences in such regulatory regimes. This is particularly the case when the strategies aim to enhance power vis-à-vis actors who cannot – or not yet – plan and organize across national frontiers, or not to the same extent as TNCs.

As we saw in Chapter 13, Zetlin (1974: 1090) argues that power (and control) 'is essentially relative and relational: how much power, with respect to whom?'. Companies' power has usually been analysed in relation to market power and, therefore, with respect to rival firms. In fact, many theories of the TNC deal – to a greater or lesser degree – with strategic behaviour towards rival firms (Vernon, 1966; Knickerbocker, 1973; Graham, 1978; 2000; Cowling and Sugden, 1987; Cantwell, 1989; 1995; Dunning, 1993b; Buckley and Casson, 1998b). However, power may also relate to other players in the economic system and specifically labour, governments, suppliers/distributors, and subcontractors.[8]

Power is used in the resolution of conflicts, particularly those over distributional issues arising from production or market conditions. In the case of conflicts with rivals, the distribution relates to market shares; in the case of labour, the conflict is over distribution between profits and wages; in the case of conflicts with governments the issue is distribution over the overall surplus and how much should go to the private sphere – companies – or public sphere – governments and taxpayers.

The first three advantages listed in Box 14.3 involve distributional issues and conflicts with labour and governments. The last two advantages can put the TNC in a better position towards rivals and therefore involve distribution over market shares. We shall consider them in the next two subsections.

Advantages towards labour

What impact does internationalization have on the balance of power between labour and capital? Can/do companies develop strategies to enhance their power? What role, if any, does internationalization play in such strategies? The international business literature has not given much weight to these issues[9] or to the possible role of such strategies in the explanation of the pattern of international production.

The concentration of the literature on strategic behaviour towards rivals and not on strategic behaviour towards labour is compatible with the assumption of imperfect products markets and perfect labour markets. The distribution elements in terms of market shares and in terms of wages/profits may be interlinked in the following sense. A stronger position vis-à-vis labour puts the company in a better position to gain a higher market share. Conversely, will a stronger market position give the company a stronger bargaining position towards labour? The acquisition of assets-specific skills – that is, of skills developed in the context of a specific organizational and technological institution – may make labour less mobile. However, asset specificity can also be the source of problems for the company: the employed labour has been trained by the company to work within a specific environment in terms of assets and organization and thus hiring fresh labour and training it is costly.

Besides, labour employed within the same ownership unit – that is, within business enterprises all belonging to the same company – may find it easier to organize and take action; easier organization may also develop when all the labour employed by the same company is concentrated in one or few countries. The growth of firms and the concentration of their production (or indeed of large parts of an industry) into the same country or region within it, may lead to an easier organization for labour and to a more powerful labour force vis-à-vis capital. Labour has, traditionally, found it easier to organize and resist when a substantial number of labourers are: (1) working for the same company/institution; and (2) working within the same country or region within it. Proximity, shared condition of labour, shared contracts and shared cultural and social environments give the labour force a stronger feeling of solidarity as well as laying the foundation for easier organization and resistance.

What strategies are open to companies that want to prevent or make it difficult for labour to increase their bargaining power? It will be in the interest of companies to try to implement strategies leading to the *fragmentation* of labour. Various types of fragmentation are possible, in particular the following:

- organizational fragmentation through the externalization of some activities within an overall strategy of control of production;
- fragmentation by nation-states through the location of production in various countries characterized by different labour and social security regulatory regimes.

These two fragmentation strategies are not incompatible and they may indeed be implemented together. The first strategy (organizational fragmentation) involves the company in the externalization of labour through outsourcing strategies (such as subcontracting arrangements) which allow the principal considerable control of production but without the responsibility for the labour employed for such production. The second strategy involves the spread of production in regions, countries, areas not linked by common labour organization regimes, i.e. having different trade unions and/or different labour and social security laws and regulations. These elements make the organization of labour and its resistance to the demands of capital more difficult. The underlying assumptions in this analysis are the following:

1   Labour organization is easier whenever labour works for the same 'ownership/ management unit'; and labour organization is more difficult whenever employment is dispersed among many smaller units – be they wholly or partially independent firms – or among some large and some small units.
2   Labour organization is easier within a single country than between different nation-states.

This does not imply that, for labour, full harmonization and homogeneity of organization and power exist within each country. Differences can arise at the level of

regions due to local conditions and institutional structures, or between different industries or due to different structural features of production in terms of
ownership/management arrangements as in (1) above.

The main point made here is that, on the whole, the differentials in the actual and
potential for labour organization and power is higher between countries separated by
institutional, political, cultural, legal and governmental borders than within each
border. We can then define areas of 'labour organization regimes' as those geographical areas within which – ceteris paribus – labour finds it easy to organize itself effectively. They are likely to be defined by the boundaries of the nation-state though it is
conceivable that they could extend only within smaller regions of the same country or
that they could theoretically extend to various nation-states (such as the European
Union) if labour manages to organize and mobilize across nation-states. Up to now
such organization and mobilization has not extended beyond the confines of single
nation-states.[10]

Two consequences derive from this, both relevant for TNCs' strategic decisions
in terms of the location of international production. First, that – ceteris paribus –
companies may seek to locate in areas of weak labour organization regimes; thus
foreign direct investment would flow – ceteris paribus – from areas of strong labour
organization regimes towards areas of weak regimes. This can help to explain the
existence and direction of FDI flows.[11] Second, even if the differentials in labour
organization regimes across nation-states are not high, the *dispersion* of employment
across many countries – though within the same company – *fragments the employed
labour force* and thus makes its organization more difficult and its bargaining position
weaker. Such dispersion gives a stronger position to capital vis-à-vis labour compared
with a situation in which the growth of production within the same company were to
occur all or mostly within a single country. Thus, we have a situation in which the
internationalization of production per se generates advantages for companies.

To the extent that a fragmentation strategy is pursued, we have the following
consequences:

1   Ceteris paribus, we can expect a considerable increase in international produc-
     tion and its geographical (by nation-state) spread as a response to the power of
     organized labour within single countries.
2   It is not easy to identify the direction of the flow since dispersion per se may
     become one of the strategic objectives.

Fragmentation can take place on the basis of organizational dispersion, thus leading to the various degrees of externalization of production: from full outsourcing and
use of market transactions to higher degrees of control through subcontracting
arrangements; from the employment of labour full-time and on permanent contracts
to the casualization of labour (Ietto-Gillies, 2002a: ch. 3). Fragmentation may also
take a geographical (by nation-states) route. This involves the dispersion of production over many nation-states, countries/areas, albeit within the internal, hierarchical
organization route. Some degree of both geographical and organizational dispersion
and fragmentation is also possible, for example, through international subcontracting.

The two strategies reinforce each other in the fragmentation potential and, therefore, in the difficulties they generate for the organization and resistance of labour in its bargaining with capital.

Moreover, a successful fragmentation strategy by large TNCs produces external effects which affect the balance of power between labour and capital not only in those firms, but also in the industry and macroenvironments in which they operate. In particular, countries with a high percentage of activities by TNCs – whether domestic or foreign – and which have developed successful fragmentation strategies towards labour, may have a more compliant workforce. This is because the fragmentation makes it more difficult for the workforce to unite but also because companies with operations in many countries have more credible relocation threats. Therefore the weakening of the contractual power of labour by the strategies of a few TNCs may have spillover effects in the whole industry and in the country.

Transnationality and power towards governments

Having production locations and business activities in several nation-states can also give the company a strong bargaining position towards governments of the nation-states and their regions. Transnational companies can – and do – play governments of different countries or regions against each other with the objective of raising the offer of incentives for the location of inward FDI (Oman, 2000; Phelps and Raines, 2002). For example, the lack of fiscal harmonization within the EU has led to competition by governments for attracting foreign companies – sometimes only nominally rather than with jobs and capital relocation – via lower and lower rates of corporation tax.[12] Moreover, if a company has production facilities in many countries its threat of re-location (Kogut, 1983) becomes very credible and can be used as bargaining power with governments to gain high incentives.

There are further advantages to be gained by a company with direct business activities in different nation-states. The latter, as loci of different governance systems and regulatory regimes, are also loci of specific taxation and currency regimes. Operating across several fiscal regimes puts the company in a position to minimize its world-wide tax liability via the manipulation of transfer prices, i.e. prices charged for the exchange of goods and services within the firm but across national frontiers, on which more in Chapter 20. As I revise this chapter (early 2011) companies drilling for oil in the North Sea are threatening to relocate in response to the British (Coalition) Government introduction of a windfall tax on oil profits. The manipulation of transfer prices can also be connected to operations across different currency regimes.[13]

Different regulatory regimes regarding environmental and safety standards between different nation-states may also lead to advantages for TNCs and to a stronger position in their negotiations over the location of FDI. *The Guardian* (2010) reports that Transocean, the owner of the rig leased by BP in the Gulf of Mexico disastrous oil exploration, was registered in the Marshall Islands and possibly responsible to their governmental institutions for environmental and safety standards.

Power towards suppliers

Operations across different nation-states can also enhance the bargaining power of companies towards their suppliers and, as a consequence, enhance its competitive power towards rivals. The existence of multiple sourcing channels (whether actual or potential) in the various countries gives the TNCs a powerful bargaining position towards suppliers. This is particularly the case because many suppliers have specific characteristics which make them liable to low bargaining power with large TNCs. In particular: (1) suppliers are often smaller companies operating in a more competitive environment than their customer; (2) they are often located in developing countries; (3) they cannot easily develop alternative international networks. In this situation it is not difficult to see how a big TNC with a large transnational network and which can rely on several actual or potential suppliers may use its international position to enhance its bargaining power towards specific suppliers.

Knowledge acquisition and risk spreading

Transnationality gives advantages to companies also in terms of: (1) the acquisition of knowledge and innovation; and (2) the spreading of risks. Unlike the issues discussed in the first two subsections, these advantages do not derive from direct conflicts over distribution. Let us discuss these two types of advantages in turn:

1   Chapters 11 and 15 discuss the knowledge acquisition and transfer via the TNCs' double network. It is an approach in which geographical diversification of production enables each unit of the TNC to learn from the environment. The acquired knowledge is then transferred to other units of the company via the internal network of subsidiaries. In this perspective, transnationality generates benefits from operating in a diverse environment with diverse knowledge and innovation histories: different nation-states with different cultural environments in terms of knowledge, innovation and technology. Moreover, Cantwell – Chapter 11 – points out how there are two-way spillover effects: from the locality to the company and from the company to the locality.

2   A further advantage of operating across several nation-states is connected with risk spreading.[14] A strategy of dispersion of production and multiple sourcing can also be a diversification strategy which allows the spread of risks of disruptions to production due, for example, to political upheavals or industrial disputes in any one country. Disruptions to production can come about also through other problems such as natural disasters. Most risks linked to the latter are not nation-specific but are more likely to be specific to the physical and geographical environment. However, the ability of countries to cope with them and to minimize risks and costs for business is, to a large extent, nation-specific and thus specific to the social, economic and governance environment and not just to the physical environment. Thus, a strategy of fragmentation by nation-states may also become a strategy of geographical diversification in order to spread risks deriving from the social and political as well as the physical environment.[15]

Before ending this section I would like to make the following points:

- All the advantages of internationalization discussed in this section put the TNCs in a stronger position vis-à-vis rivals who are not – or are less – internationalized. This comes about either because the strategies lead to lower costs (see advantages towards labour or governments or suppliers or risk spreading) or because they lead to new/better products or processes (as in the case of advantages in the acquisition of knowledge and innovation).
- In the approach highlighted so far in this chapter the decisions to decentralize production organizationally or locationally (by nation-state) are – to a considerable extent – *strategic decisions aiming at shifting the balance of power in favour of the TNC*, particularly in relation to its dealings with labour and governments. They are not efficiency-driven decisions, but decisions driven by strategies for dealing with other power-holding players in the economic system.
- We should at this point ask ourselves the following question. Do companies derive only advantages from a fragmentation strategy? Is it indeed all a bed of roses? The answer is certainly negative, because there may be problems associated with operating below the most efficient size. Moreover, the diversity of regulatory regimes across which they operate may, in itself, generate extra costs and uncertainty. For example, different currency regimes generate transaction costs; exchange rates fluctuations may bring losses as well as gains. Nonetheless, while these problems have been dealt with in the literature, the advantages of transnationalization have, on the whole, been rather neglected and this is, partly, the reason for stressing them here.

5 Advantages of multinationality as a determinant of international production

Why do we need special theories of the TNC? Can't such theories be subsumed under the theory of the firm? Or the theory of investment? We do not have special theories for companies investing in regions of the same nation-state. We do not perceive such a need; we operate within the general theory of investment and theories of location. So why TNC-specific theories? The answer – following the analysis of the previous sections – is that we need special studies of the TNCs because of the existence of nation-states with their diverse regulatory regimes.

In a hypothetical world in which no nation-states exist and all geographical areas of the world are governed as a single unit and under the same sets of regulatory regimes, we would have no need for specific theories of the TNC. We could apply the theory of the firm or theories of location to explain, for example, how the firm grows and in which part of the world it locates its activities. Were, for example, the EU to become a more political union managed with the same fiscal and social security regimes – as well as the same currency regime – we would not need TNC-specific theories to explain intra-EU FDI. Thus, we need theories of the TNC because of the specificity of nation-states and their regulatory regimes. The latter generate scope for specific strategic behaviour aiming at realizing the potential advantages. This is why we need special theories of the TNCs and their activities.

The approach outlined in this chapter helps us to explain various trends – mentioned in Chapter 1 – in international production and FDI, including the following:

1   The increase in international production worldwide. It is more difficult to explain the pace and acceleration in its growth if we start from the assumption that international production has built-in costs and disadvantages that need to be counteracted by other ex ante advantages. Therefore the emphasis on advantages of transnationality per se correspond to the reality of increased international production in the last few decades. It then helps us to focus on the sources of such advantages (as in section 4).
2   The very large – albeit declining – share of FDI directed towards developed countries.
3   The positions of several developed countries (such as the UK) that are both host and home countries.
4   Worldwide, faster growth of FDI than of trade.
5   The large amount of FDI that is intra-industry (Chapter 19).
6   The large and increasing geographical spread of activities (Ietto-Gillies, 2002a: chs 4 and 5).
7   The growing trends towards externalization and towards the establishment of external networks.

The patterns in (1) to (4) are often explained in terms of location near markets (which tend to be in the rich environment of developed countries) coupled with differentiation of products to meet the taste of sophisticated consumers (5). However, markets can be sourced through exports as well as direct production. It is usually argued that producing near the market adds some advantages. This is undoubtedly the case. However, we should also consider the fact that the entry mode via FDI has advantages on the production side as well as on the demand/market side. The added advantage on the production side has to do with the role of 'regulatory regimes' and in particular with the following. Sourcing markets via exports means concentrating production in one or few countries and thus within one or few 'labour regulatory regimes'. The dispersion of production into many countries has the advantage of fragmenting the labour force employed by the same company into different loci of regulatory regimes. This makes it more difficult for labour to organize and bargain for better conditions. Moreover, such dispersion also gives the TNCs bargaining power towards governments and scope for creating advantages from their fiscal and currency regimes.

There are many reasons why TNCs may want to locate in developed countries such as high-income markets, good infrastructure and a skilled and educated workforce. The problem may be the high degree of organization of the workforce; however, by spreading over many developed countries TNCs will face – ceteris paribus – a weaker labour force than by concentrating all their production in one or few developed countries. Moreover, in countries where many TNCs operate (whether they are national or foreign) this process may lead to an overall weaker labour force because labour employed by any one company is weakened by the ownership fragmentation across the many countries in which the TNCs operate. Moreover, locating activities in many countries generates scope for wider advantages, i.e those towards governments, suppliers, risk spreading and knowledge acquisition as argued in section 4.

It is interesting to note that some business strategists (Ohmae, 1995) favour the fragmentation of current nation-states into smaller regions each with its own regulatory regimes. Similarly the right wing political party Lega Nord (Northern League) in Italy is pursuing a policy of separate regions and weaker Italy. It is not difficult to see that the beneficiaries of such divisive policies would be large companies and particularly TNCs. They would be in a stronger position not only with respect to the nation-states but also with respect to the regions within them.

It is not claimed here that the pursuit of advantages of transnationality is the only determinant of the scale and pattern of international production. There are several other determinants. In the last analysis, in looking for determinants of international production and its geographical and modality pattern we should consider the following:

a   Industry-specific elements. Here the role of technology and created technological competitive advantages in some manufacturing industries can be very relevant as highlighted by Cantwell (Chapter 11).

b   Locational specific elements linked to resources, factor endowments, markets, and growth rates. These elements may help to predict the direction of flows (see Chapter 9).

c   Elements linked to countries/nation-states' macro characteristics such as customs, currencies and labour organization regimes, growth rates and markets. The latter contribute to the explanation of the direction of FDI flows.

d   Elements linked to advantages of multinationality per se. In particular: labour fragmentation; favourable bargaining position towards governments and towards suppliers; differentials in tax and currency regimes; spreading of risks; opportunities for knowledge acquisition.

e   The extent to which companies and industries can implement strategies of organizational dispersion in which labour fragmentation can be achieved through the outsourcing of parts of the production process.

f   In addition, another relevant element is the extent to which the two strategies of fragmentation – organizational and locational – can be combined together.

Elements in (d) above help to explain the *growth and spread* of international production and its macro trends as in (1) to (4) in the list above, not necessarily the pattern in the direction of the flow. While (b) and (c) are linked to *differentials* between countries (or areas), (d) does not depend only on differentials but also on the advantages of overall spread of activities (and this helps to explain trend 3 above). Elements in (e) and (f) help to explain the changing patterns of contractual relationships with labour as well as strategies of expansion via licensing, subcontracting and joint ventures either at home or abroad. Expansion via these market-based modalities leads to external networks (point 7 above) and are reflected in the growing academic interest in the so-called network company (see Chapter 15).

6   Comments

This chapter stresses the need to concentrate on advantages of multinationality and on strategic behaviour on the part of companies in looking for the determinants of the growth, patterns and organization of international production.

Nation-states are defined in terms of their regulatory regimes (section 3). Multinationality allows the TNC to operate across different regulatory regimes and to take advantage of the differences between them in its conflicts with labour over the distribution of profits versus wages and with governments (over, for example, tax liabilities or the size of financial incentives to attract inward FDI). There are also potential advantages towards suppliers and in terms of knowledge acquisition and risk spreading.

As regards labour, the hypothesis put forward in this chapter is that TNCs follow fragmentation strategies towards the labour force. These strategies can take a locational (by nation-states) and/or an organizational mode. In both cases they are likely to lead to the weakening of the power of labour towards capital.

What corroboration can be found for the fragmentation hypothesis? Section 4 mentioned a few examples of companies' behaviour that are in line with the theory put forward: taking advantage of different currency regimes or tax regimes or different labour and social security regimes. I would like to mention three more groups of potential or actual pieces of evidence. First, the indicators of extensive and growing locational dispersion of TNCs' direct activities by nation-state (Ietto-Gillies, 2002a: chs 4 and 5). In addition, the considerable growth in organizational fragmentation since the 1980s is now well acknowledged and supported in the literature (ibid.: ch. 3).

A second corroborative element could, theoretically, be found in analyses of the strategies of TNCs' top management. On this point the empirical evidence required for full corroboration is very difficult to come by. It would require information on ex ante strategic discussions, plans and behaviour of the top managers of TNCs. Peoples and Sugden (2000) attempt to corroborate their thesis of 'divide and rule' with some indirect evidence on strategic planning from Britain, the USA and Canada. As regards Britain they analyse the possible playing off of workers in various countries by foreign TNCs operating in Britain. For the USA they consider reports from trade unions on bargaining tactics of foreign-owned firms. For Canada they give evidence on how 'international unions might have greater bargaining strength than national unions when negotiating with a transnational corporation' (ibid.: 187). The instances they give are 'strongly suggestive' (as they repeatedly state) of their hypothesis. They are also strongly suggestive of the labour fragmentation hypothesis put forward in this chapter.

A corroborative case in point is the conflict between FIAT, the Italian motor manufacturer and its workforce. The company management has confronted its Italian labour force with the stark choice between accepting worse conditions – including some deemed unconstitutional by some lawyers – or see investment and jobs moved to Poland. The 'fragmentation' of FIAT's workforce between Poland and Italy contributed to the success of the management in its conflict with labourers in Pomigliano, Southern Italy.

Third, the fact that the approach adopted here helps to make sense of other salient features (1 to 7 in section 5) in the pattern of location of international production is a strong point in favour of the hypothesis.

Some readers may find the hypothesis of strategies to weaken the power of labour difficult to accept on the basis that during the last 30 years labour has been very weak indeed. There are many reasons for this weakness, including the technological shift we have witnessed during the same period and the related changes in the sectoral structure of employment in modern economies. However, I would maintain that the locational and organizational fragmentation strategies of TNCs have also contributed to such weakening. I would, in other words, see the weakening trend as supporting the corroboration of the hypothesis.

I should, nonetheless, like to make two further points. First, the fact that I consider that more corroboration is necessary and possible. Second, that I do not consider that 'fragmentation' and conflicts towards labour or governments are the only motivation behind the locational and organizational pattern of international production. There are many other important elements such as the search for markets, or cost-cutting or direct strategies towards rivals. However, the inclusion of issues linked to conflicts and power towards labour and governments adds an element that may help to bind together all the salient features of international production in the last 30 years.

It is always difficult to be critical and objective at the same time. When it comes to one's own work it is an almost impossible task. Nonetheless, for the sake of consistency with the structure of the other chapters, I will try. The *possible strong and novel points* of the approach presented in this chapter are the following:

* analysis that links the need for a TNC-specific theories to the existence and characteristics of nation-states;
* emphasis on advantages of multinationality rather than on its costs and disadvantages;
* created advantages and the notion of strategic behaviour of firms to realize them;[16]
* emphasis on strategies towards other players in the economic system besides rival firms; in particular, strategies towards labour, governments, suppliers as well as with regard to risk spreading and knowledge acquisition.

The *weak points* are the following:

* low direct, empirical evidence supporting the theory;
* the fact that the theory does not take account of the full range of strategies (towards rivals and other players), or of possible conflicts between strategic objectives;
* the dynamic potential of the theory is not developed.

Regarding the last point it should be noted that the approach can be made more dynamic by linking a variety of strategies towards the various players as briefly mentioned in the chapter. For example, by analysing how the outcome of strategies towards one set of players (e.g. the workforce) would affect the position towards the others (say rivals or governments) and how the possible strategies towards the latter set of players would then develop. Another example in this direction would be to analyse whether and to what extent the advantages of multinationality highlighted above might act as entry barriers (Kogut, 1983) for new and smaller companies lacking the history and experience of transnationalism. The possible interlink between such TNC strategies and the social and political environment might be an interesting area of research, one that would also inject dynamism into the theory .[17]

SUMMARY BOX 14

Review of the 'nation-states and TNCs' strategic behaviour' approach

Antecedents

Cowling and Sugden (1987 and 1998); Sugden (1991); Peoples and Sugden (2000)

Main elements of the theory

- Emphasis on advantages of transnationality linked to the existence of nation-states and their frontiers.
- Nation-states defined in terms of their 'regulatory regimes'.
- Need for TNC-specific theories linked to nation-states and their different regulatory regimes.
- The different regulatory regimes of nation-states create scope for TNCs' advantages towards labour and governments, suppliers, knowledge acquisition and risk spreading.
- TNCs act strategically to take advantage of opportunities offered by different regulatory regimes.
- TNCs can enhance their advantage towards labour via strategies of geographical (by nation-state) and/or organizational fragmentation.

Modalities

Mainly international production; indirectly licensing and exports

Level of aggregation

Mainly the firm; to a lesser extent the industry and the macroeconomy

Other relevant chapters

Cowling and Sugden (Chapter 13)

Cantwell (Chapter 11)

Throughout the chapter I have stressed the *fragmentation* role of TNCs. Yet the TNCs are often associated with an *integration* role in the context of the global economy. Do they integrate or fragment? My answer is that it all depends on the perspective from which we look at the issues.[17]

From the point of view of the labour force working for them, producing in many countries fragments it and thus affects its power to organize and resist. Another instance of fragmentation can be seen if we look at the issue from the point of view of the production process, on which more in Chapter 18.[18] Whenever production is located in many countries on the basis of a vertical division of the production process, the latter is geographically fragmented. However, from the overall perspective of countries, the increased volume and value of activities across different nation-states leads to a higher degree of integration of the countries concerned. In conclusion, we can say that the TNCs play a double contradictory role: they integrate countries while they fragment the labour force they employ or the production process they organize.

Indicative further reading

Ietto-Gillies, G. (2002a), *Transnational Corporations: Fragmentation Amidst Integration,* London: Routledge, chs 3, 4, 5 and 6.

Ietto-Gillies, G. (2002b), 'Hymer, the nation-state and the determinants of multinational corporations' activities', *Contributions to Political Economy*, **21** (1), 43–54.

Peoples, J. and Sugden, R. (2000), 'Divide and rule by transnational corporations', in C.N. Pitelis and R. Sugden (eds), *The Nature of the Transnational Firm*, London: Routledge, ch. 8, pp. 174–92.

Notes

1 A first sketch of the theory was presented in Ietto-Gillies (1992: ch. 14); a more developed version is in Ietto-Gillies (2002a: ch. 6). See also Ietto-Gillies (2011b).

2 See, for example, Zaheer (1995) and Forsgren (2008:16).

3 Hymer (1968) highlights costs and disadvantages of operating in foreign countries (ch. 5). Constraints and obstacles to investment abroad are also stressed in Johanson and Vahlne (1977), as we saw in Chapter 10. See also Krugman (1991a), as in Chapter 12, section 4.

4 Other authors who have also emphasized – to some extent – the advantages of multinationality for firms are Dunning (1980) and Cowling and Sugden (1987); see also Kogut (1983).

5 Johanson and Vahlne (1977) also see the experience in one internationalization mode as helping to branch into a different mode (Chapter 10).

6 Cf. also Giddens (1985: 121) for a similar approach to the nation-state.

7 On environmental standards and the MNEs see Rugman and Verbeke (2001).

8 Erturk (2011) discusses the increase in asymmetry of power between different stakeholders brought about by the globalization process.

9 One author who explicitly deals with distributional issues and strategies towards labour as a determinant of TNCs' activities is Sugden (1991), a work which has its origin in Cowling and Sugden (1987) and is further developed in Peoples and Sugden (2000), as we saw in Chapter 13.

10 It is interesting to note that successive British governments have always opposed the European Social Charter and any attempt at harmonizing 'labour regimes' within the EU.

11 Aliber (1970) uses currency regimes to explain the direction of the flow of FDI (see Chapter 7).

12 See, for example, the case of Ireland where very low rates of corporation tax have upset other European governments while not being much benefit in its unfolding (as I revise this chapter) economic and political crisis.

13 Cox (2000) discusses how the British American Tobacco (BAT) company in the 1930s was able to circumvent currency control via the manipulation of transfer prices for its intra-firm transfers.

14 On international business risk see Berg and Guisinger (2001).

15 Rugman (1979) suggests that the international spread of activities may be a risk diversification strategy on the part of the company. Penrose (see Chapter 15) considers international production as a diversification strategy of firms in their pursuit of growth.

16 This point is also in Cantwell (Chapter 11).

17 These points are further developed in Ietto-Gillies (2011a).

18 See also Yamashita (2010).

15 Resources, networks and the TNC

I Introduction

Most of the theoretical approaches to the transnational company discussed in the preceding chapters take for granted the theory of the firm and do not concern themselves with it. Most theories concentrate on firms' motivations, strategies, processes leading to internationalization, independently of the definition and boundaries of the firm. The possible exception is the internalization theory which takes as point of departure Coase's approach to firms and markets as we saw in Chapter 8. In it the TNC becomes part and parcel of a specific approach to the firm and its boundaries.

There are many conceptions of the firm,[1] but covering the related literature is not within the scope of this book: it would require a text of its own. The last two decades have seen a growing amount of literature on how various conceptions of the firm can be applied to TNCs. I shall concentrate here on two specific approaches: the firm as a 'bundle of resources' and the firm as a 'network'.

2 The TNC as 'bundle of resources'?

In 1959 Edith Tilton Penrose published a book called *The Theory of the Growth of the Firm*. It went unnoticed for many years but has had well-deserved recognition in the last couple of decades. The book is not about the firm as a TNC, but about the firm in general and, in fact, about a specific aspect of the firm – albeit probably the most important one – its growth. It was published before Hymer developed the first proper theory of the TNC as such. Given our historical approach to the presentation and analysis of theories, the reader might well think that Penrose's theory is misplaced and it should have been considered much earlier in Part III of this volume. However, though Penrose produced her theory of the growth of the firm in the 1950s, possible applications to the TNCs were not considered by herself and, lately, by others until more recent times.

Penrose starts by setting the boundaries of the firm: how do we know where the firm begins and when it ends? We know because the boundaries are set by the administrative coordination power – which is largely hierarchical power – of the management within it.

So, given these boundaries, what exactly is a firm? How can we define and characterize it? For Penrose 'a firm is more than an administrative unit; it is also a collection of productive resources the disposal of which between different uses and over time is determined by administrative decision' ([1959] 2009: 21).[2]

In fact, the relevant element in terms of their uses over time is not so much resources per se but the services that can be extracted from those resources. The amount of services that can be extracted from a given resource or a bundle of several resources is not fixed and immutable, neither is it context-independent. The way the resources are bundled together and the specific firm context in which they operate will provide services which are different from those obtainable in other contexts. A specific resource may also give different services according to the combination of other resources it is bundled with.

But even within a specific context and a specific collection of resources, it is always possible to extract more or different services from a given collection. Knowledge is the key element in the number and type of services that can be extracted from given resources and 'the possibility of using services change with changes in knowledge' (ibid.: 68). Moreover, knowledge itself evolves according to what use is made of resources. Knowledge and technological innovation are closely linked and the latter is the decisive element in the development of competitive advantages.

Resources are never fully utilized. It is the possibility of using existing resources more fully and in different ways in order to extract different and more services from them that is one of the keys to growth within the firm. 'Unused productive services are, for the enterprising firm, at the same time a challenge to innovate, an incentive to expand and a source of competitive advantage' (ibid.: 76). They are also 'a selective force in determining the direction of expansion' (ibid.: 77).

So, one main opportunity (or constraint) to growth is internal to the firm: its resources, the way they are utilized and the knowledge and innovation they give rise to. But there are also external opportunities and constraints, specifically those related to demand. Penrose thinks that demand: (a) can, to a large extent, be created by the entrepreneurs and managers and therefore become, to some extent, endogenous; and (b) is not such a big constraint to the modern firm. Demand might be a constraint in the single product firm; however, most modern, large corporations are diversified and thus involved in several product markets. Diversification is, indeed, the key to overcoming demand constraints. Diversification is relatively easy and part and parcel of large technological firms: they develop new products as part of their technological innovation, which, ultimately, determines the path taken by diversification. The encouragement towards diversification and thus growth comes from the existence of cash reserves as well as possible external opportunities such as opportunities for acquisitions.

The type of resources Penrose concentrates on are managerial, entrepreneurial and – to a lesser but large extent – engineering resources. They are the ones whose services are key to growth. At any given stage in the life of the firm, resources are inherited and thus '"history matters"; growth is essentially an evolutionary process and based on the cumulative growth of collective knowledge, in the context of a purposive firm' (ibid.: 237).[3]

So far for the growth of the firm. But what about the TNC? There is almost nothing in the original book about it. On page 89 there is a hint of it when she writes: 'Taking advantage of internal economies of growth, firms may go into new products or they may build (or acquire) plants in new locations at home or in foreign countries'.

She does not see anything special in having assets in foreign locations and she thinks that, once the subsidiary has been set up and running, it will have a life of its own and it will grow according to the laws highlighted in the book for the firm in general. Her 1956 article, 'Foreign investment and the growth of the firm' expressed similar views.[4] Her *New Palgrave Dictionary* article (1987) expresses the view that special studies of the MNCs are necessary. Indeed, in it Penrose criticizes the internalization/transaction cost approach to the MNC because the theory is not sufficiently linked to international issues. Moreover, she points out how FDI is not just an international movement of capital – as in the neoclassical theory (see our Chapter 3) – but should be seen as 'the movement of a bundle of resources' (ibid.: 562).

In 1995, writing the 'Foreword to the Third Edition' of *The Theory of the Growth of the Firm* she was much more aware of the need to take account of the TNC and she wrote a specific section on multinational corporations. Nonetheless, in it she seems to think that most of the theory already developed in her book would apply and only a few more assumptions might have to be added. She specifically writes that: 'Many, if not most, of these assumptions would apply equally to domestic firms expanding within the United States or other large and diverse countries'. Therefore she seems to be implying that an analysis of FDI can be largely subsumed into an analysis of investment in spatially diverse locations. Nonetheless, she finishes the section with the following passage: 'But with the advent of the very large global corporations of "firms" there spread what became effectively an extremely sophisticated, though not entirely new, form of organization requiring a different analysis of the nature of the firm and the relation between the firm and the market' (ibid.: 239).

In her entry in the *International Encyclopedia of Business and Management* (1996) she sees national frontiers as more than spatial borders – which seems to be the case in her analogy with investment within the USA as quoted above – and takes account of wider issues. She writes:

> The differences arise from the additional obstacles (or advantages) relating to culture, languages, . . . to different currencies, border controls or other type of physical or financial regulations, political attitudes of foreign or home governments, size of protected markets, the configurations of firm cultures or associations, the type of technology involved. (ibid.: 1720)

Penrose has not fully exploited the potential of her theory of the growth of the firm to explain the TNC. There are several potential lines in this direction. The main one is the diversification route: investment in foreign countries can be seen as a strategy of diversification to break through demand constraints at home. She analysed diversification in terms of products but not in terms of countries of operation.

Another line of investigation which would link her to the literature on ownership advantages – such as Hymer or Dunning – can be seen via the competitive advantages created within her firm by the specific combination of resources.

Both these lines are considered in Pitelis (2000) who concludes that Penrose's book can provide the framework for a theory of the TNC, putting together both supply- and demand-side factors.[5] Pitelis (2004) also notes how Penrose, in her limited consideration of the MNC, dealt only with the FDI modality. Penrose's

emphasis on knowledge as created resource linked to the firm's social and technological contexts has already been used in both Cantwell and Kogut and Zander's theories
(Chapter 11). There is scope for further developments along those lines.

Penrose (1996) has a final section on the 'network firm', which she sees as a new
development in the real world as well as in terms of interest by the academic community.
In the next section we shall discuss an approach that attempts to merge these two aspects.

3   Networks and the TNC

At the semantic level the expression 'network firm' describes the fact that modern
large firms comprise several units in different locations. When the locations are different countries we have the TNC. The development of the firm as a network of different units raises issues of organization of those units and of their control by the centre:
how are the units linked together? To what extent are they part of the whole or
autonomously run? Are their activities in line with a common strategy within the
company? What degree of control does HQ have over the units? What degree of
communication and interaction is there between the units?

The analysis of these issues is interesting per se and in terms of advancing
knowledge on the internal organization of companies and on their working; they are
particularly interesting and relevant when applied to companies whose network is
spread over many countries. However, the analysis of the issues only does not constitute a theory of the firm, let alone the TNC. To arrive at a theory of the TNC we need
elements related to value creation and its connection with the network structure of the
company. This is what many theorists in the managerial tradition of international business analysis have done (Hedlund, 1986; Bartlett and Ghoshal, 1988 and 1989;
Ghoshal and Nohria, 1997; Hedlund and Rolander, 1990). Indeed, Ghoshal and
Nohria (1997) start by criticizing the internalization theory for being 'in essence a
negative theory of the firm: the reason for the existence of the firm is described in
terms of its facility to avoid a stifling market failure' (p. 1). They want to move on to
a *positive* theory of the MNC; one in which 'value creation instead of value appropriation [becomes] the *raison d'être* of the multinational company' (p. 208).

A positive theory of the MNC is what all the authors cited above have in
common: a theory in which the network of subsidiaries in different countries act as
facilitator for value creation via the development and transfer of knowledge. The
development of knowledge and innovation is facilitated by the shared social context
and values (a view present also in Kogut and Zander, as we saw in Chapter 11).
Moreover, the transfer of knowledge between different units is facilitated by the internal network of the company.

There are three interlinked elements that characterize the network company as a
theory of the MNC: (a) the double network; (b) the organizational structure of the
MNC; and (c) value creation. In Chapter 1 it was mentioned that TNCs are increasingly involved in two types of networks, some of which are internal to the company
(its network of affiliates), and some which are external to it. The latter involve
contractual relationships which may be at various degrees of arm's length. The double

network was also discussed in connection with Cantwell's theory in Chapter 11 and in Chapter 14 in relation to advantages of multinationality.

The double network model sees potential for knowledge acquisition in the following process. Each subsidiary develops knowledge and it also acquires some from contacts with its external environment – customers, suppliers, collaborative partners including universities. The diversity of knowledge and innovation environments in which the various geographically dispersed subsidiaries operate becomes an advantage in terms of the acquisition of knowledge and innovation. The internal networks of HQ and all subsidiaries will then facilitate the transfers of knowledge to other parts of the company. Thus, the double network leads to value creation.[6]

How easy is the acquisition of knowledge by each subsidiary and then its transfer to other parts of the company? The answer depends on the internal organization of the TNC (Hedlund, 1986; Bartlett and Ghoshal, 1989; Hedlund and Rolander, 1990; Gupta and Govindarajan, 1991, 2000). If we have a very centralized structure in which control by HQ is very tight and the degree of autonomy of the subsidiary very limited then the subsidiaries may find it difficult to interact with their local environment and thus acquire knowledge from it. Thus, a more decentralized structure would help in the acquisition of knowledge. However, the more decentralized the structure is – and thus the more autonomous and independent the units are – the more difficult it is for knowledge to be transferred from unit to unit, internally to the company. This is how the internal organization of the company and value creation interact.

In the last analysis it is the connection between value creation and (a) the double network and (b) the organizational structure of the company that leads to theories of the TNC as a network company. There are several such theories and it is not possible here to do justice to this rich literature. The book by Forsgren, Holm and Johanson (2005) falls within this tradition. It has been chosen for more detailed treatment here partly because it is the most recent and partly because in their treatment the various issues presented above are well integrated.

Forsgren et al. – from now on FHJ – recognize the importance of looking at the MNC as an organization; however, their great emphasis is on the environment in which the TNC operates. The following three points are key to their theory:

- The firm's relation to the environment is essential to an understanding of what goes on within it and to an understanding of how advantages are created.
- Cooperation at all levels is paramount independently of its degree of arm's length. Specifically, cooperation between: (a) subsidiaries and their suppliers, their customers, partners involved in joint ventures or the government institutions they have dealings with; (b) subsidiaries of the same TNC; (c) each subsidiary and HQ.
- Knowledge acquisition – both via transfer and via own development – is key to the creation of value and competitive advantages. Therefore the TNC must be seen in the context of – and in relation to its ability to foster – knowledge acquisition. Knowledge acquisition cannot be understood without reference to the external environment, i.e to the external networks within which each subsidiary operates.

FHJ have a distinct definition of the MNC; one that focuses on two elements: (a) the network of business relationships both internal and external to the company; and (b) embeddedness. They write: 'doing business is not only a matter of selling and purchasing; it also means establishing and developing business relationships with important customers or intermediaries, and suppliers' (ibid.: 15).

Moreover, the partners' commitment to the relationship is not static and is likely to increase with time. A business relationship develops through the years, is long-lasting and difficult to replace in the short term. It may involve any unit of the TNC in exchanges with customers or suppliers or public institutions or indeed other units within the TNC. The authors emphasize that they see business relationships as exchange relationships between business partners, not production relationships.

What about embeddedness? What is it? The basic concept is taken from Granovetter (1985)'s idea that social structure is very relevant and plays a big role in economic behaviour. Nonetheless, embeddedness is a concept that is fluid and difficult to measure; it is also a multidimensional concept. Embeddedness takes time to develop and therefore our embedded TNC is a company with a history through which business relationships have evolved. For our authors an 'embedded business relationship [is] a relationship characterized by a high degree of mutual, long-lasting adaptation in terms of relation-specific investment. The Embedded Multinational thus signifies a MNC whose subsidiaries operate in different business networks that, to a notable extent, consist of highly embedded relationships' (ibid.: 103).

Network embeddedness can operate at two levels: (1) a subsidiary may be more or less embedded in the external environment via exchanges with customers, suppliers and other actors; (2) a subsidiary may be more or less embedded in the corporation via its exchanges with sister subsidiaries or with HQ. As many of these relationships are specific to a TNC, it follows that the transnational is a heterogeneous institution.

There are analogies – highlighted by FHJ in Chapter 5 of their book – between their approach and the one by the Scandinavian School (see our Chapter 10).[7] In both approaches experience and commitment are relevant. However, the Scandinavian School takes the country as the unit of analysis and of boundaries; in the embedded multinational's approach the focus of analysis and of boundaries move from country to business relationships.

FHJ consider three dimensions on internationalization of the MNC. First, the number of countries it has units in: the ownership dimension. Second, in relation to each subsidiary, in terms of where its business partners are located. Third, how well integrated the overall business network is across countries. In terms of measurement, they accept the measure of internationalization developed by the UNCTAD *World Investment Report*,[8] which focuses on degree of foreignness: what percentage of activities is located abroad, where abroad could be any number of countries.[9]

According to FHJ, learning and knowledge acquisition are essential elements in value creation within the MNC. Subsidiaries acquire knowledge via (a) transfers from external business partners; (b) transfers between internal units (other subsidiaries or HQ) within the MNC; and (b) their own knowledge development. The network becomes essential in both the transfer and development of knowledge. Regarding the latter mode the authors show how, often, new products and processes are developed collaboratively between the subsidiary and its suppliers or customers. The acquisition of knowledge – be it by transfer or development – can take place whether the partners in the business relationship operate in similar products or processes or in complementary ones.

Two consequences derive from the embeddedness approach to the MNC. First, hierarchy does not necessarily imply control. There are two aspects of control: (a) the administrative aspect – formal control – that is exercised through the hierarchy; and (b) actual influence on what the subsidiaries do and how they develop their objectives and strategies, which may not, necessarily, coincide with those of HQ. The more a subsidiary is embedded (i.e. very involved in long-lasting relationships) the more its behaviour is affected by these relationships. This means that the subsidiary's business relationships may be a source of power for the subsidiary itself and a source of diminished power for HQ. The latter can exercise power on the subsidiary by controlling the funds for investment, but once these are released there may be little power in terms of affecting how they are used and what specific objectives the subsidiary managers assign to them. There is asymmetry of information between HQ and subsidiaries and the more embedded the subsidiary is, the more asymmetric the information relationship becomes.

The overall view that comes across is of the MNC that, far from being a monolithic institution, is one which is divided, difficult to control and where conflicts between HQ and subsidiaries are common in the power struggle for control of resources and strategies. The more embedded the MNC is the more difficult for HQ to exercise control. The best way for HQ to exercise control is to become involved in business relationships with its own subsidiaries.

The authors conclude by writing:

> [B]eing the HQ of an Embedded MNC involves a never-ending process of seeking to understand what is going on in different parts of the organization, and a continuous struggle for influence in competition with other MNC units. It is an interesting paradox that this is what occurs just when the perception of the general public embraces the idea of a powerful and dominating HQ that exerts more or less full control over the MNC's operations. This paradox deserves a study of its own! (ibid.: 192–3)

The second consequence of the embeddedness approach is that ownership advantages and value creation of each subsidiary and of the company as a whole depend on knowledge acquisition – via own development and/or transfer. This in turn depends on the degree of embeddedness of the subsidiaries into their business networks and on the power[10] and control relationships within the MNC.

4   Comments

This chapter has presented two approaches to the TNC: the first one should be seen as a potential development more than a fully developed theory. In the second approach – network theory – there are many theoretical and applied works; however, the approach as a whole is still in the process of development.

The starting point for the first approach is now well established and recognized: the resource-based theory of the firm. The extension to the TNC is very tentative and based on the following: (a) relationship between resources – and the variable services that can be extracted from them – knowledge and competitive advantages; and (b) growth in demand via diversification.

This is a theory that is very dynamic and deals with processes: the firm is never in a state of equilibrium but always on the move: it is a welcome, realistic approach to the firm. In analysing growth, more emphasis is given to the resources side than to the demand side; not because the latter is not considered important but because it is seen as a problem with a solution: diversification. It should be pointed out that when the theory was developed, demand in western economies was certainly not a problem: in post-WWII there was plenty of pent-up demand and plenty of investment opportunities. The constraints may have been more on the supply and resources side. Penrose's theory reflects this historical fact. This means that applications of the original theory to the contemporary firm need to play more attention to problems of demand deriving not – or not only – from the position of specific firms and industries but from the global macroenvironment as a whole.

Penrose's emphasis on the firm rather than the product is a welcome and realistic move from Vernon's emphasis on the product. Penrose's early approach with emphasis on spatial distance between countries – and the similarities between FDI and investments in different regions of the same country (the USA) – recalls the new trade theory approach to the MNC. However, she later (1996) brought in differentials in regimes of different countries and here there is an analogy with some of the elements developed in our Chapter 14.

Attempts to extend Penrose's theory to the TNC are welcome though still largely undeveloped. The emphasis on the demand side has a clear path in the original theory in terms of diversification: it is easy to see the extension from diversification by product to diversification by country. However, this demand side leaves unsolved the problem of explaining large amounts of FDI that are not motivated by demand-side elements but more by problems and opportunities on the production side, such as those aiming at international vertical integration of production. It also begs the question of modality: why not meet foreign demand via exports rather than direct production abroad? Penrose's emphasis on the enhancement of resources via knowledge creation is an area where further research is possible and is likely to prove fruitful.

Unlike Penrose, the second approach discussed in this chapter relates not to the firm in general, but to the MNC; in fact a multinational whose units in different countries are all set up and fully operational. It is not, therefore, a theory of why and where the company invests and sets up subsidiaries abroad but of business relationships once those units are up and running. It links value creation to knowledge development and transfer: the latter are related to the internal and external networks of the MNC as well as to the internal organization of the company.

In FHJ's theory the boundaries of the TNC are seen as set by the business relationships more than by the countries in which they operate or by geographical distance. In common with the resource-based theory, it emphasizes processes as well as knowledge acquisition. The embedded multinational theory develops a good case for conflicts within the TNCs: between its constituent parts. This point makes it more realistic than Kogut and Zander's assumptions of harmonious relationships within the TNC (see Chapter 11). However, the FHJ approach overlooks possible conflicts and indeed opportunities generated by management's dealings with labour: yet such conflicts may be at the root of why specific types of business relationships are created, for example many of those with subcontractors. It may also be at the root of why embeddedness develops in some cases and not others.

Both theories (Penrose's and FHJ's) consider management as a – the? – key resource. Neither of them gives much attention to work force lower down in the hierarchical scale. In the case of Penrose we can think that availability of labour and compliance of labour was not a problem in the years when she was writing. For

---

SUMMARY BOX 15A

From Penrose's growth of the firm to the TNC?

Aims of theory

Penrose is interested in explaining the growth of the firm.

Conception of the firm

Firm as a bundle of resources; its boundaries set by administrative coordination

Knowledge and innovation

Knowledge and innovation are endogenously generated because they are the result of how the resources are exploited within the firm.

Workforce and stakeholders

Key role for managers, entrepreneurs and technologists

Transnationality

Penrose's theory is fully developed as a theory of the growth of the firm but not as a theory of why multinationals come into being and why they develop or how they function.

Theory development

Penrose's theory applied to the TNC is still in its infancy. Scope for development by using Penrose's approach to resources and to knowledge and/or to growth via diversification.

Level of aggregation

The firm

Other relevant chapters

Cantwell and Kogut and Zander's theories (Chapter 11)

SUMMARY BOX 15B

• •

Network theory and the embedded multinational

Object of study

The fully developed MNC with its business relationships; issues of control between head-quarters and subsidiaries

Boundaries of the MNC

Set by the extent of embedded business relationships

Knowledge and innovation

Linked to business relationships; essential to the development of competitive advantages

Level of aggregation

The firm

Other relevant chapters

Cantwell and Kogut and Zander's theories (Chapter 11)

Penrose, administrative coordination is enough to give strategic control. For FHJ it is not: the subsidiaries' involvement in business relationships may stand in the way of HQ strategic control.

FHJ specifically reject the notion that their theory relates to production: they are only interested in business relationships, not in production relationships. This is a point in common with the Scandinavian School theory (our Chapter 10)[11] and it may be a limitation which, perhaps, the same or other researchers can overcome. It would be interesting to see FHJ's theory extended to an analysis of the 'production' side of embeddedness: what role does labour play in the embeddedness of subsidiaries in specific countries or relationships? What are the links and mutual effects of international, vertically-integrated production systems and embeddedness?

In both theories knowledge and innovation are endogenously determined and are very relevant in the development of competitive advantages, in growth and value creation. There is an analogy here with the theories considered in Chapter 11.

A last point that should be made is that both theories draw, in different ways on case studies to support their theoretical assumptions. Both approaches leave scope for further empirical applications and testing as well as for further theory development.

Indicative further reading on Penrose

Penrose, E.T. ([1959] 2009), *The Theory of the Growth of the Firm. With an Introduction by Christos Pitelis*, 4th edn, Oxford: Blackwell, chs I, II, and pp. 229–33; Foreword to the Third Edition (p. 234). The Introduction by Pitelis is recommended reading.

Penrose, E.T. (1996), 'Growth of the firm and networking', in *International Encyclopedia of Business and Management*, London: Routledge, pp. 1716–24.

Indicative reading on the network theory

Bartlett, C.A. and Ghoshal, S. (1988), 'Organizing for worldwide effectiveness: the transnational solution', *California Management Review*, **31** (1), 1–21; reprinted in P.J. Buckley and P.N. Ghauri (1999), *The Internationalization of the Firm. A Reader*, London: International Thomson Business Press, pp. 295–311.

Forsgren, M., Holm, U. and Johanson, J. (2005), *Managing the Embedded Multinational. A Business Network View*, Cheltenham, UK and Northampton, MA, USA: Edward Elgar, chs 1, 2, 5, 6, 7, 13.

Forsgren, M. (2008), *Theories of the Multinational Firm. A Multidimensional Creature in the Global Economy*, Cheltenham, UK and Northampton, MA, USA: Edward Elgar, ch. 6.

Ghoshal, S. and Nohria, N. (1997), *The Differentiated MNC: Organizing Multinational Corporations for Value Creation*, San Francisco, CA: Jossey-Bass.

Hedlund, G. and Rolander, D. (1990), 'Action in heterarchies: new approaches to managing the MNC', in C.A. Bartlett, Y. Doz and G. Hedlund (eds), *Managing the Global Firm*, London: Routledge, pp. 1–15.

Notes

1 See Dietrich (2006) and Dietrich and Krafft (2012, forthcoming).

2 All references are to the fourth edition (Oxford University Press) unless otherwise indicated.

3 This quote comes from Penrose's 'Foreword to the Third Edition' of her book, reproduced as an Appendix in the fourth edition.

4 This work deals mainly with the issue of funding method for FDI and its impact on the host economy.

5 See also Pitelis' excellent Introduction to the fourth edition of *The Theory of the Growth of the Firm*, as well as Pitelis (2002b).

6 The double network impact on knowledge and innovation acquisition has been used in several researches: (Zanfei, 2000; Castellani and Zanfei, 2002 and 2004; Frenz et al., 2005; Frenz and Ietto-Gillies, 2007 and 2009; Filippetti et al., 2011).

7 Nonetheless, the Scandinavian School approach seems to be more rooted in the process – how the firm moves from one internationalization mode to another – than the embedded multinational approach. In the latter the history of the company and its business relationships lead to a particular state and depth of relationships which affects the company's strategies and performance.

8 See UNCTAD (1995) and following years.
9 Acceptance of this measure is at odds with their first dimension of internationalization: the number of countries in which the company is involved. For a discussion of different conceptual approaches to the degree of internationalization see Ietto-Gillies (2009).
10 Dorrenbacher and Gammelgaard (2011) analyse four types of power and how they affect the bargaining between subsidiary and HQ.
11 One of the three authors of the book is also a contributor to the Scandinavian School approach.

PART IV • EFFECTS

● ●

Introduction to Part IV

> The coming of age of multinational corporations should represent a great step forward in the efficiency with which the world uses its economic resources, but it will create grave social and political problems and will be very uneven in exploiting and distributing the benefits of modern science and technology. In a word, the multinational corporation reveals the power of size and the danger of leaving it uncontrolled.
>
> (Stephen Hymer, 1970: 53)

This final part is devoted to the effects of the activities of transnational corporations and, in particular, of their international production. The part is structured in five chapters dealing respectively with issues of boundaries in the assessment of effects (Chapter 16) and with specific effects on innovation, labour, international trade and the balance of payments (Chapters 17, 18, 19 and 20).

The aim of these five chapters is to set out the *analytical framework* which will, hopefully, enable students and scholars to see through the myriad of problems and issues facing the researcher, business person or politician when attempting to assess the effects of TNCs' activities.

I deliberately refrain from dealing with details of empirical evidence on which there is, indeed, a large amount of research related to specific firms or industries or to the macroeconomy of specific countries/regions.[1]

There are various reasons why I do not want to immerse the student, and the readers in general, in detailed empirical studies within the context of this book. The main reason is that I think it is useful to give students an analytical framework to be used as a kind of backcloth on which to position any specific empirical study they may come across later, or indeed undertake themselves. Didactically, I feel that it is better to give the student a general analytical framework to be used in a variety of international business studies, rather than the results of specific studies without the general theoretical skills needed to evaluate them. Another reason for this didactic strategy is the fact that there are just too many empirical studies around and picking on a few might not do justice to the many which would have to be left out for reasons of space. Moreover, empirical studies tend to become outdated fairly quickly as new research is undertaken.

Analysis of the effects raises the issue of policies to enhance positive effects and avoid negative ones. Policy issues are outside the scope of this book, though some will be touched on here and there in the following chapters.

Though I am well aware of the wide-ranging effects of TNCs' activities, the following chapters concentrate mainly on the economic domain. Other effects on society or politics or the environment or the military or population movements across frontiers are very relevant. However, a proper treatment of these issues might require separate volumes of their own. They are not the subject of this book; nonetheless, some will be touched on from time to time when we discuss specific effects in the next four chapters.

Note

1 A survey of empirical results on effects is in Barba Navaretti and Venables (2004: chs 7, 8, 9).

16 Boundaries in the assessment of effects

1 Introduction

The activities of transnational corporations in all their modalities and manifestations, produce a variety of effects. Though the media and politicians often present us with hasty, clear-cut conclusions, in reality the effects are far from easy to evaluate.

In the assessment of effects there are general methodological issues in relation to the development of specific models and to their empirical corroboration. In particular, what sort of factual evidence one uses and how the data is to be elaborated. These are, of course, very important issues in the methodology of research and those students who will go on to develop research in the field will have to confront them. They are, however, largely, outside the scope of this book, partly because they are general issues of research methods, not specific to international business or the TNCs.

The issues I want to tackle in the present chapter relate to the boundaries of the validity of effects. Understanding the boundaries within which the assessment of effects applies is relevant both in terms of the development of research projects on effects and in terms of the interpretation of results of existing research. The boundaries we are going to consider are mostly specific to the TNCs and their activities. As listed in Box 16.1 there are several dimensions ranging from underlying assumptions to time period to people and institutions affected.

2 Effects on whom?

The question in the title of this section can be approached from a variety of perspectives (see Box 16.2). We may be interested in the effects on the company – its market share, sales or profits – or the industry of which the company is part. It should be remembered that, in our increasingly integrated world, many industries are global. Therefore, looking at the effect on an industry may, at times, require us to look outside the home country of the TNC. We may also be interested in macroeconomic effects. The borderline between *micro, meso and macro* is blurred when we deal with economies in which TNCs play a considerable role because many TNCs are very large and dominate industries or greatly affect macroeconomies. Moreover, macro-economics is, largely, based on the nation-state in terms of the accounting system underlying theories and policies; however, TNCs operate *across* nation-states and this adds to the difficulties of aggregation from the micro to the macro systems.[1]

We may want to consider effects on various *groups, stakeholders, or social classes* within or across countries. Are workers being affected differently from the shareholders of a company? For example, it may be more profitable for the company

---

Box 16.1   *Boundaries dimensions*

- The effects usually span more than the purely economic *domain*. There are effects on society in general, on politics, on the environment, on culture. However, these will not be considered in the following chapters.

- *Effects on whom?* Different companies, people, groups, classes, stakeholders are likely to be affected differently. We must be clear which affected stakeholders we want to concentrate on.

- What *time period* are we considering in relation to the effects? Short-term effects may not be the same as long-term ones. An example of this will be given in Chapter 20.

- At what *level of aggregation* are we considering our analysis of the effects? Company or industry level or the macroeconomy? The effects may include spillover elements and externalities, and this means that the aggregation or disaggregation from one level to the other is not linear: the industry may get effects which are not just the sum of the effects on the companies which form the industry.

- Besides some obvious direct effects, there are many effects that come about in more indirect ways; examples of this will be given in the following chapters. Both *direct and indirect effects* should be considered.

- The full assessment of the effects requires the analysis of the *underlying assumptions* and of possible alternatives.

- While the nationality of the investor may be relevant for some effects, there are many effects that are linked to *multinationality per se* independently of the companies' country of origin and independently of whether the FDI we are assessing the effects of, is inward or outward.

- The assessment of effects tends to be closely *linked to the theoretical explanation* on why TNCs invest or engage in specific modalities. This is why in discussing specific effects I shall now and then make a brief reference to the various theories discussed in Part III.

– and therefore better for shareholders and managers – to source a foreign market via foreign investment and direct production abroad rather than by producing at home and then exporting. However, this may not be in the best interest of workers in the home country who may see themselves being deprived of job opportunities. Moreover, with respect to the workforce are we interested only of workers in the home country?[2] In fact, in the example just given, the workers in the host country may benefit from a company's strategy of direct production.

This takes us to a major issue in the assessment of the effects of TNCs' activities: the specific *type of country* we want to consider. When dealing with international issues it is common to consider effects on various countries or nation-states; this implies taking 'the nation-state' as the most important unit of analysis and, particularly, it implies considering it as a homogeneous block of common interests.

In reality there are conflicts of interests between workers and capital and within each of these categories: workers in different sectors (say manufacturing versus services) may have conflicting interests; similarly, the interests of national capital may not coincide with the interests of international capital. Conflicts may also arise between industrial and finance capital or between managers and shareholders of a particular company.

Moreover, TNCs' strategies have considerable effects on governments and their policies. As the activities affect the economy and various agents within it, the overall context of policy is influenced. There are also more direct effects on governments' budgets first of all via the impact on state revenues of possible additional incomes linked to TNCs' activities. This is a general effect of investment whether undertaken by TNCs or UNCs. However, some effects are specific to TNCs' activities. On the revenue side the manipulation of transfer prices on the part of TNCs leads to distortions in tax revenues and to the transfer of surplus from the public to the private sphere, as we shall discuss in Chapter 20. On the expenditure side, governments often give financial as well as other incentives (such as 'tax breaks') to induce companies to locate their inward investment in their country/region. This affects the expenditure and/or the revenue side of government budgets.

Most of the effects we have considered in this section are direct effects of TNCs' activities on home or host countries or on the investing company and industry. However, there are also considerable indirect effects. Among the latter, two categories are of particular relevance in the context of international business.

First, the impact of FDI on third countries and on other firms. The literature on FDI and international production usually deals with the effects by dividing them into effects on the home country and effects on the host country.[3] However, an excessive emphasis on *home/host country dichotomy* may be misleading for various reasons. In particular:

1   Home and host countries are not the only two types of countries involved in the effects. Third countries, where a given TNC already has production facilities, are likely to be affected by the company's overall strategy with regard to the sourcing of markets and/or the location of production or of segments of the production process. What I mean here is the following: let us assume that company Z, originating in country A and with existing production activities in countries B, C and D, decides to invest in country X (where X could be any country including A, B, C and D). The effects of this decision will be felt – in a variety of ways – not only in the host and home country (X and A) but also in all the other countries in which the company has production facilities (B, C and D). With the increase in the spread of TNCs' internal and external networks, the need to account for effects on 'third' countries is becoming more and more relevant.

2   Third countries may be affected even if they are not – and never have been – host to direct production by a specific TNC. For example, Japanese investment in the UK motor industry affected other European countries because it led to – and was indeed partly motivated by – exports from the UK to other EC/EU countries.

Similarly, a TNC's investment decision may affect the position of other companies either because they are rivals competing in the same markets or because they are or can become part of the supply chain of the investing company.

A second type of indirect effects is due to externalities of business activities, i.e. to the impact that activities in one company have on other businesses and the economy in general. The effects spill over from company to company, industry to industry and country to country. These spillover effects can be positive or negative. A company may pollute the environment with negative consequences for other companies and for the macroenvironment. Another company absorbs a large share of the locality's skilled workforce, thus creating skills shortages in the industry, with high costs for other firms. On the positive side, the training programmes of a particular firm may have positive effects on the industry as the trained employees relocate to other firms. The externalities may then result in the growth of productivity for the industry as a whole. Moreover, there may be positive spillover effects on the diffusion of knowledge and innovation as we shall argue in the next chapter. The spillover effects can be felt by other firms within the same industry or indeed in different industries. Effects can also spill over from locality to locality via the companies' networks of linkages with suppliers, customers, partners or their own subsidiaries.[4]

Box 16.2   *Effects on whom: a variety of perspectives*

- Firms, industries, local economies, macroeconomies: distinctions are sometimes blurred

- Groups/classes/stakeholders: workers, managers, shareholders, consumers, other firms

- Countries: home and host countries; third countries

Indirect effects
- Effects on third countries

- Spillover effects

---

3   The relevance of multinationality per se

The home versus host country dichotomy assumes that the effects are linked entirely to the direction of the flow of investment. It implies, for example, that outward FDI produces positive employment effects on the host country and possibly negative ones on the home country.[5] Emphasis on the direction of the flow of FDI may sometimes be misplaced. *Multinationality in itself* may be responsible for some effects and here are some examples.

If a TNC operating, say, in Britain has activities in many other countries, this may affect the direction and structure of British *trade*, because the company may have specific strategies as to where to export to or which country to import from. These strategies and the related effects are independent of whether the company originates from Britain or is a foreign company operating in Britain as a host country: the relevant point is the fact that the company is a TNC and, as such, has operations in many countries. This is a particularly important issue because many companies engage in strategic planning of their production process and the possible location of its segments. Various components may be located in different countries and this requires the movement of components from country to country for further processing, with effects on the structure and volume of trade. This issue is reconsidered in the following chapters, particularly for its specific effects on trade and the balance of payments (Chapters 19 and 20).

A second example derives from the possible *manipulation of transfer prices*, that is, prices charged for transfers of goods and services internally to firms, though across national borders, on which more in Chapter 20. The possible effects are on a variety of areas including the balance of payments and the distribution of economic surplus between various countries and between private and public domains. As we shall see, the manipulation of transfer prices – made possible because the company operates in many nations – is almost entirely independent of the nationality of the company: it depends on the fact that the company operates across several countries and fiscal regimes.

Another area of potential effects of multinationality is *knowledge and innovation*, on which more in Chapter 17. Moreover, in Chapter 14 I put forward the view that multinationality creates a variety of advantages for TNCs, including advantages in the *bargaining power with labour, governments and suppliers*.

There is another issue emerging in the literature which is connected to multinationality. As already mentioned in section 2, standard macroeconomics and the related *accounting system* are based on the nation-state. We calculate the domestic product on the basis of production activities in the country, collect trade statistics on the basis of exports and imports of the country, and record transactions in the balance of payments of the country on the same basis.

Yet some of the production abroad and the assets and sales of foreign affiliates of domestic TNCs belong to these domestic TNCs. As these foreign activities have been increasing through time, some authors have expressed doubts about our current accounting systems based on the *residency principle*. Some voices have been raised in favour of an accounting system – particularly for trade/foreign sales and for the balance of payments – based on the *ownership principle*. This would mean moving from the idea of accounting on the basis of where the activity takes place, to accounting on the basis of which company owns the assets and is responsible for the activities in the various countries. Another proposal is for the collection and publication of statistics based both on residency and ownership in order to give researchers and the public a clear view of the situation.[6] (See Box 16.3 for a summary of areas of relevance of multinationality.)

> **Box 16.3**   *Areas of relevance of 'multinationality per se' on effects*
>
> • Direction and structure of international trade (Chapter 19)
>
> • Scope for the manipulation of transfer prices and related impact on the balance of payments and on the distribution of economic surplus (Chapter 20)
>
> • Development and diffusion of knowledge and innovation (Chapters 11, 14, 15 and 17)
>
> • Possible increase in bargaining power towards labour and governments (Chapter 14).

4   Assumptions and alternatives

In economics, as in all the social sciences and indeed to a very large extent the natural sciences, research requires looking for causes or assessing effects in situations in which there are many elements influencing the outcomes. Any economic problem we study is filled with an enormous amount of possible elements/variables influencing the outcome. In order to begin to understand what is going on, researchers have to make assumptions about some of those elements. These elements are often related to the behaviour of other agents in the economic system, be they other companies, consumers, workforces or governments.

In the specific case we are interested in, when we research the effects of FDI, we have to make implicit or explicit assumptions about the behaviour of other firms when faced with foreign investment by a TNC, or about the behaviour of governments. For example, does FDI affect the investment plans of other firms in either/or the home and host country? Does the foreign investment substitute for domestic investment or is it an addition to it? It all depends on what assumptions we make about the behaviour of other firms and about the level of capacity and its degree of utilization in the country, be it home or host country. Thus, the question is closely linked to the issue of whether FDI is a substitute for, or additional to, domestic investment in the host country, and whether it is a substitute for or an addition to investment in the home country.

Hufbauer and Adler (1968), in an early study of the effects on foreign investment on the US economy, organize the various alternatives into three sets of assumptions which they call: *classical, reverse classical* and *anticlassical*. The *classical hypothesis* assumes that FDI adds productive capacity to the host country and detracts from home country investment. The result is a territorial shift in investment and productive capacity: the home country is deprived of productive capacity while the host country's domestic firms are not crowded out of investment opportunities. The *reverse classical hypothesis* assumes that foreign investment does not deprive the home country of productive capacity since other firms supplement and take up any investment opportunity; however, FDI makes no net addition to the productive capacity of the host country because it crowds out investment by domestic and other firms or because the economy is running near full capacity and the new investment can only be accommodated by crowding out other investment plans. The *anticlassical hypothesis* assumes that no substitution takes place at home or abroad; therefore, FDI increases productive capacity in the host country without decreasing it at home.

In the last analysis, under the classical and reverse classical assumptions, the total world volume of capital expenditure remains the same whether FDI takes place or not. Under anticlassical assumption the total volume of capital expenditure increases because of FDI as shown in Table 16.1.

It should, however, be noted that these three hypotheses are developed under the general assumption that FDI takes the greenfield rather than the mergers and acquisitions mode. In the latter case there would not be any increase in the world's productive capacity as we argued in Chapter 1, section 6.

These three hypotheses are clearly crucial in the assessment of balance of payments, employment and growth effects in the host and home countries. In spite of the clarity with which they have originally been expressed, they are not easy to handle in practice. This is because each of them involves a full set of sub-assumptions about, for example: investment opportunities in the host and home countries; the availability of funds for investment; the method of financing the FDI; the behaviour of other investors in the two countries; the market structure of the relevant industry; the level of employment and capacity utilization in the two countries. No a priori generalization can be made regarding the applicability of the three assumptions. Each case – country and sector – must be considered on its own and the plausibility of each assumption must be assessed according to the prevailing conditions. What is important is to realize that conclusions about effects are always based on many underlying assumptions. These assumptions are sometimes made explicit by the researchers; at other times they are implicit. However, we must always take account of them in interpreting the results; this may require bringing to light implicit assumptions.

Table 16.1   *Impact of greenfield FDI on the productive capacity of home, host countries and world total under three hypotheses*

| Hypothesis | Productive capacity | | World total |
	In home country	*In host country*	
Classical	Detraction	Addition	Unchanged
Reverse classical	Unchanged	Unchanged	Unchanged
Anticlassical	Unchanged	Addition	Addition

5   The next chapters

In the next four chapters we shall consider the following specific areas: innovation; labour; trade and the balance of payments. The following points will be common to all the chapters:

- The chosen topics will be dealt with not so much in their own right – a situation which would require a book for each topic – but in relation to the impact that the TNCs and their activities may have on them.
- A discussion of how the boundaries discussed in the present chapter apply to each area considered.
- Whether and how any of the theories considered in Part III has anything to say in relation to that specific area.
- Reference, here and there, to some empirics. However, none of the chapters should be seen as a survey of empirical evidence.

Regarding the last two points I would like to make the following remarks. The effects are not – and indeed cannot be – evaluated in a theoretical vacuum, independently of theories. The assessment of effects is done – whether in a conscious or unconscious way – within the framework of theories. The latter influences the type of effects we are interested in, the models we develop to assess them, how we interpret the results and, therefore, the conclusions we reach. Since a theoretical framework tends to be present in the assessment of effects, I feel that it is better to make it explicit and thus allow the reader or policy-maker to draw wider conclusions. In the next four chapters the links between theories and effects will be highlighted.

SUMMARY BOX 16

Boundaries in the assessment of effects: key elements

Domain

Economy; society; culture; politics; environment etc.

Effects on whom/what

Groups; stakeholders; social classes; enterprises; sectors; macroeconomy

Short- and long-term effects

May, sometimes, go in opposite directions

Host and home countries; third countries

Direct and indirect effects; spillover effects

Relevance of multinationality per se

Alternative assumptions and related hypotheses

Classical, reverse classical, anticlassical

Other relevant chapters

Chapters on specific effects (17 to 20)
Chapters 11, 14 and 15

The availability of information for certain specific effects or theories affects the boundaries of corroboration for them. It could be argued that this problem is disappearing in our era of information and communication technologies. The ICTs have indeed unleashed a tremendous amount of data often available in large databases. However, this in itself creates problems ranging from the reliability of the datasets – often produced by private commercial firms – to difficulties in choosing from a variety of data sources. Moreover, in spite of this large wealth of data, some key information is missing usually because companies or governments in various countries have restrictions on what is to be made publicly available and they impose a variety of confidentiality clauses. An important example in this field is the case of intra-firm trade for which only a few countries (the USA, Sweden, Japan and France) release selected data.

Even when evidence is fully available and reliable, we still face the problem of the relationship between observations and theory. Philosophers of science maintain that there is no such thing as objective empirical evidence and that all evidence is theory-laden (Gillies, 1993: pt III); i.e. our evidence is affected by the theoretical background we – consciously or unconsciously – use to gather, select and process data and information.

Notes

1 This issue was raised in Chapter 1, section 6 in relation to differences between FDI and GDFCF.
2 See discussion of FIAT's strategies regarding Italian and Polish workers in Chapter 14, section 6.
3 See Barba Navaretti and Venables (2004).
4 On spillover effects particularly with regard to productivity and innovation see Castellani and Zanfei (2006).
5 This is a simplification that may not hold as we discuss in Chapter 18.
6 The approach based on ownership has been proposed – in different forms – by the US National Academy of Science and by Julius (1990). The proposal for two parallel systems based on residency and ownership has been put forward by the US Department of Commerce. Details of these debates are in Landefeld et al. (1993) and in UNCTAD (1994: 153–4). I have not seen any recent follow up to these debates.

17 Innovation and the TNCs

I Introduction

Innovation activities and innovation performance can be considered at the level of firms, industries or countries. The effects of innovation are both direct and indirect; the latter take place via spillover effects from one company to others in the industry and the economies as a whole. Innovation leads to high productivity and competitiveness, thus to good export performance and thus to high profits and more investment in a cumulative cycle. It is the best element for generating long-term cumulative causation processes for both firms and countries (Archibugi and Michie, 1997).

Innovation may be in relation to products or to production processes or to both. Moreover, innovation may refer to the introduction of a product and/or process that is new to the firm as well as the industry and the economy; or to products and/or processes new only to the firm as the latter introduces into its operations something already established in the industry or the economy. In the former case we talk of *radical* innovation; in the latter of *incremental or imitative* innovation (Tushman and Anderson, 1986; Henderson and Clark, 1990).

The issue of *short- versus long-term performance* is very important in the field of innovation. Some elements of expenditure on innovation lead to high costs in the short run but are likely to lead to – and are usually made on the expectation of – better performance in the long run. The case of expenditure on R&D is relevant here. In the short term this expenditure is a cost that may affect the profitability of the company negatively. However, in the long run the investment in R&D may lead to new products or production processes that are likely to make the company more competitive and profitable.

One unfortunate side of the working of the market economy is that the stock market expects good performance in the short or medium term. This is particularly the case in countries (such as the USA or the UK) where the highly advanced and sophisticated financial markets tend to rule the rest of the economy and businesses. If the good performance does not manifest quickly, the company's share price may fall, with negative consequences for the company, its management and shareholders. This means that there is a bias against expenditure whose benefits are felt in the long run, and particularly R&D; however, a strategy of innovation – and thus of R&D expenditure – is the best way to achieve long-term competitiveness and good performance.

Innovation figures prominently in the theories we discussed in Part III. The first theory of international production that is specifically related to innovation and technology is Vernon's international product life cycle theory (Chapter 5). In it the phases and modalities of internationalization are directly related to the fact that we deal with an innovative product. The innovative firm has a monopolistic advantage which it exploits at home and abroad via exports and FDI considered sequentially. Knowledge and technology are gradually transferred from country to country and firm to firm as imitation processes set in. There is a clear hierarchy of firms and countries in terms of their innovation capabilities. This theory was later criticized by Vernon himself (1979) and by Cantwell (1995) as we saw in Chapters 5 and 11 respectively. Innovation comes in more indirectly in Dunning's theory (see Chapter 9) and in the internalization theory (see Chapter 8). In the former it plays a role as ownership advantage; in the latter, it affects the organization of production across countries in terms of the company's ability to appropriate the results of its own innovation efforts.

Knowledge and innovation play a very direct role in the development of the evolutionary theories of Cantwell and of Kogut and Zander (Chapter 11). It also plays a strong role in the network theories of the TNC as well as in the development of resources in Penrose's theory (Chapter 15). Some of these points will be dealt with more extensively in the next section.

2   Knowledge, innovation and the TNCs

Causation involving internationalization and innovation is a two-way process. Innovative companies are more likely to compete successfully via exports and/or via direct production in foreign countries (Amendola et al., 1993; Carlsson, 2006; Filippetti et al., 2009) as in Vernon's theory. The same countries may also be sought-after partners for international joint ventures. Conversely, the international environment may enhance knowledge and innovation for companies and countries as envisaged in the evolutionary and network theories of the TNCs.[1] We shall confine ourselves here to internationalization via direct activities of TNCs and to the impact of TNCs on innovation.

There are several issues in relation to innovation and the TNC ranging from the location of research laboratories (Patel and Pavitt, 1994; Pearce and Papanastasiou, 1999) to the growth of research-related inter-firm partnerships (Cohen, 1995; Hagedoorn, 1996; Tether, 2002) to impact on home and host countries' innovation capabilities (Castellani and Zanfei, 2006).

Moreover, the TNCs raise specific questions in relation to innovation such as the following. Are TNCs more or less innovative than uninational companies (see Box 17.1)? Are their activities likely to produce negative or positive effects on the innovation intensity of the industry and the macroeconomy? Arguments in favour of a negative attitude towards the innovation potential of TNCs and their activities stress the following elements:

1   The TNCs increase the *degree of monopoly* in the industry and this reduces the incentive to invest and innovate (Cowling and Sugden, 1987, as we saw in Chapter 13; Schenk, 1999).

2   Moreover, local business in the host countries may be *crowded out* and their innovation potential linked to the local economies will be lost.

However, there are many arguments for the claim that TNCs may increase the innovation potential in industries to which they belong and in the localities in which they operate. A first argument has to do with *size and availability of resources*: TNCs tend to be large companies and large companies tend to spend more on research and development and to be more innovative. Several studies point to considerable R&D expenditure on the part of TNCs; Narula and Zanfei (2004) in particular give evidence on their expenditure in both the home and host countries.

Box 17.1   *Are TNCs more or less innovative than UNCs?*

They are more innovative because

- their large size gives them the resources for R&D expenditure and innovation;

- multinationality per se favours the development and spread of knowledge and innovation.

They are less innovative because

- their activities increase the degree of monopoly in the industries and this lowers the incentive to innovate;

- local businesses and their innovative potential in host countries are crowded out.

Are TNCs in a special position regarding knowledge and innovation? In other words does *multinationality per se* and the fact TNCs operate in many countries have an effect on knowledge and innovation?. The theoretical and empirical linkages between innovation and multinationality have been the subject of several studies, culminating in the evolutionary theories and in the network theories as in Chapter 11 and 15. In this theoretical approach, multinationality per se has positive effects on knowledge and innovation. In this respect, the role of the networks that the TNCs are involved in becomes crucial. Such networks can be internal and external, and knowledge – which is part and parcel of innovation – is transferred within each of these networks and between them. Transnationality facilitates the transfer of knowledge and innovation internally to the company and from country to country according to where the various units of the company operate. There are also transfers of knowledge and innovation from company to company. Business units learn from the environment in which they operate, absorb knowledge and – if they are part of a TNC – transmit it to other parts of the company. There are innovation spillovers from one firm to others. Moreover, in Cantwell's theory (Chapter 11) the activities of the units affect the innovation environment of the localities in which they operate and allow other firms to learn from them.

Various questions emerge in relation to this framework:

1   How is knowledge transferred within internal or external networks and between them? What are the mechanisms that allow/facilitate the transfer?

2   What are the possible constraints to internal or external knowledge transfer?
3   What are the possible facilitators of such transfer?

As regards the first question we must distinguish between *codified* and *uncodified –*
tacit – knowledge (Polanyi, 1966; 1967). The former is the type of knowledge that can
be written down in clear instructions and codes and this means that people in different localities can acquire knowledge and use it to innovate. Uncodified knowledge
cannot be written down in clear instructions because much of it is embodied in what
workers do in their everyday tasks and in the way they work together as a group. The
latter point forms the basis of Kogut and Zander's (1993) analysis of the TNC as a
social community as we saw in Chapter 11.

People and their expertise are essential for the development, use and transfer of
both types of knowledge and the innovations linked to it. In the case of uncodified
knowledge, transmission via people is the only effective way for it to spread from one
business unit to another. The mobility of skilled labour is an excellent vehicle for
knowledge and innovation transfers. Such mobility can take place on an intra- or
inter-company basis. In the former, the skilled labour moves from subsidiary to
subsidiary within the same country or between different countries. The latter means
that the transfer of knowledge, innovation and technology can operate in both directions: the firm transfers to the local environment and receives from it. The transfers
can be deliberate and planned or they can be accidental. The latter can occur via external labour markets: as labourers move from firm to firm they take their knowledge and
experience with them. Nonetheless there can also be other channels of knowledge
transfer, for example, via the interaction of the subsidiary with local customers or
suppliers or distributors.

The degree to which a firm contributes and receives innovation to and from the
environment depends on the following:

- To what extent is the subsidiary of the company *embedded in the locality*? For
  example, to what extent are its suppliers chosen from the local community? If
  they are, this facilitates the spillover process as the suppliers learn from the
  company while the company learns about the knowledge environment and about
  the requirements of the local markets (see Chapter 15).
- To what extent can the locality absorb innovation (Cohen and Levinthal 1989;
  1990)? Indicators of high *absorption capacity* may be the levels of labour skills
  and education of the local labour force or the number of research laboratories and
  the related expenditure on R&D in the area. High absorptive capacity allows the
  locality to take advantage of spillovers; indeed, it may be a condition for
  spillovers from a foreign TNC to local firms to take place. It may also become
  an attractive locational advantage which encourages foreign firms to invest in
  that particular area.[2] Agglomeration effects set in motion cumulative processes
  (see Chapters 11 and 12). Therefore the initial location advantages in terms of
  elements of absorption capacity, may lead to further location advantages and to
  the enhancement of absorptive capacity. Moreover, it also leads to increased
  ownership advantages in the innovation field for the companies that invest in –

and learn from – the locality. Thus, both locational and ownership advantages become – to a certain degree – endogenous.

- What is the *degree of autonomy* that the subsidiary has in dealing with the local environment, for example in dealing with suppliers and distributors? A relatively decentralized structure with little control from the centre may favour local embeddedness and therefore external knowledge spillovers. However, a more centralized structure may favour the internal transfer of knowledge (see Chapter 15).
- The *mode of entry* can affect the speed of learning about market and production conditions in host countries. Indeed, sometimes entry via acquisition of local firms is justified in terms of the knowledge acquisition it facilitates. Conversely, entry via joint ventures may facilitate the learning process and spillover knowledge from the foreign TNC to the firms in host countries. This is usually considered as a main reason why some developing countries' governments require that foreign investors enter into partnerships with domestic firms: the joint venture modality may therefore lead to higher absorptive capacity in the medium to long term.

In summary, the extent to which knowledge is transferred within internal and/or external networks may depend on: the balance between the organizational structure of the company and its degree of centralization; the degree of embeddedness of the subsidiary into the local economy; and the absorption capacity of the locality (see Box 17.2).

Box 17.2   *Transnationality and innovation*

Transfer of knowledge and innovation within and between internal and external networks

Labour and the internal or external labour markets as vehicles of transfer

Transfers within internal networks is affected by

- the organizational structure of the company;
- the degree of centralization and control of subsidiaries by headquarters.

Transfers from and to the external environment is affected by

- degree of embeddedness of the subsidiary into the local economy;
- absorption capacity of the local economy;
- the mode of entry of the TNC into the local economy.

The balance between degree of decentralization and control, the degree of embeddedness and the absorption capacity of the locality are relevant elements in the development and transfer of knowledge, innovation and technology.

The approach presented here does not take the home versus host country dichotomy as the basis for assessing the effects. Instead it considers the company's international network as a whole in which each unit can contribute to knowledge and innovation and can also benefit from knowledge and innovation developed by other units: in other words, when it comes to the acquisition of innovation, multinationality matters.

SUMMARY BOX 17

TNCs and innovation

Theories where innovation figures prominently

Vernon's IPLC; evolutionary theories; network theories

TNCs' activities enhance innovation via the availability of resources for R&D

Multinationality favours acquisition of knowledge via

- internal networks across countries;
- external networks.

Labour mobility as a vehicle for the transfer of knowledge and innovation

Level of analysis

Company and macro level

Other relevant chapters

5, 11, 15 and 16

Indicative further reading

Cantwell, J. (1992), 'Innovation and technological competitiveness', in P.J. Buckley and M. Casson (eds), *Multinational Enterprises in the World Economy: Essays in Honour of John Dunning*, Aldershot, UK and Brookfield, VT, USA: Edward Elgar, ch. 2, pp. 20–40.

Castellani, D. and Zanfei, A. (2006), *Multinational Firms, Innovation and Productivity*, Cheltenham, UK and Northampton, MA, USA: Edward Elgar, chs 1 and 2.

Filippetti, A., Frenz, M. and Ietto-Gillies, G. (2011), 'Are innovation and internationalization related? A comparative analysis of European countries', *Industry and Innovation*, **18** (5).

Narula, R. and Zanfei, A. (2004), 'Globalization of innovation: the role of multinational enterprises', in J. Fageberger, D.C. Mowery and R.R. Nelson (eds), *The Oxford Handbook of Innovation*, Oxford: Oxford University Press, ch. 12, pp. 318–46.

Notes

1 Empirical evidence for 32 countries support this statement (Filippetti et al., 2009 and 2011).
2 See Cantwell and Iammarino (2003) and Driffield and Love (2003).

18 Effects on labour

· ·

I Introduction

The effects of the activities of transnational corporations on labour are very wide. They range from effects on employment, job creation and opportunities to wider aspects related to the location of employment or the quality of labour and its re- muneration (such as skills development, productivity and wages), or to the bargain- ing power of labour with employers. In most of these elements the conclusion that can be reached depends on the sector one is dealing with, on the technological and organizational context in which the investment takes place, and on the specific conditions of the country(ies) we are interested in.

Most of the issues considered in Chapter 16 are relevant for the assessment of the effects on labour, and I shall highlight them as we go along. The next section deals with employment effects; the wider effects are dealt with in section 3. Section 4 analyses some recent developments due to activities of TNCs in the international division of labour.[1]

2 Direct and indirect employment effects

Direct employment effects

Worldwide the TNCs appear to be responsible for the employment of over 77 million people (UNCTAD, 2009a: xxi). The previous edition of this book gave a figure of 86 million based on UNCTAD (1995). The drop in employment of circa 9 million in a decade may appear puzzling particularly in the face of a considerable increase in the number of TNCs worldwide (from almost 60 000 in the late 1990s to almost 104 000 twenty years later. The decline in employment must, however, be seen in the context of changes in the organization of production with increase in outsourcing: the total production controlled by TNCs (see Chapter 13) is likely to have increased while the number of workers for which they have direct responsibil- ity has declined.

The more recent figure in itself tells us nothing about the potential for job creation of TNCs as such. Is their potential for job creation higher than that of uninational companies? This is a purely theoretical question which involves us in a counterfactual argument: what might happen if reality were different? Nonetheless it is possible to argue about it on the basis of the factual elements we have. We know that, on average, transnational companies are bigger and more capital and technology intensive than uninational companies. This means that they also tend to be less labour intensive and therefore – ceteris paribus – to use less labour per unit of output. Therefore the answer to the above question is very likely to be negative.

Though TNCs have a high potential for capacity creation per unit of investment expenditure, their potential for job creation is not – ceteris paribus – as high as that of smaller less capital-intensive uninational companies. However, I should point out that the ceteris paribus clause is unlikely to apply. It is far-fetched to assume that the level of investment in any economy with smaller UNCs would be the same as in one where large TNCs operate. The TNC may well exploit investment opportunities which are open only to large technological and integrated companies and not to smaller ones. In this case the TNCs' FDI – of the greenfield type – adds to both capacity and employment in the country in which they invest.

The contribution of TNCs to job creation (or in some cases job destruction) can come about through a variety of activities from exports to imports to joint ventures to direct production. The job creation/opportunities of foreign direct investment is the issue that tends to hit the headlines. Media people and politicians are usually quick to reach conclusions about the number of jobs created/destroyed by specific strategies of TNCs, particularly in relation to FDI. Yet, as already mentioned, the assessment of employment effects is far from easy.

The first point to note is the fact that the majority of FDI in the last 30 years has taken the form of *mergers and acquisitions*; approximate estimates point to M&As being almost 80 per cent of total FDI in some years. This type of investment generates extra capacity for the acquiring company but not for the host country or the world as a whole. All we have is a change in the ownership of a company and of the productive capacity of the acquiring company, not the creation of new capacity for the world as a whole: this applies to the acquisition of private companies as well as that of privatized public institutions. In this situation the new FDI does not create jobs in the short run. In the medium term it is likely to cut jobs as restructuring and rationalization take place after the acquisition/merger.[2] This means that the reorganization may lead to an increase in productivity. In the longer run the company might invest organically and this would lead to the creation of new jobs. Moreover, the position of the new company – worldwide and in terms of its specific industry – may generate further investment opportunities which might not have existed in the old company.

Greenfield FDI does generate new capacity and therefore has the potential for extra jobs creation in the host country. Nonetheless, it is possible to increase capacity while creating few job opportunities. Whenever the production process is very capital intensive, it leads to so-called 'jobless growth'. Foreign investment in developed countries tends, on the whole, to lead to capital-intensive production, while in developing countries, where unskilled labour is plentiful and cheap, labour-intensive methods are likely to be used. Thus, the potential for greenfield FDI to generate employment opportunities may be higher when investment takes place in developing countries compared to developed countries.

More caveats are needed before we can reach any conclusions about job creations in host countries by inward FDI. We have so far concluded that greenfield inward FDI adds to capacity and thus, very likely, to job creation. This conclusion is based on the assumption that foreign investment adds to the existing investment plans in the country. But what if it substitutes for it? Foreign direct investment and international production could, in fact, just replace planned domestic investment and production in the host country. This may happen because domestic firms cannot compete with foreign firms and would go out of business or would have to curtail their investment plans when faced with foreign competition. This issue relates to the assessment of alternatives discussed in Chapter 16, section 4, and it is a case of the reverse classical hypothesis (Table 16.1). Whether the new greenfield investment generates extra jobs or not, depends to a large extent on the assumptions we make about the reactions of other firms within the industry.

What about effects on the *home country*? Would a domestic TNC investing abroad detract from job creation in the home country? The answer, as usual, depends on the specific situation and on the assumptions we make about the behaviour of other agents. If we are dealing with a case of relocation of production, i.e. closing down a factory and relocating it somewhere else, the answer seems fairly clear-cut. Jobs are destroyed in the home country, unless the production opportunities are taken up by other firms whether domestic or foreign.[3] If we are not talking of relocation, but of new investment abroad, then it is difficult to see a reduction in employment levels at home; however, if the economy is below the full employment level, it might be claimed that the domestic TNC is not taking up possible opportunities for capacity and job creation at home and favouring foreign locations instead. Very much depends on our assessment of the alternatives and on the assumptions/ reality regarding the existing level of employment and capacity utilization. As explained in Chapter 16, Table 16.1, any of the hypotheses (classical, reverse classical or anticlassical) might apply; it all depends on the actual circumstances.

Indirect employment effects

So far we have considered direct employment effects. However, in Chapter 16 we mentioned that many effects are indirect. Indirect employment effects can come about through the following. First, the trade effects of FDI. If outward FDI increases exports opportunities, this may lead to additional job creation. On the other hand, if outward FDI leads to extra importation, it may detract from employment creation in the home country.

Indirect employment effects can also come about through the vertical production chain (some upstream – e.g. the supply of raw materials – and some downstream – e.g. distribution activities). If the supply chain operates within the country, the indirect employment effects will be positive because the supplier/distributor are nationals. If it extends abroad, there may not be many positive effects. Nonetheless Yamashita (2010) in a study of the impact of international outsourcing – by Japanese TNCs – on the Japanese economy finds that it contributes positively to both employment and skills upgrading.

In Chapter 16 we mentioned that some effects may be independent of the direction of the flow and may have more to do with multinationality per se. This is the case of some trade effects or some effects on the supply chain. This means that the activities of a TNC in a country may have trade effects – which result in employ-ment effects – independently of whether the firm is domestic or foreign. For example, if the TNC has specific strategies for the supply of foreign markets, this will have repercussions for the export potential and pattern of the country it oper-ates in, whether the country is home or host to the TNC. Similarly with supply chain issues. If the company has a strategy of location of different components in differ-ent countries, this will have trade and employment effects on the countries it oper-ates in, independently of whether the countries are home or host countries. These are effects linked to multinationality per se rather than to the direction of the flow of investment.

There are also indirect macroeconomic effects. The effects of the Keynes/Kahn income and employment multiplier may operate in the case of greenfield FDI. As is well known, the multiplier effects tend to be checked by high import propensities as well as other possible leakages such as taxes. These are not indirect effects specific to foreign investment; they apply to all investment of the capacity creation type, whether domestic or foreign.

The general points on the employment effects (both direct and indirect) made in this section are illustrated by the first row of Table 18.1 adapted from UNCTAD (1994: 167). Table 18.1 deals with two 'areas of impact' on employment: quantity and quality. It divides the effects into those deriving from inward FDI, and those from outward FDI and therefore follows a traditional distinction between effects on home and host country. In each case we can have direct and indirect effects each of which can generate positive and negative effects.

3   Wider effects on labour: quality issues

Table 18.1 considers under 'Area of impact' the quality as well as the quantity of employment. We have considered the 'quantity' area in the previous section and we now turn to the quality area. The quality effects on labour relate to: wages, produc-tivity and skills as well as the bargaining power of labour.

There is evidence that *productivity levels* are higher in TNCs' production than in production by smaller uninational companies. There may be several reasons for this pattern. The TNCs' production process may operate with higher levels of capital per unit of output. On balance, the TNCs are larger and tend to use more capital-intensive production techniques than UNCs. This goes hand in hand with the use of more advanced technologies. The higher levels of productivity allow the company to pay higher than average wages. The higher productivity levels may also be achieved through staff training programmes that lead to the *upgrading of skills*. There is evidence of higher spending on training and development by TNCs (UNCTAD/DTCI, 1994: ch. V). Moreover, TNCs tend to be more innovative in terms of products, processes and the organization of production, all of which elements may have posi-tive impact on productivity. The large size of many TNCs may also generate scale economies.[4]

Table 18.1 (second row) deals with wages, skills and labour organization

Table 18.1 *Potential effects of FDI on the quantity and quality of employment*

| Area of impact | Inward foreign direct investment/host country | | | | Outward FDI/home country effects | | | |
| | Direct effects | | Indirect effects | | Direct effects | | Indirect effects | |
	Positive	Negative	Positive	Negative	Positive	Negative	Positive	Negative
Quantity	Greenfield FDI adds to net capital; creates jobs in expanding industries	FDI through M&As may result in rationalization and job losses. May crowd out local firms	Creates jobs through forward and backward linkages and multiplier effects	Reliance on imports or displacement of existing firms results in job losses	Some jobs serving the needs of affiliates abroad may be preserved.	Relocation or 'job export' if foreign affiliates substitute for production at home	Some jobs in supplier industries that cater for foreign affiliates may be preserved	Loss of jobs in the industry due to value chain effects. Negative multiplier effects
Quality	Pays higher wages and has higher productivity	May introduce undesirable labour practices	Spillover of 'best practice' work organization to domestic firms	Erodes wage levels as domestic firms try to compete	In the long run restructuring may lead to skills upgrading and to higher value production*	'Give backs' or lower wages to keep jobs at home	May boost sophisticated industries*	Downward pressure on wages and labour standards may flow on to suppliers

Note: *These effects are unlikely to manifest even in the long run without a specific, targeted strategic policy by the government. The underlying assumption seems to be that the losses are always in the unskilled jobs; this is not always the case in the real world.

Source: Adapted from UNCTAD/DTCI (1994: Table IV.1, p. 167).

issues. As regards wages, a direct effect of TNCs activities is likely to be higher wages paid by TNCs. However, to this may correspond an indirect effect on wages: smaller firms in host countries – particularly the developing ones – may try to compete with TNCs through cost-cutting and thus offer lower wages to their employees. As regards the effects on the home country, the conclusions in Table 18.1 are, in fact, partly based on various assumptions about the possible reactions by other companies, as argued in Chapter 16, section 4.

Some of the spillover effects discussed in Chapter 17 will have an impact on labour in terms of employment as well as quality elements. Labour trained in one company may be beneficial to other companies and to the locality because the labour force often moves from company to company. There are considerable spillover effects on skills, including management and organization skills and practices. The spin-off productivity effects on the local economy may be substantial as Castellani and Zanfei (2003) found in relation to foreign TNCs investing in Italy, France and Spain. There may also result negative spillover elements such as crowding out of local firms, pollution of the environment, excess demand on local services and infrastructures with negative effects on employment structure or the quality of life.

The geographical structure of employment is also affected by the activities of transnational companies (Van den Berghe, 2003). There is also some evidence of effects on the gender pattern of employment as a result of both activities of TNCs and use of information and communication technologies. More women can work from home; more women are involved in the international chain of production; at the same time more women are migrating from developing and CEE countries to developed ones in response to increased demand for caring jobs (Braunstein, 2003). [5]

What about the bargaining power of labour towards capital? Do the activities of TNCs make labour stronger or weaker? Chapter 14 presented a theory of TNCs' location strategies in which the fragmentation of labour confronting capital is a very important element in such strategies. The activities of TNCs can lead to various types of fragmentation which are not incompatible and indeed reinforce each other. They are, specifically: organizational fragmentation; geographical (by nation-states) fragmentation; and fragmentation of the production process (Yamashita, 2010), which results in the international location of different components of manufacturing or services products in different countries.

All these fragmentation elements have been increasing in the last 35 years. They all result in the fragmentation of the labour force employed by the same company and thus in difficulties for labour to organize itself effectively in its bargaining with the company(ies). This is an issue where multinationality per se is relevant more than the direction of the flow of FDI. As argued in Chapter 14, it does not matter whether the company is a domestic TNC or a foreign one. What matters for this particular effect are the strategies of the companies: how many countries they operate in; what strategies they follow for their location of production; and what their strategies are regarding in-house or outsourcing of parts and components.

4   The new international division of labour[6]

The strategies of transnational companies regarding the international location of production processes are also having a major impact on the international division of labour, that is, on employment opportunities and structure across the world.

The 1970s saw the development of the so-called new international division of labour (NIDL; see also Box 18.1) generated by the TNCs' strategies of international location of production. The latest technologies and organizational methods were used to divide the production process into different components requiring different levels of skills for their production (Frobel et al., 1980;[7] Yamashita, 2010): for example, design of products in a developed country – thus using its skilled labour – and the location of routine work (such as sewing garments) in developing countries where it is possible to use cheap labour often in combination with old machinery. The so-called Export Processing Zones (EPZs) were and are used for this type of production in developing countries.[8] These are designated areas in which foreign TNCs invest and produce for exportation only. The production processes in the EPZs tend to be labour intensive. The host governments see these activities as beneficial in terms of employment creation as well as exports opportunities. The latter opportunities bring into the country much needed foreign currencies with which to pay for imports. In order to attract TNCs towards these activities, governments usually give special incentives in a variety of forms, from free land usage to tax breaks.

For the company, a strategy of fragmentation of the production process for location in various countries allows the utilization of the minimum required skilled and expensive labour in developed countries, while using the cheaper labour of developing countries for the unskilled part of the production process. The total unit costs of production of the final product are therefore minimized.

The design of the production process to fit this overall cost minimization strategy is possible thanks to: (a) the latest technologies and organizational methods; and (b) the considerable decrease in transportation costs. The latter allows the movements of components from country to country for further processing and for the final assembly, without excessive additions to the total unit cost.

Various economic and social consequences follow from strategies of international vertical integration. First, the volume of world trade increases as components are moved from country to country. Second, the production process becomes locationally and operationally fragmented. This, in turn, also fragments the labour force employed in it. These fragmentations are, paradoxically, accompanied by a higher level of integration. Production and production processes become vertically integrated across nation-states. National economies become more interlinked by working towards the same final product; by the movement of international managers who organize and monitor the process; and by the imports and exports that this international location strategy generates. Industries also become more internationally integrated as a result of this strategy by TNCs. Both integration and fragmentation coexist and are aspects of the same strategies and processes.

The NIDL in the electronic age

A key role in the NIDL is played by new methods of organization of production made possible by the development and diffusion of information and communication technologies. Moreover, the last two decades have seen further technological progress which has led to a further development in the new international division of labour. The possibility of transmission of data and documents in real time through-out the world is creating a completely new internationalization mode: components or final products of some information services can be transmitted electronically within and across borders. This new mode can be used to trade final products (for example, to deliver a final report or music or script to be prepared for publication) or it can be used to transmit component(s) of a service product that can be further processed in the different location – within the same country or abroad – and returned electronically to base. We can therefore talk of a NIDL for the electronic age.

Why would a firm want to have part of information-intense products processed in other location(s)? There are two main reasons: (1) in order to use labour which is skilled though cheaper than in the main production location; and (2) in order to access specific highly skilled labour which is unavailable in the main production location. Either of these two reasons apply within and across nation-states. Many developing countries have pockets of skilled labour which can be bought at much cheaper rates than the corresponding labour in developed countries: they range from accountants to software engineers to data and text processors to copy editors. This creates incentives for splitting the production process of many services into discrete components, some of which can be downloaded and processed by pockets of skilled specialists in developing or intermediate countries.[9]

We can begin to talk of an electronic-age 'new international division of labour' (E-NIDL) in which the information and communication technologies allow increased scope for the conditions which led to the NIDL. In the E-NIDL the scope for division of the manufactured products into appropriate components is still applicable. However, to this we must now add the scope for division of services into components, some of which can be transmitted electronically for further processing in other locations. Thus, the E-NIDL comprises two elements: a manufacturing element to which the NIDL applies, and an information service element to which the e-transmission mode applies.

There are many similarities and differences between the NIDL and the E-NIDL. As regards similarities, both originate through the activities of TNCs; both involve division of the production process into discrete components and an appro-priate organization of production within and across countries; both involve activi-ties in developed and developing countries; and both impact on the international division of labour and on trade; both are likely to give rise to intra-firm and intra-industry trade.

However, there are also some major differences. The NIDL refers to manufac-tures while the E-NIDL applies to services or services components of manufactures. The scope for internationalization increases in the E-NIDL as new forms and modes (through e-transmission) are added in the E-NIDL to the traditional imports and exports of the NIDL. In the NIDL the division of the production process into various components is done in such a way as to allow the *utilization of cheap unskilled labour*. In the E-NIDL the strategic element in the design of the production process for information services is the *utilization of cheap skilled labour*. Pockets of such labour can, in fact, be found in developing or intermediate countries (such as India or Ireland) at much lower rates than in developed countries. There are two major consequences in relation to labour: (1) the fact that skilled labourers in developing and intermediate countries can be employed to do skilled jobs in their own country rather than migrating to a developed country; and (2) the fact that these jobs compete with similar ones in developed countries.

Box 18.1   *The new international division of labour: for manufacturing and services*

Common elements to the production of both goods and services

- Use of new technologies to organize the production process most efficiently.

- Division of the production process into components, some to be located in developed and others in developing countries, with the overall aim to minimize the costs of production.

- The countries' economies become more integrated while the production process becomes fragmented.

- The labour employed by the same company also becomes fragmented.

- There are effects on the structure of trade: they both give rise to intra-firm and intra-industry trade (see Chapter 19).

Specific to manufacturing: the NIDL

- The division of the production process leads to demand for skilled labour in developed countries and for unskilled labour in the developing countries.

- Establishment of Export Processing Zones.

Specific to information services: the E-NIDL

- Demand for skilled operatives in developing countries where there are pockets of cheap skilled labour.

- This generates demand for skilled labour directly in the developing countries, thus avoiding the migration of such labour.

- Competition for skilled jobs between developed and developing countries.

- Electronic transmission of the product and/or its components: a new international division of labour.

Though stress is laid here on the international division of labour, some of the points made are more general and apply to the spatial division of labour. They therefore apply to regions – within nation-states – as well as between nation-states. Thus, for example, the new technologies allow the location of call centres in places within the nation-state spatially separated from the headquarters of the business or its main production location(s).

Many of the developments mentioned in this section are still at the initial stage. Nonetheless we already see some clear signs now: pockets of specialization in relatively high skills are to be found in Singapore (financial services), in India (software) and Brazil (engineering) (Miozzo and Soete, 2001). Scotland and the North of England seem to have the lead on call centres within the UK; however, their comparative advantages are rapidly being eroded by competition from English-

---

SUMMARY BOX 18

· ·

Effects of international production on labour: key points

Employment effects

Direct

- Greenfield versus mergers and acquisitions FDI
- Host and home country effects
- Relevance of alternative hypotheses (classical, reverse classical and anti-classical)

Indirect

- Value chain: repercussions on the vertical and horizontal chains
- Income and employment multiplier effects
- Via effects on exports and imports

Wider effects on labour

Quality of labour

- Productivity levels
- Skills development
- Organization of labour
- Wages

Labour fragmentation and its bargaining power

The New International Division of Labour (NIDL)

Manufacturing and e-services (Cf. Box 18.1)

Other relevant chapters

Chapters 13, 14, 16, 17, 19 and 20

speaking developing countries. The rapid diffusion of the new technologies and the coming on-stream of the full effects of these developments are likely to increase their relevance in the years to come.

The NIDL and the E-NIDL emanate from companies' strategies. However, their effects are felt on the companies and their profitability; on the industries which become more internationally integrated; and on the macroeconomies because they affect employment levels and structures. The effects on labour manifest in terms of the structure of employment in developed and developing countries – and on the division of labour between them – as well as in terms of the overall employment potential. Some of their specific effects on trade will be considered in the next two chapters.

A more recent development is taking place in the health care industry. It is linked again to the existence of pockets of cheap skilled labour in developing countries as well as to low transportation costs. There is a growing demand for the services of health professionals from developing countries, but while till recently the professionals would emigrate to developed countries in search of job opportunities, more recently, developed countries have created capacity at home – often via the investment by healthcare TNCs from developed countries – and the traveller now is often the patient, not the doctor and nurse.

Indicative further reading

Barba Navaretti G. and Venables, A.J. (2004), *Multinational Firms in the World Economy*, Princeton and Oxford: Princeton University Press, chs 7, 8, 9.

Blomstrom, M., Fors, G. and Lipsey, R.E. (1997), 'Foreign direct investment and employment: home country experience in the United States and Sweden', *Economic Journal*, **107** (445), 1787–97.

Buckley, P.J. and Mucchielli, J.L. (eds) (1997), *Multinational Firms and International Relocation*, Cheltenham, UK and Lyme, NH, USA: Edward Elgar.

OECD (1994), *The Performance of Foreign Affiliates in OECD Countries*, Paris: OECD, ch. 3.

UNCTAD/DTCI (1994), *World Investment Report 1994: Transnational Corporations, Employment and the Workplace*, Geneva: United Nations, chs IV, V and VI.

Notes

1 Results of specific empirical studies on the impact of FDI on host and home countries can be found in Barba Navaretti and Venables (2004: chs 7 and 9).

2 It might be argued that, if the acquired company was failing and unviable, jobs losses would have been inevitable even without the acquisition. But why would a failing firm be acquired? For asset-stripping purposes? Or because synergies with the acquiring company may make it viable?

3 A useful source on relocation strategies and their effects is Buckley and Mucchielli (1997).

4 On the impact of TNCs on productivity see Castellani and Zanfei (2006: Part II).

5 This picture may have changed post 2007 financial crisis.

6 More on this issue in Ietto-Gillies (2002c).

7 A brief summary of Frobel et al.'s position is in Ietto-Gillies (1992: ch. 5).

8 As I revise this chapter the current Coalition Government is planning the establishment of Export Processing Zones in the UK.

9 The internationalization of business service firms and the role played by the ICTs is clearly analysed in Roberts (1998). See also Inoue (2010).

19 Effects on trade

●●●

1   Introduction

International trade is the exchange of goods and non-factor services[1] across national frontiers. Transnational companies are responsible for very large amounts of world trade. UNCTAD (1996) distinguishes between TNC-initiated trade, intra-firm trade and arm's-length trade. It estimates that, approximately, two-thirds of world trade is the responsibility of TNCs. Moreover, a third of world trade is estimated to take place on an intra-firm basis.

Payments for imports and exports are still the major component of international financial transactions. However, trade is not the fastest-growing transaction. The growth rate of trade has been overtaken by other components, particularly those related to portfolio investment but also to FDI.

We know that TNCs are responsible for very large amounts of world trade and that trade and FDI are very closely linked. But what are the theoretical and/or structural reasons for such linkages? This forms the subject of the next section, while section 3 deals with effects of TNCs' activities on the patterns of trade.

In terms of connections between the theories in Part III and trade effects, the following are relevant. Vernon (Chapter 5) considers exports as one of the main modalities for the sourcing of foreign markets prior to direct production. Similarly, exports are considered also in the dynamic sequence of modalities by the Scandinavian School (Chapter 10). The new trade theories apply the same methodologies and similar static models to both trade and FDI and analyse the trade-off between exports and direct production.

2   Trade and international production

What is the relationship between international production or FDI – as a proxy for international production – and trade?[2]

There is a considerable body of literature on the issue of complementarity versus substitution between trade and international production (Molle and Morsink, 1991; Thomsen and Woolcock, 1993; Cantwell, 1994; Petri, 1994; UNCTAD, 1996). To what extent does direct production in a host country substitute for exports to it? To what extent do the strategies of international vertical integration – discussed in Chapter 18 – generate more trade? Under the neoclassical framework the relationship between trade and FDI is analysed by considering possible impediments to trade or to FDI. Trade impediments – that is, obstacles to the movements of material and non-material products – stimulate factors' movements – that is, the movements of labour and capital across frontiers – and therefore stimulate FDI and international production. In summary, if companies cannot source a market via export, they will produce where the market opportunities are. On the other hand, restrictions to the movements of factors of production – specifically capital in our case – are likely to stimulate production at home and the sourcing of foreign markets via trade. In this framework, trade and FDI/international production are substitutes for each other (Mundell, 1957). This is, to a large extent, due to the fact that they are analysed only in their role as sources of supply for markets.

However, this is not the only role of FDI/international production whose relationship to trade may emerge from strategic rather than efficiency objectives on the part of TNCs (Acocella, 1992). Cantwell (1994) makes a comprehensive and detailed analysis of the relationship between trade and international production using the following three categories of production:

1   resource-based production, that is, production aiming at the acquisition of raw materials;
2   market-oriented production, that is, production designed to provide products (whether material or immaterial, i.e. services) for the local market;
3   rationalized or integrated international production which results from a strategy of vertical integration of the production process across countries leading to a new international division of labour (as discussed in Chapter 18).

Cantwell considers the issue of *substitution versus complementarity* between FDI and trade arising from these three cases.[3]

In case (1) the resource-based international production leads to the specialization of countries into resource-based economies and manufacturing- and/or services-based ones. This specialization pattern generates an increase in trade in the world as a whole because the raw materials are transported from one country – or set of countries – to another or set of others. The first set of countries tends to be developing ones and the second set tends to be developed countries. Thus, the first type of international production (1) is trade-creating. Moreover, developed countries are likely to be suppliers of equipment and machinery needed for the extraction of raw materials (as, for example, in the case of oil extraction) and this leads to further trade enhancement.

In case (2), international production appears to replace exports as a means of sourcing foreign markets. Nonetheless, some trade creation is possible if production in the host country enhances the scope for the export of related products from the home country and/or if it gives scope for penetration via exports into third countries. An example of the first type could be the exportation of goods and services to be used in the production process abroad. An example of the second type is the case – already mentioned – of investment into the UK by US and Japanese companies in view of penetrating wider European (EC/EU) markets through exports. If there are legal barriers to imports, companies are led to use direct production to source markets which – in the absence of trade barriers and ceteris paribus – they might have sourced via home production and exports. There is therefore substitution of international production for trade. This is the case also considered in the neoclassical literature as mentioned above.

Various interlinked issues arise in connection with the possible substitution between trade and direct production. Regional areas of integration (such as the North American Free Trade Agreement [NAFTA] or the EU) stimulate trade as barriers between member countries come down. Moreover, they attract inward FDI from non-member countries' TNCs who want to have the benefits of free trade in the region. We have already noted the case of Japanese FDI into the UK as a strategy of penetration of wider European markets.

It should also be noted that some products are not tradable, such as hotel services; they cannot be produced in one location/country for use in another location; they must be produced where the consumers are. In this case the only way of sourcing a foreign market is, therefore, direct foreign production.

Substitution in the opposite direction may occur if there are impediments to the transfer of capital and thus FDI across frontiers but not to the movements of products; this leads to the sourcing of the foreign market via exports.

In case (3), vertically integrated international manufacturing production, the strategy definitely leads to the creation of trade as components are moved from country to country for further processing and final assembly. In this case international production and trade are complementary. Both exports and imports increase due to the movements of components for further processing across the world.

In Chapter 18, alongside the NIDL for manufacturing, we discussed what I called the E-NIDL, that is, a new international division of labour for the electronic age. As noted, the E-NIDL is still at relatively early stages of development and will, no doubt, grow considerably in the next decades. It is therefore interesting to analyse its current and possible trade effects.

The ICTs have in effect allowed the development of a new internationalization mode in which service components of a final product – in the form of data or documents – can be made available to a distant location – whether in the same country or in a foreign one – at a very low cost and in real time. This new form is neither international production nor trade of the traditional type. It is a new mode of international activity made possible by the ICTs. Nonetheless, some FDI is likely to take place in order to set up the business structure – as either a single or joint venture – that will carry on the processing activity.

The substitution versus complementarity issue between trade and international production raises a variety of collateral issues. First, whatever the time sequence between FDI and trade, many authors agree that the first mode of market penetration is likely to lead to lower transaction costs for the other: it is easier to operate in a market via a second mode (say direct production) once the company has operated via a different mode (say exports). Once knowledge of the physical, business and governmental or bureaucratic environment has been acquired via the first mode, it makes operations through the second mode easier and cheaper. Whichever comes first, there is likely to be a sharing of transaction and information costs between trade and FDI for any given company (Thomsen and Woolcock, 1993; Petri, 1994).

Second, the time linearity – that is, the time sequence trade followed by FDI – of the relationship may not necessarily imply linearity with respect to the quantum, i.e. the volume or value of exports or international production. Molle and Morsink (1991) find a non-linear relationship between the size of trade and FDI within the EC/EU. They write: 'The relationship between trade and DI appeared to be non-linear; for foreign DI to occur, the trade relations need to reach a minimum level. Beyond that level, more trade integration in the EC does not seem to give rise to larger EDIE flows' (ibid.: 98).[4]

Market-sourcing strategies are more likely to follow a 'linear sequence' in which exports from home production are followed by direct investment and production in the foreign countries where the markets are. The framework is similar to the one set in the international product life cycle model (Vernon, 1966): the initial sourcing via exports is followed by direct production leading to substitution between the two. The substitution must be seen dynamically, as a substitution in time and according to specific market-sourcing strategies. The sequence deals with finished consumer products. In the case of intermediate manufactured products we must consider the location strategies followed by the TNCs. If the companies operate a vertically-integrated international production strategy for manufactured products this will result in trade creation as noted above.

Third, we should account for dynamic choices and sequences. Some of the considerations made here on complementarity versus substitution between trade and international production imply static ex ante choices between the two types of market sourcing: ex ante the firm has the choice of either producing at home and exporting or of producing directly abroad. Other strategies imply a dynamic time sequence. The market-oriented manufacturing output implies a linear time sequence which goes from exports to FDI as in Vernon (1966), considered in Chapter 5. However, the speed with which the sequence is implemented depends on many elements, in partic-ular: the life cycle of the product; the competitive structure of the industry and the position of the company within it; the cost structure of production and in particular the structure of transportation and other spatial costs; the costs of acquiring information on the local markets and local production conditions; the technology used and the evolution of the technology in the life of the product; and the relationship between technology and tradability of the product.

Time and history (for both trade and FDI) as well as the vintage of FDI – how long ago the FDI was made – seem relevant in stimulating further complementarities between them. Time is also of relevance in another aspect of FDI. A large share of world FDI increasingly takes the form of mergers and acquisitions as already mentioned. Among the characteristics of acquisitions compared with other forms of penetration into a market and country, is the fact that they are a speedy form of pene-tration; companies can acquire new capacity very quickly by buying up existing firms in host countries. Moreover, the restructuring which inevitably follows mergers and acquisitions may involve changes in the structure of international suppliers and customers with effects on the trade pattern of countries.

Fourth, we should take account of possible trade creation due to other inter-nationalization modes and particularly to joint ventures. The latter mode may facilitate the exportation of products produced by the local joint venture partners who might – before the venture – have found it difficult to branch out into foreign markets.

The issue of complementarity versus substitution (see Box 19.1) may also be specific to either the industry and/or countries of origin or destination of the FDI. For example, Kojima (1978) and Ozawa (1979) maintain that Japanese outward FDI is trade-creating.

The above discussion is based on the standard macroeconomic accounting system based on residency as we discussed in the methodological chapter. However, it is worth noting that the proponents of an ownership system for national accounting under conditions of large activities by TNCs would want to see the computation of sales as a whole. Sales by a particular country would group together both exports and sales by foreign affiliates of domestic TNCs. More on this in the next chapter.

Box 19.1   *Trade and international production: complements or substitutes?*

Resource-based international production
Specialization between countries generates trade, therefore there is complementarity between trade and FDI.

Market-oriented international production
Substitution between exports and FDI either as ex ante strategy or as time sequence.

Trade barriers stimulate direct production to penetrate markets

Internationally vertically-integrated production processes
FDI leads to international trade as components are moved from country to country for further processing.

---

3   Effects on the pattern of trade

Over and above the impact that the activities of TNCs have on the volume of trade mentioned in the introduction to this chapter and whose theoretical bases we analysed in section 2, there is also a considerable impact on the pattern/structure of trade.

Three types of patterns are particularly relevant (see Box 19.2):

- the geographical pattern/structure of trade;
- intra-firm trade;
- intra-industry trade.

Geographical structure of trade

The activities of TNCs have considerable impact on the geography of trade: which countries/regions export or import to or from whom, what products, how much. This is connected to the strategies of TNCs with regard to market penetration and sourcing. For example, Japanese investment in the UK motor industry was partly motivated by the desire to overcome trade barriers to imports from Japan. If production takes place in an EC/EU country (such as the UK) then the trade barriers would not apply. One consequence of these strategies was the exports of motor products from the UK to other European countries.

A second example may derive from the considerable increase in exports from China. These are, usually, attributed to low wages in China which do indeed play a major role. What should, however, also be mentioned is the fact that, at the micro level, these exports usually originate with international production in China by western TNCs. It may indeed be US TNCs investing in China that end up exporting from China to the USA. A pattern of imports into the USA of products produced by US TNCs investing abroad emerges also from the third phase of Vernon's IPLC model (see Chapter 5).

Moreover, the strategies of TNCs regarding the international vertically-integrated process and the related location of components affect the geography of trade because it affects which components are moved between which countries/regions. Yamashita (2010) points out (pp. 34–40) that developing countries are increasing their share of world trade in components on both the exports and imports side.[5]

Intra-firm trade

Intra-firm trade (IFT) is the exchange of goods and services between parts of the same firm that operate across different nations. It is therefore an exchange internal to the firm though external to the countries.

The amount of intra-firm trade is very substantial. It is estimated to be no less than a third of world trade and to be increasing. These estimates are extrapolations from data of specific countries as there are no comprehensive data on the extent of this phenomenon, particularly on the import side. Some countries – namely the USA, Sweden, Japan and France – collect data on both imports and exports within companies. We can only rely on estimates because hard statistical facts are not available due to confidentiality clauses imposed by firms and governments. The confidentiality is usually connected with the fact that companies do not want to disclose their internal exchanges for two reasons: first, because they may fear criticism at the possible high levels of imports they are involved with in any one country. Indeed, data on imports of IFT[6] are considerably scarcer than data on exports. A second and important reason may be due to the fact that disclosures on the volume and geographical structure of IFT may assist government revenue authorities in different countries in detecting the possible manipulation of transfer prices, on which more in the next chapter.

Internal transfers within companies at the international level involve not only goods and services but also technology. There is scant evidence on the transfer of technology whether at arm's length, through internal transfers or via collaborative agreements. Some evidence can be drawn from the cross-countries payments for technology services available for some countries. We must, however, remember that technology transfer is probably the area which gives most scope for transfer price manipulation, given the difficulty of finding exact correspondence between the service transferred internally and the one available on the market. Thus, the receipts may not fully reflect the actual arm's-length value of the service transferred.

Two questions arise from this picture. First, why is intra-firm trade so large and increasing? Second, why is it important? The answer to the first question can be found in the strategies of TNCs as regards the location of production worldwide and particularly their strategies of vertically integrated international production, which – as mentioned in Chapter 18 – leads to the new international division of labour. Under the NIDL, different parts of the production process are located in different countries to take advantage of different skills availability and costs of labour. This leads to the need to move components from country to country for further processing and, eventually, for final assembly. The movement of components is internal to the firm but takes place across countries and therefore generates intra-firm international trade.

Is IFT important and should we, therefore, be worried about the lack of reliable statistics? The answers to these questions are positive for the following reasons. First, because the TNCs' strategies affect the overall geographical pattern of trade; governments need to have a clear picture of the possible determinants of trade patterns of their countries if they are to develop and implement appropriate policies. Second, because IFT gives scope for the manipulation of transfer prices, that is, of prices of components transferred internally to the firm though across national frontiers. The manipulation of prices in the invoicing of internal transfers refers to the fact that such prices may be set at a different level from the ones which would operate if the exchange were between two separate and independent firms, that is, different from arm's-length prices. In the next chapter I discuss the reasons why TNCs might manipulate transfer prices and the possible effects of such manipulations.

Intra-industry trade

Intra-industry trade (IIT) refers to the exports and imports of products that belong to the same industrial category. Such trade seems to contradict a main pillar of neoclassical trade theory, i.e. that trade is the outcome of specialization in production by the various trading countries. If the countries produce similar products or, in any case, products belonging to the same industrial groups, it would appear that their structure of production is not different but similar and trade emerges not from specialization but in spite of the lack of specialization.

Intra-industry trade poses several questions for economists over and above the possible conflict with the neoclassical trade theory. The first issue relates to measurements and the construction of indicators. How do we assess and measure IIT and therefore how do we know its size and relevance? Various indicators have been proposed,[7] the main ones by Balassa (1974), Grubel and Lloyd (1975) and Aquino (1978). The basic problem in the measurement issue is the fact that estimates partly depend on our chosen yardstick and definition of industrial category. If the chosen industrial category is very large, then almost all trade is intra-industry. If it is very fine, then the amount of IIT is small.

The second question refers to reasons why IIT is large and increasing. Various theories have been proposed on the determinants of IIT, some stressing consumers'

Box 19.2   *International production and the pattern of international trade*

International production affects

The geographical structure of trade

Intra-firm trade
Relevance of international vertically-integrated production processes

Intra-industry trade
Can have various causes including the TNCs' strategy of international vertically-integrated production processes

---

preferences for differentiated products, some looking at the structure of the markets or at the production side for explanations of the determinants of IIT.

Among those that stress the production side, we can place the strategies of TNCs and in particular, once again, the strategy of international vertically integrated production. The components being moved from country to country for further processing not only increase the volume of intra-firm trade (as we saw above), they also contribute to intra-industry trade. This is because the various components which are imported, processed and exported all belong to the same industrial category(ies), therefore they are part of IIT.

SUMMARY BOX 19

Effects of international production on trade: key elements

Trade and international production: substitutes or complements? (See Box 19.1)

- Resource-based production
- Market-oriented production
- International vertically-integrated production

Effects on trade patterns (see Box 19.2)

- Geographical pattern
- Intra-firm trade: causes; relevance and impact
- Intra-industry trade: measurement issues and difficulties; possible explanations for its existence and growth

Relevant chapters

Chapters 5, 10, 12 and 16

In conclusion, trade, this most traditional mechanism of international integration, is now largely initiated by transnational companies. The TNCs' international production and trade activities are closely interlinked and indeed about one-third of world trade takes place on an internal intra-firm basis. Moreover, the strategies of TNCs also affect the geographical pattern as well as the patterns of intra-firm and intra-industry trade. In summary, the TNCs affect both the volume and the patterns of world trade.

Indicative further reading

Barry, F. and Bradley, J. (1997), 'FDI and trade: the Irish host-country experience', *The Economic Journal*, **107** (445), 1798–11.

Cantwell, J. (1994), 'The relationship between international trade and international production', in D. Greenway and I.A. Winters (eds), *Surveys in International Trade*, Oxford: Blackwell, ch. 11, pp. 303–28.

Chesnais, F. and Saillou, A. (2000), 'Foreign direct investment and European trade', in F. Chesnais, G. Ietto-Gillies and R. Simonetti (eds), *European Integration and Global Corporate Strategies*, London: Routledge, ch. 2, pp. 25–51.

Gray, P.H. (1992), 'The interface between the theories of international trade and production', in P.J. Buckley and M. Casson (eds), *Multinational Enterprises in the World Economy*: *Essays in Honour of John Dunning*, Aldershot, UK and Brookfield, VT, USA: Edward Elgar, ch. 3, pp. 41–53.

Grimwade, N. (2000), *International Trade*: *New Patterns of Trade, Production and Investment*, London: Routledge, chs 3 and 4.

OECD (1994), *The Performance of Foreign Affiliates in OECD Countries*, Paris: OECD, ch. 5.

Sutcliffe, B. and Glyn, A. (2003), 'Measures of globalisation and their misinterpretation', in J. Michie (ed.), *The Handbook of Globalisation*, Cheltenham, UK and Northampton, MA, USA: Edward Elgar, ch. 3, pp. 61–78.

UNCTAD (2002), *World Investment Report 2002*: *Transnational Corporations and Export Competitiveness*, Geneva: United Nations, ch. 6 and pp. 243–8.

Notes

1 Non-factor services are services as products rather than the services of labour or of capital as part of the production process.

2 As pointed out in Chapter 1, international production and FDI do not coincide because a considerable amount of production abroad is carried out without FDI as mature affiliates can rely on local sources of funding rather than investment from the parent company. Nonetheless, FDI can be taken as a very good proxy for international production and the two will be used interchangeably here, though the reader is warned about possible discrepancies.

3 Cantwell's analysis is wider than the one mentioned here. He considers the pattern of trade (intra- versus inter-firm trade and intra- versus inter-industry trade) as well as the applicability of the traditional factor endowment (Heckscher–Ohlin–Samuelson) framework for the explanation of trade.

4 In this passage DI stands for direct investment and EDIE for European Direct Investment in Europe.

5 See also World Trade Organization (2005) on outsourcing and trade issues.

6 Keith Cowling has kindly pointed out to me that the availability of data on the licensing of vehicles by country of origin allows the calculation of some intra-firm statistics on the motor industry (cf. Cowling et al., 2000).

7 A clear review of theories, measurements and related problems of intra-industry trade is in Grimwade (2000: ch. 3).

20 Effects on the balance of payments

1 Introduction

The balance of payments of a country records the summary value of transactions between residents in that country and residents of foreign countries. The transactions may be undertaken by individual citizens or by institutions of the private or public sector. The transactions are grouped under current and financial accounts.

The activities of TNCs have considerable effects on the balance of payments of a country. There have been some major studies of balance of payments effects – particularly on developed home countries – with a view to the formulation of appropriate policies (Reddaway et al., 1967; 1968; Hufbauer and Adler, 1968).

Some balance of payments effects are *direct* and others are *indirect*. The next section considers the main direct balance of payment effects. Section 3 considers indirect effects. It specifically discusses transfer prices manipulation and its economic effects including effects on the balance of payments. The last section emphasizes methodological issues.

None of the theories considered in Parts II and III deal with balance of payments issues. There may be a tenuous connection between Aliber's theory (Chapter 7) and the effects in this chapter: in that theory the exchange rate and the value of currencies and the movements of financial capital between countries do play a major role.

2 The direct effects on the balance of payments

Whenever the foreign activities of a TNC are financed via the transfer of funds from the home country, they give rise to balance of payments transactions. This is the case of FDI funded by the headquarters of the company, which results in a transaction between the home and host country: the home country will register a negative value on the *financial account of the balance of payments* – as investment funds leave the country – and the host country will record a corresponding positive value. The transaction is recorded in the same way, whether the funding is for a joint or sole venture or whether it is for an acquisition or a greenfield activity. Indeed, the overall effects on the balance of payments are the same whether the capital outlay is for portfolio or direct investment.

It should, however, be remembered that not all foreign assets and related international production – whatever the setting up mode – are funded via the transfer of funds from the home country. Some are funded via retained profits from pre-existing activities in the country or via the raising of funds in the host country. These funding modes do not give rise to records in the balance of payments because they do not involve movements of funds from one country to another.

The investment abroad – whether FDI or portfolio – will, in due course, produce profits and dividends for the investor. Many of these will find their way back into the home country. There will therefore be a flow of funds going in the opposite direction from the capital funds. These transactions will be recorded in the *balance of payments current account*.

Here we have an example of an important time-boundary issue which I promised the reader I would go back to when I first introduced it in Chapter 16: the different effects in the short and long run. In the short run, financial capital may leave the home country in order to fund the investment in the host country: a positive score for the host country's balance of payments, on its financial account, and a negative one for the home country.

However, the initial investment is likely to give rise to a flow of profits for many years to come. The flow of repatriated profits/dividends is recorded as a positive value in the balance of payments current account for the home country and as a negative value for the host country. Here is the case of effects that go in opposite directions in the short versus the medium to long term.

Moreover, as the flow of profits continues for many years, countries with a long history of outward foreign investment may have very substantial cumulative yearly profits. Their cumulative sums may in some cases be as large or larger than the new annual outflow of funds for new investment abroad. This means that the new vintage FDI can be funded – in terms of the overall balance of payments position – from the profits of past investment. Countries such as the UK or the Netherlands who have been large outward investors for many years are indeed in this position (Ietto-Gillies, 2000b). Countries that are mainly host countries are likely to find themselves in the opposite situation. It should, however, be noted that – as mentioned in Chapter 1 – many developed countries, and in particular the UK, have in the last few decades become heavily involved in both inward and outward FDI.

3   The indirect effects on the balance of payments

In Chapter 19 we discussed the trade effects of TNCs' activities. *International trade* transactions give rise to corresponding balance of payments transactions with the flow of currency going in the opposite direction to the flow of goods and services as the imports have to be paid for and the exporters will receive payments. This means that any foreign investment that produces trade effects will indirectly also produce balance of payments effects. The trade effects of TNCs' activities relate to both the volume and the geographical structure, as we discussed in the previous chapter. The corresponding effects on the balance of payments are both in terms of volume of funds moving from country to country and in terms of the geographical structure. The latter refers to the fact that as the TNCs may affect the direction of trade, the balance of payments between any two countries may be correspondingly affected.

Another major indirect effect may come about via the *manipulation of transfer prices*, to which we now turn.[1] What are transfer prices? They are prices charged by one part of the company (headquarters or one of the subsidiaries) to another part (any of the subsidiaries or headquarters) for the internal transfer of goods and services. Essentially, we are talking about pricing for internal markets, a feature of many private and public institutions. For example in the UK, in the last two decades of the twentieth century, there has been much discussion about internal markets and internal pricing within the National Health Service. The internal prices may or may not reflect actual costs and scarcity, and therefore they may or may not be set at the same level as market prices, i.e. the prices that are actually – or could potentially be – charged to independent, external clients.

When the internal transfer of goods and services takes place across borders as part of transnational activities, the corporations have the opportunity to develop pricing strategies that maximize the overall returns for the company as a whole. Such strategies may lead to the so-called 'manipulation of transfer prices'. The word manipulation refers to the setting of prices for internal transfers at different levels compared with the prices which might be charged for arm's-length transactions, i.e. different levels compared with the actual or potential market prices. Why would a company want to manipulate transfer prices? In what conditions and for what reasons would such a manipulation lead to higher overall profits? The reasons and conditions are highlighted in Box 20.1.

The manipulation of internal prices that these reasons may lead to are the following: lower transfer prices than the possible arm's-length market price, if the company wants to declare higher profits in the country receiving the components (goods or services); and higher prices in the opposite situation. It should, therefore, be stressed that the manipulation of transfer prices can go in either direction: it can lead to higher or lower internal charges than the arm's-length prices according to the overall company's specific interests and strategy.

The most common – and best known – reason for the manipulation of transfer prices is the minimization of the overall tax liability of the company. A company faced with tax liabilities in many countries is also likely to be faced with different tax rates in different countries. If the company can disclose most of its profits in the country with the lowest tax rate, it will avoid the charge of higher tax rates on some of its profits. Such a strategy will minimize the overall tax liability of the company as a whole. This aim can partly be achieved by a strategy of transfer prices manipulation that leads to the recording of higher profits in the country with the lowest tax rate, and very low profits in countries with high tax rates.

One thing to keep in mind is that this issue is not one of home versus host country: the lowest tax regime country could be the home or a host country. The direction of possible transfer of profits depends on the tax rate of the countries, not on whether they are host or home or whether they are developed or developing countries.

It should be noted that the effects here are linked to *multinationality per se* and not to the direction of the flow of investment, inward or outward. It is the fact that the company operates in many countries that allows it to implement transfer prices manipulation, independent of which country is its home or host country.

Companies that engage in international vertically integrated strategies have wide scope for transfer of components across countries and therefore have wide scope for manipulating transfer prices. However, such a manipulation can also occur

---

Box 20.1 *Possible reasons for the manipulation of transfer prices*

- The minimization of tax liabilities for the whole company.

- The circumvention of restrictions to the transfer of profits from host country(ies) which pose strict ceilings and constraints to such transfers.

- To take advantages of expected appreciation or depreciation of currencies.

- To record low costs of components in a country/market that the company wants to penetrate through low prices. This is essentially a strategy of disguised dumping to gain competitive advantages over rivals.

- To record relatively low profits in countries where it is feared labour and its trade unions might demand wage increases if high profits were disclosed.

---

in the pricing of services transferred between different parts of the company. These can be factor services – like the services of a highly-skilled technical expert or manager – or product services.

The manipulation of transfer prices is not without problems for the company. First, the practice is illegal and no company would own to using such a strategy. However, for most services and components transferred internally to a company, no external market exists and therefore it is difficult for governments to compare prices and thus have evidence that manipulation takes place. Nonetheless, if the practice is discovered the company may have to pay large fines. Second, it is not as easy to implement as it might appear at first sight. It may require some type of double accounting; moreover, it may lead to conflicts between managers of different units. The Organisation for Economic Co-operation and Development (2010) gives detailed guidelines for companies and tax administrators on how to – respectively – set and monitor transfer prices. These guidelines can be of use to other stakeholders and general policy-makers.

There are important effects of this practice at the macro level as well as at the micro, company level. The strategy leads to minimization of overall tax revenue for the company; the other side of this is that there is a transfer of surplus from the international public domain to the private domain. Essentially, in the world as a whole less will go to the public sphere as tax revenues, and more will be kept in the private sphere of companies who will pay an overall lower tax bill.[2] Moreover, a transfer of surplus takes place between countries because of this practice. The countries with high tax rates will see their tax revenue siphoned off towards low tax rate countries. In the last analysis the practice leads to divergence between private and social benefits worldwide and to the redistribution of surplus between different countries.

If the strategy is used for market penetration reasons, there are issues of possible unfair competition and therefore effects on the market structure of the industry in which the company operates.

Last but not least, there are effects on the volumes and structures of the balance of payments of the various countries involved in the transfers as the recorded values of the transactions are different from the value that should have been invoiced on the basis of arm's-length prices.

4   Boundary and methodology issues

The assessment of the balance of payments effects raises a variety of methodological issues, most of which are already mentioned in this chapter. However, as they are very important, it is worth summarizing them here as well as adding another issue.

SUMMARY BOX 20

Balance of payments effects: a summary of the issues

Direct effects

• Financial account transactions
• Current account transactions

Indirect effects

• Trade effects
• Effects via the manipulation of transfer prices

What are transfer prices and why companies may want to manipulate them

(cf. Box 20.1)

Effects of transfer prices manipulation

• Transfer of surplus from the public to the private domain, worldwide
• Redistribution of surplus between countries
• Impact on the countries' balance of payments

Boundaries/methodological issues

• Short- versus long-term effects
• Direct versus indirect effects
• Impact of multinationality per se
• Balance of payments records on the basis of *residence* or *ownership* principle.

Other relevant chapters

Chapters 7, 16 and 18

I have already mentioned the possible divergence between short- and long-run effects due to profits going in the opposite direction from the investment funds. A major issue is that linked to direct versus indirect effects. The latter are due to trade effects of international production or to effects of the manipulation of transfer prices. On this question, the reader is reminded that the effects are linked to multinationality per se rather than to the direction of the flow of investment and therefore rather than to a country being home or host to FDI. They are also dependent on whether the countries involved are developed or developing: it all depends on their tax rates or other elements, as in Box 20.1.

Moreover, there is a further major methodological issue arising specifically with reference to the balance of payments. The large and increasing impact of TNCs' activities on the balance of payments is raising questions on whether the recording of the latter should be done on the basis of *residence* (as is indeed the practice at present) or on the basis of *ownership*, as mentioned in Chapter 16, section 3.

The latter principle would involve recording on the basis of which country – through being home to specific TNCs – has the ownership rights to certain flows of transactions. Thus, the sales of affiliates abroad of a TNC based in the country would give rise to a balance of payments record under the ownership principle even if no flow of funds takes place across nation-states. Under the current residency principle no such recording takes place. As mentioned, these proposals are tentative and they have, so far, not given rise to changes in the balance of payments recording system which is based on residence.

Indicative further reading

Dunning, J.H. (1993), *Multinational Enterprises and the Global Economy*, Wokingham: Addison-Wesley.

Eden, L. (2001), 'Taxes, transfer pricing, and the multinational enterprise', in A.M. Rugman and T.L. Brewer (eds), *The Oxford Handbook of International Business*, Oxford: Oxford University Press, ch. 21, pp. 591–619.

Note

1 On transfer prices see also Eden (2001).
2 See Christensen (2011) on the relationship between developed countries, companies and tax havens.

References

Acocella, N. (1992), 'The multinational firm and the theory of industrial organization', in A. Del Monte (ed.), *Recent Developments in the Theory of Industrial Organization*, London: Macmillan.

Aharoni, Y. (1966), *The Foreign Investment Decision Process*, Cambridge, MA: Harvard University Press.

Aliber, R.Z. (1970), 'A theory of direct foreign investment', in C.P. Kindleberger (ed.), *The International Corporation*, Cambridge, MA: MIT Press, pp. 17–34.

Aliber, R.Z. (1971), 'The multinational enterprise in a multiple currency world', in J.H. Dunning (ed.), *The Multinational Enterprise*, London: Allen and Unwin, pp. 49–60.

Aliber, R.Z. (1993), *The Multinational Paradigm*, Cambridge, MA: MIT Press.

Amendola, G., Dosi, G. and Papagni, E. (1993), 'The dynamics of international competitiveness, *Review of World Economics*, **129** (3), 451–71.

Andersson, U. and Forsgren, M. (1996), 'Subsidiary embeddedness and control in the multinational corporation', *International Business Review*, **5** (5), 487–508.

Aquino, A. (1978), 'Intra-industry trade and inter-industry specialisation as concurrent sources of international trade in manufactures', *Weltwirtschaftliches Archiv*, **114** (2), 275–96.

Archibugi, D. and Michie, J. (1997), *Technology, Globalization and Economic Performance*, Cambridge: Cambridge University Press.

Auerbach, P. (1988), *Competition: the Economics of Industrial Change*, Oxford: Blackwell.

Auerbach, P. (1989), 'Review of *Transnational Monopoly Capitalism* by K. Cowling and R. Sugden (1987)', *International Review of Applied Economics*, **3** (1), 115–21.

Balassa, B. (1974), 'Trade creation and trade diversion in the European Common Market', *Manchester School*, **92** (2), 93–135.

Balcet, G. and Evangelista, R. (2005), 'Global technology: innovative strategies of multinational affiliates, *Transnational Corporations*', **14** (2), 10–20.

Baran, P.A. and Sweezy, P.M. (1966a), *Monopoly Capital: An Essay on the American Economic and Social Order* (1968 edition), Harmondsworth: Penguin.

Baran, P.A. and Sweezy, P.M. (1966b), 'Notes on the theory of imperialism', *Monthly Review*, March, 15–31.

Barba Navaretti, G. and Venables, A.J. (2004), *Multinational Firms in the World Economy*, Princeton and Oxford: Princeton University Press.

Barrell, R. and Pain, N. (1997), 'Foreign direct investment, technological change and economic growth within Europe', *The Economic Journal*, **107** (445), 1770–86.

Barry, F. and Bradley, J. (1997), 'FDI and trade: the Irish host-country experience', *The Economic Journal*, **107** (445), 1798–811.

Bartlett, C.A. and Ghoshal, S. (1988), 'Organizing for worldwide effectiveness: the transnational solution', *California Management Review*, **31** (1), 1–21; reprinted in P.J. Buckley and P.N. Ghauri (1999), *The Internationalization of the Firm: A Reader*, London: International Thomson Business Press, pp. 295–311.

Bartlett, C.A. and Ghoshal, S. (1989), *Managing Across Borders: The Transnational Solution*, Boston, MA: Harvard Business School Press.

Bartlett, C.A. and Ghoshal, S. (1991), *The Transnational Solution*, Cambridge, MA: Harvard Business School Press.

Berg, D.M. and Guisinger, S.E. (2001), 'Capital flows, capital controls and international business risk', in A.M. Rugman and T.L. Brewer (eds), *The Oxford Handbook of International Business*, Oxford: Oxford University Press, ch. 10, pp. 259–81.

Bhagwati, J.N. (1973), 'The theory of immiserizing growth: further applications', in M.B. Connolly and A.K. Swoboda (eds), *International Trade and Money*, Toronto: University of Toronto Press, pp. 45–54.

Blomstrom, M., Fors, G. and Lipsey, R.E. (1997), 'Foreign direct investment and employment: home country experience in the United States and Sweden', *The Economic Journal*, **107** (445), 1787–97.

Branston, R.J., Cowling, K. and Sugden, R. (2003), 'Corporate governance and the public interest', Warwick Economic Research Papers n. 626, Department of Economics, The University of Warwick.

Braunstein, E. (2003), 'Gender and foreign direct investment', in J. Michie (ed.), *The Handbook of Globalization*, Cheltenham, UK and Northampton, MA, USA: Edward Elgar, pp. 165–75.

Brecher, R.A. and Diaz Alejandro, C.F. (1977), 'Tariffs, foreign capital and immiserizing growth', *Journal of International Economics*, **7**, 317–22; reprinted in J.N. Bhagwati (ed.) (1981), *International Trade: Selected Readings*, Cambridge, MA: MIT Press.

Buckley, P.J. (1983), 'New theories of international business: some unresolved issues', in M.C. Casson (ed.), *The Growth of International Business*, Boston, MA: Allen and Unwin, pp. 34–50.

Buckley, P.J. and Casson, M.C. (1976), 'A long-run theory of the multinational enterprise', in P.J. Buckley and M.C. Casson (eds), *The Future of the Multinational Enterprise*, London: Macmillan, pp. 32–65.

Buckley, P.J. and Casson, M.C. (1998a), 'Models of the multinational enterprise', *Journal of International Business Studies*, **29** (1), 21–44.

Buckley, P.J. and Casson, M.C. (1998b), 'Analyzing foreign market entry strategies: extending the internalization approach', *Journal of International Business Studies*, **29** (3), 539–62.

Buckley, P.J. and Casson, M.C. (1999), 'A theory of international operation', in P.J. Buckley and P.N. Ghauri (eds), *The Internationalization of the Firm: A Reader*, London: ITBP, pp. 55–60.

Buckley, P. and Casson, M.C. (2001), 'Strategic complexity in international business', in A.M. Rugman and T.L. Brewer (eds), *The Oxford Handbook of International Business*, Oxford: Oxford University Press, pp. 88–126.

Buckley, P.J. and Ghauri, P.N. (1999), *The Internationalization of the Firm: A Reader*, London: ITBP.

Buckley, P.J. and Mucchielli, J.-L. (eds) (1997), *Multinational Firms and International Relocation*, Cheltenham, UK and Lyme, NH, USA: Edward Elgar.

Bukharin, N. (1917), *Imperialism and World Economy* (1987 edition), London: Merlin Press.

Cantwell, J. (1989), *Technological Innovation and Multinational Corporations*, Oxford: Blackwell.

Cantwell, J.A. (1991), 'The theory of technological competence and its application to international production', in D. McFetridge (ed.), *Foreign Investment, Technology and Economic Growth*, Calgary: University of Calgary Press.

Cantwell, J. (1992), 'Innovation and technological competitiveness', in P.J. Buckley and M. Casson (eds), *Multinational Enterprises in the World Economy: Essays in Honour of John Dunning*, Aldershot, UK and Brookfield, VT, USA: Edward Elgar, pp. 20–40.

Cantwell, J. (1994), 'The relationship between international trade and international production', in D. Greenway and L.A. Winters (eds), *Surveys in International Trade*, Oxford: Blackwell, pp. 303–28.

Cantwell, J. (1995), 'The globalisation of technology: what remains of the product cycle model?', *Cambridge Journal of Economics*, **19** (1), 155–74.

Cantwell, J. (2000), 'A survey of theories of international production', in C.N. Pitelis and R. Sugden (eds), *The Nature of the Transnational Firm*, London: Routledge, pp. 10–56.

Cantwell, J. (2003), 'Innovation and information technology in the MNE', in A.M. Rugman and T.L. Brewer (eds), *The Oxford Handbook of International Business*, Oxford: Oxford University Press, pp. 431–56.

Cantwell, J. (2009), Location and the multinational enterprise, *Journal of International Business Studies*, **40**, 35–41.

Cantwell, J. and Bellak, C. (1998), 'How important is foreign direct investment?', *Oxford Bulletin of Economics and Statistics*, **60** (1), 99–106.

Cantwell, J. and Fai, F. (1999), 'Firms as the source of innovation and growth: the evolution of technological competence', *Journal of Evolutionary Economics*, **9** (3), 331–66.

Cantwell, J. and Iammarino, S. (1998), 'MNCs, technological innovation and regional systems in the EU: some evidence in the Italian case', *International Journal of the Economics of Business*, **5** (3), 383–408.

Cantwell, J. and Iammarino, S. (2003), *Multinational Corporations and European Regional Systems of Innovation*, London: Routledge.

Cantwell, J. and Narula, R. (2001), 'The eclectic paradigm in the global economy', *International Journal of the Economics of Business*, **8** (2), 155–72.

Cantwell, J. and Piscitello, L. (2000), 'Accumulating technological competence: its changing impact on corporate diversification and internationalization', *Industrial and Corporate Change*, **9** (1), 21–51.

Cantwell, J. and Santangelo, G. (2000), 'Capitalism, innovation and profits in the new technoeconomic paradigm', *Journal of Evolutionary Economics*, **10** (1–2), 131–57.

Carlsson, B. (2006), 'Internationalization of innovation systems: a survey of the literature', *Research Policy*, **35** (1), 56–67.

Casson, M.C. (1982), 'Transaction costs and the theory of the multinational enterprise', in A.M. Rugman (ed.), *New Theories of the Multinational Enterprise*, London: Croom Helm, pp. 24–43.

Casson, M.C. (1990), Introduction to 'The large multinational "corporation": an analysis of some motives for the international integration of business', by Stephen H. Hymer, in M. Casson (ed.), *Multinational Corporations*, Aldershot, UK and Brookfield, VT, USA: Edward Elgar, pp. 1–7.

Casson, M.C. (1997), *Information and Organization: A New Perspective on the Theory of the Firm*, Oxford: Oxford University Press.

Casson, M.C. and associates (1986), *Multinationals and World Trade*, London: Allen and Unwin.

Castellani, D. and Zanfei, A. (2002), 'Multinational experience and the creation of linkages with local firms: evidence from the electronics industry', *Cambridge Journal of Economics*, **26** (1), 1–25.

Castellani, D. and Zanfei, A. (2003), 'Technology gaps, absorptive capacity and the impact of inward investments on productivity of European firms', *Economics of Innovation and New Technology*, **21** (6), 555–76.

Castellani, D. and Zanfei, A. (2004), 'Choosing international linkage strategies in the electronic industry: the role of multinational experience', *Journal of Behaviour and Organization*, **53**, 447–75.

Castellani, D. and Zanfei, A. (2006), *Multinational Firms, Innovation and Productivity*, Cheltenham, UK and Northampton, MA, USA: Edward Elgar.

Caves, R.E. (1971), 'International corporations: the industrial economics of foreign investment', *Economica*, **38**, 1–27; reprinted in J.H. Dunning (ed.) (1972), *International Investment*, Harmondsworth: Penguin, pp. 265–301.

Caves, R.E. (1982), *Multinational Enterprise and Economic Analysis*, Cambridge: Cambridge University Press.

Caves, R.E. (1996), *Multinational Enterprise and Economic Analysis*, 2nd edition, Cambridge, Cambridge University Press.

Chandler, A.D. (1962), *Strategy and Structure: Chapters in the History of the Industrial Enterprise*, Cambridge, MA: MIT Press.

Chang, H.-J. (2002), *Kicking Away the Ladder: Development Strategy in Historical Perspective*, London: Anthem Press.

Chesnais, F. and Saillou, A. (2000), 'Foreign direct investment and European trade', in F. Chesnais, G. Ietto-Gillies and R. Simonetti (eds), *European Integration and Global Corporate Strategies*, London: Routledge, ch. 2.

Christensen, J. (2011), 'The looting continues: tax havens and corruption', *Critical Perspectives on International Business*, **7** (2), 177–96.

Coase, R.H. (1937), 'The nature of the firm', *Economica*, **4**, 386–405; reprinted in G.J. Stigler and K.E. Boulding (eds) (1953), *Readings in Price Theory*, London: Allen and Unwin, pp. 331–51.

Coase, R.H. (1960), 'The problem of social cost', *Journal of Law and Economics*, **16** (3), 1–10.

Coase, R.H. (1991), 'The nature of the firm: origin, meaning and influence', in O. Williamson and S. Winter (eds), *The Nature of the Firm*, Oxford: Oxford University Press, pp. 34–74.

Cohen, W. (1995) 'Empirical studies of innovative activity', in P. Stoneman (ed.), *Handbook of the Economics of Innovation and Technological Change*, Blackwell, Oxford, pp. 182–264.

Cohen, W.M. and Levinthal, D.A. (1989), 'Innovation and learning: the two faces of R&D', *Economic Journal*, **99** (397), 569–96.

Cohen, W.M. and Levinthal, D.A. (1990), 'Absorptive capacity: a new perspective on learning and innovation', *Administrative Science Quarterly*, **35**, 128–95.

Cohen, R.B., Felton, N., van Liere, J. and Nkosi, M. (eds) (1979), *The Multinational Corporations: A Radical Approach. Papers by Stephen Herbert Hymer*, Cambridge: Cambridge University Press.

Contributions to Political Economy (2002), **21**.

Cowling, K. (1982), *Monopoly Capitalism*, London: Macmillan.

Cowling, K. (1999), 'Introduction', in K. Cowling (ed.), *Industrial Policy in Europe*, London: Routledge, pp. 3–16.

Cowling, K. and Sugden, R. (1987), *Transnational Monopoly Capitalism*, Brighton: Wheatsheaf.

Cowling, K. and Sugden, R. (1990), *A New Economic Policy for Britain*, Manchester: Manchester University Press.

Cowling, K. and Sugden, R. (1993), 'Industrial strategy: a missing link in British economic policy', *Oxford Review of Economic Policy*, **9** (3), 83–100.

Cowling, K. and Sugden, R. (1994), 'Industrial strategy: guiding principles and European context', in P. Bianchi, K. Cowling and R. Sugden (eds), *Europe's Economic Challenge: Analyses of Industrial Strategy and Agenda for the 1990s*, London: Routledge, pp. 37–59.

Cowling, K. and Sugden, R. (1998a), 'The essence of the modern corporation: markets, strategic decision-making and the theory of the firm', *The Manchester School*, **66** (1), 59–86.

Cowling, K. and Sugden, R. (1998b), 'Strategic trade policy reconsidered: national rivalry vs free trade vs international cooperation', *Kyklos*, **51**, 339–57.

Cowling, K. and Tomlinson, P.R. (2000), 'The Japanese crisis: a case of strategic failure', *The Economic Journal*, **110** (464), 358–81.

Cowling, K., Yusof, F.M. and Vernon, G. (2000), 'Declining concentration in UK manufacturing? A problem of measurement', *International Review of Applied Economics*, **14** (1), 45–54.

Cox, H. (1997), 'The evolution of international business enterprise', in R. John, G. Ietto-Gillies, H. Cox and N. Grimwade (eds), *Global Business Strategy*, London: International Thomson Business Press, pp. 9–46.

Cox, H. (2000), *The Global Cigarette. Origins and Evolution of British American Tobacco, 1880–1945*, Oxford: Oxford University Press.

Cyert, R.M. and March, J.G. (1963), *A Behavioral Theory of the Firm*, Englewood Cliffs, NJ: Prentice-Hall.

Dawes, B. (1995), *International Business: A European Perspective*, Cheltenham: Stanley Thornes.

Dicken, P. (1993), *Global Shift: Reshaping the Global Economic Map in the 21st Century*, 4th edition, London: Sage Publications.

Dicken, P. (2003), *Global Shift. Reshaping the Global Economic Map in the XXI Century*, London: Sage Publications.

Dietrich, M. (ed.) (2006), *The Economics of the Firm: Analysis, Evolution, History*, London: Routledge.

Dietrich, M. and Krafft, J. (eds) (2012), *Handbook of the Economics and Theory of the Firm*, Cheltenham, UK and Northampton, MA, USA: Edward Elgar (forthcoming).

DiMaggio, P.J. and Powell, W. (1983), 'The iron cage revisited: institutional isomorphism and collective rationality in organizational fields', *American Sociological Review*, **48**, 147–60.

Dixit, A. and Stiglitz, J. (1977), 'Monopolistic competition and optimum product diversity', *The American Economic Review*, **67**, 297–308.

Dorrenbacher, C. and Gammelgaard, J. (2011), 'Subsidiary power in multinational corporations: the subtle role of micro-political bargaining power', *Critical Perspectives on International Business*, **7** (1), 30–47.

Driffield, N. and Love, J.H. (2003), 'FDI, technology sourcing and reverse spillovers', *The Manchester School*, **71** (6), 659–72.

Duhem, P. (1905), *The Aim and Structure of Physical Theory*, English edition (1962), New York: Atheneum.

Dun and Bradstreet (2002), *Who Owns Whom, Worldwide Corporate Structure*, High Wycombe: Dun and Bradstreet.

Dunning, J.H. (1971), 'Comment on the chapter by Professor Aliber', in J.H. Dunning (ed.), *The Multinational Enterprise*, London: Allen and Unwin, pp. 57–60.

Dunning, J.H. (1977), 'Trade, location of economic activity and the MNE: a search for an eclectic approach', in B. Ohlin, P.O. Hesselborn and P.M. Wijkman (eds), *The International Allocation of Economic Activity*, London: Macmillan, pp. 395–431.

Dunning, J.H. (1980), 'Explaining changing patterns of international production: in defense of the eclectic theory', *Oxford Bulletin of Economics and Statistics*, **41** (4), 269–95.

Dunning, J.H. (1981), *International Production and the Multinational Enterprise*, London: Allen and Unwin.

Dunning, J.H. (1983), 'Changes in the level and growth of international production: the last 100 years', in M. Casson (ed.), *The Growth of International Business*, London: Allen and Unwin, pp. 84–139.

Dunning, J.H. (1993a), *Multinational Enterprises and the Global Economy*, Wokingham: Addison Wesley.

Dunning, J.H. (1993b), *The Globalization of Business*, London: Routledge.

Dunning, J.H. (1995), 'What is wrong – and right – with trade theory?', *International Trade Journal*, **9** (2), 163–202.

Dunning, J.H. (1997), *Alliance Capitalism and Global Business*, London: Routledge.

Dunning, J.H. (1998), 'Location and the multinational enterprise: a neglected factor?', *Journal of International Business Studies*, **29** (1), 45–66.

Dunning, J.H. (1999), 'Trade, location of economic activity and the multinational enterprise: a search for an eclectic approach', in P.J. Buckley and P.N. Ghauri (eds), *The Internationalization of the Firm: A Reader*, London: ITBP, pp. 61–79.

Dunning, J.H. (2000a), 'The eclectic paradigm as an envelope for economic and business theories of MNE activity', *International Business Review*, **9**, 163–90.

Dunning, J.H. (2000b), 'The eclectic paradigm of international production: a personal perspective', in C. Pitelis and R. Sugden (eds), *The Nature of the Transnational Firm*, London: Routledge, pp. 119–39.

Dunning, J.H. and Narula, R. (1996), 'The investment development path revisited: some emerging issues', in J.H. Dunning and R. Narula (eds), *Foreign Direct Investment and Governments, Catalysts for Economic Restructuring*, London: Routledge.

Dunning, J.H and Pitelis, C.N. (2008), 'Stephen Hymer's contribution to international business scholarship: an assessment and extension', *Journal of International Business Studies*, **39** (1), 167–76.

Dunning, J.H. and Wymbs, C. (1999), 'The geographical sourcing of technology-based assets by multinational enterprises', in D. Archibugi, J. Howells and J. Michie (eds), *Innovation Policy in a Global Economy*, Cambridge: Cambridge University Press, pp. 184–224.

Eden, L. (2001), 'Taxes, transfer pricing, and the multinational enterprise', in A.M. Rugman and T.L. Brewer (eds), *The Oxford Handbook of International Business*, Oxford: Oxford University Press, ch. 21, pp. 591–619.

Epstein, G. (2003), 'The role and control of multinational corporations in the world economy', in J. Michie (ed.), *The Handbook of Globalisation*, Cheltenham, UK and Northampton, MA, USA: Edward Elgar, pp. 150–64.

Erturk, K. (2011), 'Governance and asymmetric power', in M. Ugur and D. Sunderland (eds), *Does Economic Governance Matter? Governance Institutions and Outcomes*, Cheltenham, UK and Northampton, MA, USA: Edward Elgar, ch. 2.

Filippetti, A., Frenz, M. and Ietto-Gillies, G. (2009), 'Is the innovation performance of countries related to their internationalization?', thematic paper to the European Innovation Scoreboard, prepared for European Commission – DG Enterprise and Innovation.

Filippetti, A., Frenz, M. and Ietto-Gillies, G. (2011), 'Are innovation and internationalization related? An analysis of European countries', *Industry and Innovation*, **18** (5), 437–59.

Fine, B. and Harris, L. (1985), *The Peculiarities of the British Economy*, London: Lawrence and Wishart.

Forsgren, M. (2008), *Theories of the Multinational Firm. A Multidimensional Creature in the Global* Economy, Cheltenham, UK and Northampton, MA, USA: Edward Elgar.

Forsgren, M., Holm, U. and Johanson, J. (2005), *Managing the Embedded Multinational. A Business Network View*, Cheltenham, UK and Northampton, MA, USA: Edward Elgar.

Frenz, M. and Ietto-Gillies, G. (2007), 'Does multinationality affect the propensity to innovate? An analysis of the third UK Community Innovation Survey', *International Review of Applied Economics*, **21** (1), 99–117.

Frenz, M. and Ietto-Gillies, G. (2009), 'The impact on innovation performance of different sources of knowledge: evidence from the UK Community Innovation Survey', *Research Policy*, **38** (7), 1125–35.

Frenz, M., Girardone, C. and Ietto-Gillies, G. (2005), 'Multinationality matters in innovation. The case of the UK financial services', *Industry and Innovation*, **12** (1), 1–28.

Friedman, M. (1953), *Essays in Positive Economics*, Chicago: University of Chicago Press.

Frobel, F., Heinricks, J. and Kreye, O. (1980), *The New International Division of Labour*, Cambridge and Paris: Cambridge University Press and Editions de la Maison des Sciences de l'Homme.

Ghoshal, S. and Bartlett, C.A. (1988), 'Innovation processes in multinational corporations', in M.L. Tushman and W.L. Moore (eds), *Readings in the Management of Innovation*, Cambridge, MA: Ballinger, pp. 499–518.

Ghoshal, S. and Nohria, N. (1997), *The Differentiated MNC: Organizing Multinational Corporations for Value Creation*, San Francisco, CA: Jossey-Bass.

Giddens, A. (1985), *A Contemporary Critique of Historical Materialism, Vol. II: The Nation-State and Violence*, Berkeley, CA: University of California Press.

Gillies, D.A. (1989), 'Non-Bayesian confirmation theory, and the principle of explanatory surplus', in A. Fine and J. Leplin (eds), *Proceedings of the 1988 Biennial Meeting of the Philosophy of Science Association*, **2** (12), 373–80.

Gillies, D.A. (1993), *Philosophy of Science in the Twentieth Century: Four Central Themes*, Oxford and Cambridge: Blackwell.

Graham, E.M. (1978), 'Transatlantic investment by multinational firms: a rivalristic phenomenon?', *Journal of Post-Keynesian Economics*, **1** (1), 82–99.

Graham, E.M. (1985), 'Intra-industry direct investment, market structure, firm rivalry and technological performance', in E. Erdilek (ed.), *Multinationals as Mutual Invaders: Intra-Industry Direct Foreign Investment*, London: Croom Helm.

Graham, E.M. (1990), 'Exchange of threats between multinational firms as an infinitely repeated non-cooperative game', *International Trade Journal*, **4** (3), 259–77.

Graham, E.M. (1992), 'Direct investment between the United States and the European Community post-1986 and pre-1992', in J. Cantwell (ed.), *Multinational Investment in Modern Europe: Strategic Interaction in the Integrated Community*, Aldershot, UK and Brookfield, VT, USA: Edward Elgar.

Graham, E.M. (1998), 'Market structure and the multinational enterprise: a game-theoretic approach', *Journal of International Business Studies*, **29**, 67–83.

Graham, E.M. (2000), 'Strategic mangement and transnational firm behaviour: a formal approach', in C.M. Pitelis and R. Sugden (eds), *The Nature of the Transnational Firm*, 2nd edition, London: Routledge, ch. 7, pp. 162–73.

Graham, E.M. (2002), 'The contributions of Stephen Hymer: one view', *Contributions to Political Economy*, **21**, 27–42.

Granovetter, M. (1985), 'Economic action and social structure: the problem of embeddedness', *American Journal of Sociology*, **78** (3), 3–30.

Gray, P.H. (1992), 'The interface between the theories of international trade and production', in P.J. Buckley and M. Casson (eds), *Multinational Enterprises in the World Economy: Essays in Honour of John Dunning*, Aldershot, UK and Brookfield, VT, USA: Edward Elgar.

Greaver II, Maurice F. (1999), *Strategic Outsourcing. A Structural Approach to Outsourcing Decisions and Initiatives*, New York: American Management Association.

Grimwade, N. (2000), *International Trade: New Patterns of Trade, Production and Investment*, 2nd edition, London: Routledge.

Grubel, H.G. and Lloyd, P.J. (1975), *Intra-Industry Trade*, London: Macmillan.

Gruber, W., Mehta, D. and Vernon, R. (1967), 'The R&D factor in international trade and international investment of United States industries', *Journal of Political Economy*, **75** (1), 20–37.

Gupta, A.K. and Govindarajan, V. (1991), 'Knowledge flows and the structure of control within multinational corporations', *Academy of Management Review*, **16** (4), 768–92.

Gupta, A.K. and Govindarajan, V. (2000), 'Knowledge flows within multinational corporations', *Strategic Management Journal*, **21** (4), 473–96.

Hagedoorn, J. (1996), 'Trends and patterns in strategic technology partnering since the early seventies', *Review of Industrial Organization*, **11**, 601–16.

Hansen, A. (1938), *Full recovery or stagnation?*, New York: Norton.

Hatzichronoglou, T. (1997), 'The impact of foreign investment on domestic manufacturing industry of OECD countries', in P.J. Buckley and J.-L. Mucchielli (eds), *Multinational Firms and International Relocation*, Cheltenham, UK and Lyme, NH, USA: Edward Elgar, pp. 123–60.

Heckscher, E. (1919), 'The effect of foreign trade on the distribution of income', in H. Ellis and L.A. Metzler (eds) (1950), *Readings in the Theory of International Trade*, London: Allen and Unwin, pp. 272–300.

Hedlund, G. (1986), 'The hypermodern MNC – a heterarchy?', *Human Resource Management*, **25** (1), 9–35.

Hedlund, G. and Rolander, D. (1990), 'Action in heterarchies: new approaches to managing the MNC', in C.A. Bartlett, Y. Doz and G. Hedlund (eds), *Managing the Global Firm*, London: Routledge, pp. 1–15.

Helpman, E. (1984), 'A simple theory of international trade with multinational corporations', *Journal of Political Economy*, **92** (3), 451–71.

Helpman, E. (1985), 'Multinational corporations and trade structure', *Review of Economic Studies*, July, 443–58.

Helpman, E. and Krugman, P. (1985), *Market Structures and Foreign Trade: Increasing Returns, Imperfect Competition and the International Economy*, Cambridge, MA: MIT Press.

Henderson, R.M. and Clark, K.B. (1990), 'Architectural innovation: the reconfiguration of existing product technologies and the failure of established firms', *Administrative Science Quarterly*, **35** (1), 9–30.

Hennart, J.-F. (1982), *A Theory of Multinational Enterprise*, Ann Arbor, MI: University of Michigan Press.

Hennart, J.-F. (2000), 'Transaction costs theory and the multinational enterprise', in C.N. Pitelis and R. Sugden (eds), *The Nature of the Transnational Firm*, London: Routledge, pp. 72–118.

Hennart, J.-F. (2001), 'Theories of the multinational enterprise', in A.M. Rugman and T.L. Brewer (eds), *The Oxford Handbook of International Business*, Oxford: Oxford University Press, pp. 127–49.

Hilferding, R. (1912), *Das FinanzKapital*, Vienna: Wiener Volksbuchhandlung.

Hirsch, S. (1965), 'The United States' electronics industry in international trade', *National Institute Economic Review*, **24**, 92–7.

Hirsch, S. (1967), *Location of Industry and International Competitiveness*, Oxford: Clarendon Press.

Hobson, J.A. (1902), *Imperialism: a Study*, 1988 edition, London: Unwin-Hyman.

Hodgson, G.M. (1998), 'Evolutionary and competence-based theories of the firm', *Journal of Economic Studies*, **25** (1), 25–56.

Holm, U. and Pedersen, T. (eds) (2000), *The Emergence and Impact of MNC Centres of Excellence – a Subsidiary Perspective*, Houndmills, Basingstoke: Macmillan.

Hood, N. and Young, S. (1979), *The Economics of Multinational Enterprise*, London: Longman.

Hufbauer, G.C. (1966), *Synthetic Materials and the Theory of International Trade*, London: Duckworth.

Hufbauer, G.C. and Adler, M. (1968), *Overseas Manufacturing Investment and the Balance of Payments*, Washington, DC: US Treasury Department.

Hymer, S.H. (1960), *The International Operations of National Firms: A Study of Direct Foreign Investment*, 1976 edition, Cambridge, MA: MIT Press.

Hymer, S.H. (1966), 'Direct foreign investment and the national economic interest', in P. Russell (ed.), *Nationalism in Canada*, Toronto: McGraw-Hill, pp. 191–202.

Hymer, S.H. (1968), 'La grande "corporation" multinationale: analyse de certaines raisons qui poussent à l'integration internationale des affaires', *Revue Economique*, **14** (6), 949–73; English version ('The large multinational "corporation": an analysis of some motives for the international integration of business') in M. Casson (ed.) (1990), *Multinational Corporations*, Aldershot, UK and Brookfield, VT, USA: Edward Elgar, pp. 6–31.

Hymer, S.H. (1970), 'The efficiency (contradictions) of multinational corporations', *American Economic Review*, **60** (2), 411–18; reprinted in R.B. Cohen, N. Felton, J. Van Liere and M. Nkosi (eds) (1979), *The Multinational Corporation: A Radical Approach, Papers by S.H. Hymer*, Cambridge: Cambridge University Press, pp. 41–53.

Hymer, S.H. (1971), 'The multinational corporation and the law of uneven development', in J.W. Bhagwati (ed.), *Economics and World Order*, London: Macmillan, pp. 113–40; reproduced in H. Radice (ed.) (1975), *International Firms and Modern Imperialism*, Harmondsworth: Penguin, pp. 113–35.

Hymer, S.H. (1972), 'The internationalisation of capital', *The Journal of Economic Issues*, **6** (1), 91–111.

Hymer, S.H. (1975), 'The multinational corporation and the law of uneven development', in H. Radice (ed.), *International Firms and Modern Imperialism*, Harmondsworth: Penguin Books, pp. 113–35.

Ietto-Gillies, G. (1983), 'Monopoly capitalism and the UK economy: a review article', *Studi Economici*, **21**, 57–75.

Ietto-Gillies, G. (1992), *International Production: Trends, Theories, Effects*, Cambridge: Polity Press.

Ietto-Gillies, G. (1997), 'The environment of international business', in R. John, G. Ietto-Gillies, H. Cox and N. Grimwade (eds), *Global Business Strategy*, London: International Thomson Business Press, pp. 73–89.

Ietto-Gillies, G. (2000a), 'What role for multinationals in the new theories of trade and location?', *International Review of Applied Economics*, **14** (4), 413–26.

Ietto-Gillies, G. (2000b), 'Profits from foreign direct investment', in F. Chesnais, G. Ietto-Gillies and R. Simonetti (eds), *European Integration and Global Corporate Strategies*, London: Routledge, pp. 71–91.

Ietto-Gillies, G. (2002a), *Transnational Corporations. Fragmentation amidst Integration*, London: Routledge.

Ietto-Gillies, G. (2002b), 'Hymer, the nation-state and the determinants of multi-national corporations' activities', *Contributions to Political Economy*, **21**, 43–54.

Ietto-Gillies, G. (2002c), 'Internationalization and the demarcation between services and manufactures: a theoretical and empirical analysis', in M. Miozzo and I. Miles (eds), *Internationalization, Technology and Services*, Cheltenham, UK and Northampton, MA, USA: Edward Elgar.

Ietto-Gillies, G. (2004), 'Should the study of transnational corporations be part of the economics syllabus?', *A Guide to What is Wrong with Economics*, London: Wimbledon Publishing.

Ietto-Gillies, G. (2007), 'Theories of international production: a critical perspective', in *Critical Perspectives on International Business*, **3** (3), 196–210.

Ietto-Gillies, G. (2009), 'Conceptual issues behind the assessment of the degree of internationalization', *Transnational Corporations*, **18** (3), 59–83, December.

Ietto-Gillies, G. (2010), 'The economic crisis of 2008 and international business. Can we say anything meaningful about future scenarios?', *Futures*, **42** (9), 910–19, November.

Ietto-Gillies, G. (2011a), 'The integration and fragmentation roles of transnational companies', in M.N. Jovanovic (ed.), *International Handbook on the Economics of Integration, Vol. III*, Cheltenham, UK and Northampton, MA, USA: Edward Elgar, pp. 56–72.

Ietto-Gillies, G. (2011b), 'Strategies of transnational companies in the context of the governance systems of nation-states', in M. Ugur and D. Sunderland (eds), *Does Economic Governance Matter? Governance Institutions and Outcomes*, Cheltenham, UK and Northampton, MA, USA: Edward Elgar, ch. 5.

Ietto-Gillies, G. and Meschi, M. (1999), 'The characteristics, performance and strategic behaviour of merged versus non-merged establishments in Britain', *Review of Industrial Organization*, **15** (1), 1–24.

Inkpen, A.C. (2001), 'Strategic alliances', in A.M. Rugman and T.L. Brewer (eds), *The Oxford Handbook of International Business*, Oxford: Oxford University Press, ch. 15, pp. 402–27.

Inoue, H. (2010), 'Several characteristics of service multinational corporations', Centre for International Business Studies Research Working Papers, No. 1-10.

International Monetary Fund (IMF) (1977), *Balance of Payments Manual*, 4th edition, Washington, DC: IMF.

International Monetary Fund (IMF) (1993), *Balance of Payments Manual*, 5th edition, Washington, DC: IMF.

Iversen, C. (1935), *International Capital Movements*, 1967 edition, London: Frank Cass.

Johanson, J. and Vahlne, J.-E. (1977), 'The internationalization process of the firm – a model of knowledge development and increasing foreign market commitment', *Journal of International Business Studies*, **8** (1), 23–32.

Johanson, J. and Vahlne, J.-E. (1990), 'The mechanism of internationalization', *International Marketing Review*, **7** (4), 11–24.

Johanson, J. and Wiedersheim-Paul, F. (1975), 'The internationalization of the firm: four Swedish cases', *Journal of Management Studies*, **12** (3), 305–22.

John, R., Ietto-Gillies, G., Cox, H. and Grimwade, N. (1997), *Global Business Strategy*, London: International Thomson Business Press.

Jones, G. (2002), *Merchants to Multinationals: British Trading Companies in the Nineteenth and Twentieth Centuries*, Oxford: Oxford University Press.

Julius, D. (1990), *Global Companies and Public Policy: The Growing Challenge of Foreign Direct Investment*, London: Royal Institute of International Affairs and Pinter Publishers.

Kaldor, N. (1967), 'The role of increasing returns to industry', *Strategic Factors in Economic Development*, New York: New York State School of Industrial and Labour Relations, pp. 3–23.

Kalecki, M. (1939), *Essays in the Theory of Economic Fluctuations*, London: Allen and Unwin.

Kalecki, M. (1954), *Theory of Economic Dynamics*, London: Allen and Unwin.

Kalecki, M. (1971), *Dynamics of the Capitalist Economy*, Cambridge: Cambridge University Press.

Keat, R. and Urry, J. (1975), *Social Theory as Science*, London: Routledge and Kegan Paul.

Kindleberger, C.P. (1969), *American Business Abroad*, New Haven, CT: Yale University Press.

Knickerbocker, F.T. (1973), *Oligopolistic Reaction and Multinational Enterprise*, Cambridge, MA: Division of Research, Graduate School of Business Administration, Harvard University.

Knight, G.A. and Cavusgil, S.T. (1996), *The Born Global Firm: A Challenge to Traditional Internationalization Theory*, Advances in International Marketing, Greenwich, CT: JAI Press.

Kogut, B. (1983), 'Foreign direct investment as a sequential process', in C. Kindleberger and D. Andretsh (eds), *The Multinational Corporation in the 1980s*, Cambridge, MA: MIT Press.

Kogut, B. and Zander, U. (1993), 'Knowledge of the firm and the evolutionary theory of the multinational corporation', *Journal of International Business Studies*, 4th quarter, 625–45.

Kogut, B. and Zander, U. (2003), 'A memoir and reflection: knowledge and an evolutionary theory of the multinational firm 10 years later', *Journal of International Business Studies*, **34**, 505–15.

Kojima, K. (1978), *Direct Foreign Investment: A Japanese Model of Multinational Business Operations*, London: Croom Helm.

Krugman, P. (1985), 'Increasing returns and the theory of international trade', *National Bureau of Economic Research Working Papers*, No. 1752, November.

Krugman, P. (1987), 'The narrow moving band, the Dutch disease and the competitive consequences of Mrs Thatcher: notes on trade in the presence of dynamic scale economies', *Journal of Development Economics*, **27**, 41–55.

Krugman, P. (1991a), *Geography and Trade*, Cambridge, MA: MIT Press.

Krugman, P. (1991b), 'Increasing returns and economic geography', *Journal of Political Economy*, **99**, 483–99.

Krugman, P. (1998), 'What's new about the new economic geography?', *Oxford Review of Economic Policy*, **14** (2), 7–17.

Krugman, P. and Venables, A. (1995), 'Globalization and the inequality of nations', *Quarterly Journal of Economics*, **110** (4), 857–80.

Krugman, P. and Venables, A. (1996), 'Integration, specialisation and adjustment', *European Economic Review*, **40**, 959–67.

Kutznets, S. (1953), *Economic Change*, New York: W.W. Norton.

Lakatos, I. (1978), *The Methodology of Scientific Research Programmes*, Cambridge: Cambridge University Press.

Landefeld, S.J., Wichard, O. and Lowe, J. (1993), 'Alternative frameworks for U.S. international transactions', *Survey of Current Business*, **73**, December, 50–61.

Lazonick, W. (1994), 'The integration of theory and history: methodology and ideology in Schumpeter's economics', in L. Magnusson (ed.), *Evolutionary and Neo-Schumpeterian Approaches to Economics*, Boston, MA: Kluwer, pp. 245–63.

Lenin, V.I. (1917), *Imperialism, the Highest Stage of Capitalism*, 1970 edition, Moscow: Progress.

Leontief, W. (1953), 'Domestic production and foreign trade: the American capital position re-examined', *Proceedings of the American Philosophical Society*, **97**, 332–49.

Leontief, W. (1956), 'Factor proportions and the structure of American trade: further theoretical and empirical analysis', *Review of Economics and Statistics*, **38**, 386–407.

Luxemburg, R. (1913), *The Accumulation of Capital*, 1971 edition, London: Routledge and Kegan Paul.

Markusen, J.R. (1984), 'Multinationals, multiplant economies and the gains from trade', *Journal of International Economics*, **16** (3/4), 205–24.

Markusen, J.R. (1995), 'The boundaries of multinational enterprises, and the theory of international trade', *Journal of Economic Perspectives*, **9** (2), 169–89.

Markusen, J.R. (1997), 'Trade versus investment liberalisation', *National Bureau of Economic Research Working Paper Series*, No. 6231, October.

Markusen, J.R. (1998), 'Multinational firms, location and trade', *The World Economy*, **21** (6), 733–56.

Marshall, A. (1920), *Principles of Economics*, London: Macmillan.

McDonald, F. and Burton, F. (2002), *International Business*, London: Thomson.

McManus, J. (1972), 'The theory of the international firm', in Gilles Paquet (ed.), *The Multinational Firm and the Nation State*, Don Mills, Ontario: Collier-Macmillan, pp. 66–93.

Meschi, M.M. (1997), 'Analytical perspectives on mergers and acquisitions: a survey', *Centre for International Business Studies, Research Papers in International Business*, London: South Bank University, pp. 5–97.

Michalet, C.A. (1980), 'International sub-contracting. A state-of-the-art', in D. Germidis (ed.), *International Sub-Contracting. A New Form of Investment*, Paris: OECD, pp. 38–70.

Miller, N.C. (1968), 'A general equilibrium theory of international capital flows', *The Economic Journal*, **78**, June, 312–20.

Miozzo, M. and Soete, L. (2001), 'Internationalization of services: a technological perspective', *Technological Forecasting and Social Change*, **67** (2), 159–85.

Molle, W. and Morsink, R. (1991), 'Intra-European direct investment', in B. Burgenmeier and J.L. Mucchielli (eds), *Multinationals and Europe 1992: Strategies for the Future*, London: Routledge, pp. 81–101.

Mundell, R.A. (1957), 'International trade and factor mobility', *American Economic Review*, **47**, 321–35; reprinted in J.N. Bhagwati (ed.) (1981), *International Trade: Selected Readings*, Cambridge, MA: MIT Press, pp. 21–36.

Musgrave, A. (1981), 'Unreal assumptions in economic theory: the F twist untwisted', *Kyklos*, **34** (3), 377–87.

Narula, R. (2000), 'Strategic technology alliances by European firms since 1980: questioning integration?', in F. Chesnais, G. Ietto-Gillies and R. Simonetti (eds), *European Integration and Global Business Strategies*, London: Routledge, pp. 178–91.

Narula, R and Duyster, G. (2004), 'Globalization and trends in international R&D alliances', *Journal of International Management*, **10**, 199–218.

Narula, R. and Zanfei, A. (2004), 'Globalization of innovation: the role of multi-national enterprises', in J. Fageberger, D.C. Mowery and R.R. Nelson (eds), *The Oxford Handbook of Innovation*, Oxford: Oxford University Press, pp. 318–46.

Nelson, R.R. and Winter, S.G. (1982), *An Evolutionary Theory of Economic Change*, Cambridge, MA: Harvard University Press.

Nurkse, R. (1933), 'Causes and effects of capital movements', in J.H. Dunning (ed.) (1972), *International Investment*, Harmondsworth: Penguin, pp. 97–116.

Ohlin, B. (1933), *Interregional and International Trade*, 1967 edition, Cambridge, MA: Harvard University Press.

Ohmae, K. (1995), *The End of the Nation State. The Rise of Regional Economies*, New York: Free Press.

Oman, C.P. (2000), 'Policy competition for foreign direct investment: a study of competition among governments to attract FDI', OECD Development Centre, Paris: OECD.

Organisation for Economic Co-operation and Development (OECD) (1970), *Gaps in Technology – Comparisons Between Member Countries in Education, Research & Development, Technological Innovation, International Economic Exchanges*, Paris: OECD.

Organisation for Economic Co-operation and Development (OECD) (1992), *Globalisation of Industrial Activities. Four Case Studies: AutoParts, Chemicals, Construction and Semiconductors*, Paris: OECD.

Organisation for Economic Co-operation and Development (OECD) (1994), *The Performance of Foreign Affiliates in OECD Countries*, Paris: OECD, ch. 3.

Organisation for Economic Co-operation and Development (OECD) (1996), *Detailed Benchmark Definition of Foreign Direct Investment*, 3rd edition, Paris: OECD.

Organisation for Economic Co-operation and Development (OECD) (2008), *Benchmark Definition of Foreign Direct Investment*, 4th edition, Paris: OECD.

Organisation for Economic Co-operation and Development (OECD) (2010), *Transfer Pricing Guidelines for Multinational Enterprises and Tax Administrators*, Paris: OECD.

Oviatt, B.M. and McDougall, P.P. (1994) 'Towards a theory of international new ventures', *Journal of International Business Studies*, **25**, 45–64.

Ozawa, T. (1979), *Multinationalism, Japanese Style*, Princeton, NJ: Princeton University Press.

Patel, P. and Pavitt, K. (1994), 'National innovation systems: why they are important, and how they might be measured and compared', *Economics of Innovation and New Technology*, **3** (1), 77–95.

Pearce, R. and Papanastasiou, M. (1999), 'Overseas R&D and the strategic evolution of MNEs: evidence from laboratories in the UK', *Research Policy*, **28** (1), 23–41.

Penrose, E.T. (1956), 'Foreign investment and the growth of the firm', *The Economic Journal*, **66** (262), 220–35.

Penrose, E.T. ([1959] 2009), *The Theory of the Growth of the Firm. With an Introduction by Christos Pitelis*, 4th edition, Oxford: Oxford University Press.

Penrose, E.T. (1987), 'Multinational corporations', in *The New Palgrave: A Dictionary of Economics*, London: Macmillan, pp. 562–4.

Penrose, E.T. (1996), 'Growth of the firm and networking', in *International Encyclopedia of Business and Management*, London: Routledge, pp. 1716–24.

Peoples, J. and Sugden, R. (2000), 'Divide and rule by transnational corporations', in C.N. Pitelis and R. Sugden (eds), *The Nature of the Transnational Firm*, 2nd edition, London: Routledge, pp. 174–92.

Petri, P.A. (1994), 'The regional clustering of foreign direct investment and trade', *Transnational Corporations*, **3** (3), 1–24.

Phelps, N. and Raines, P. (eds) (2002), *The New Competition for Inward Investment*, Cheltenham, UK and Northampton, MA, USA: Edward Elgar.

Phelps, N.A., Mackinnon, D., Stone, I. and Braidford, P. (2003), 'Embedding the multinationals? Institutions and the development of overseas manufacturing affiliates in Wales and North East England', *Regional Studies*, **37**(1), 27–40.

Pitelis, C.N. (ed.) (1993), *Transaction Costs, Markets and Hierarchies*, Oxford: Blackwell.

Pitelis, C.N. (2000), 'A theory of the (growth of the) transnational firm: a Penrosian perspective', *Contributions to Political Economy*, **19**, 71–89.

Pitelis, C.N. (2002a), 'Stephen Hymer: life and the political economy of multinational corporate capital', *Contributions to Political Economy*, **21**, 9–26.

Pitelis, C.N. (2002b), *The Growth of the Firm: the Legacy of Edith Penrose*, Oxford: Oxford University Press.

Pitelis, C.N. (2004), 'Edith Penrose and the resource-based view of (international) business strategy', *International Business Review*, **13**, 523–32.

Pitelis, C. (2005), 'Stephen Herbert Hymer and/on the (theory of) the MNE and international business', *International Business Review*, **15** (2), 103–10.

Polanyi, M. (1966), 'The logic of tacit inference', *Philosophy*, **41**, 1–18.

Polanyi, M. (1967), *The Tacit Dimension*, London: Routledge.

Popper, K.R. (1959), *The Logic of Scientific Discovery*, London: Hutchinson.

Popper, K.R. (1963), *Conjectures and Refutations*, London: Routledge and Kegan Paul.

Posner, M.V. (1961), 'International trade and technical change', *Oxford Economic Papers*, **13**, 323–41.

Quine, W.V.O. (1951), 'Two dogmas of empiricism'; reprinted in *From a Logical Point of View* (1963), New York: Harper Torchbooks.

Reddaway, W.B. with Perkins, J.O.N., Potter, S.J. and Taylor, C.T. (1967), *Effects of UK Direct Investment Overseas: An Interim Report*, Cambridge: Cambridge University Press.

Reddaway, W.B. with Potter, S.J. and Taylor, C.T. (1968), *Effects of UK Direct Investment Overseas: Final Report*, Cambridge: Cambridge University Press.

Ricardo, D. (1817), *On the Principles of Political Economy and Taxation*, online version available at: http://www.econlib.org/library/Ricardo/ricP.html; accessed 24 August 2011.

Roberts, J. (1998), *Multinational Business Service Firms*, Aldershot: Ashgate.

Rowthorn, R.E. and Wells, J.R. (1987), *De-Industrialization and Foreign Trade*, Cambridge: Cambridge University Press.

Rugman, A.M. (1979), *International Diversification and the Multinational Enterprise*, Lexington, MA: Lexington Books.

Rugman, A.M. (1981), *Inside the Multinationals: The Economics of the Multinational Enterprise*, New York: Columbia University Press.

Rugman, A.M. (ed.) (1982), *New Theories of the Multinational Enterprise*, London: Croom Helm.

Rugman, A.M. and Verbeke, A. (2001), 'Environmental policy and international business', in A.M. Rugman and T.L. Brewer (eds), *The Oxford Handbook of International Business*, Oxford: Oxford University Press, ch. 19, pp. 537–57.

Rybczynski, T.M. (1955), 'Factor endowment and relative commodity prices', *Economica*, **23**, 352–9.

Salt, J. (1997), 'International movements of the highly skilled', Directorate for Education, Employment, Labour and Social Affairs. International Migration Unit: Occasional Papers No. 3, Paris: OECD/GD (97), 169.

Samuelson, P.A. (1948), 'International trade and the equalization of factor prices', *The Economic Journal*, **58**, 163–84.

Samuelson, P.A. (1949), 'International factor-price equalization once again', *The Economic Journal*, **59**, 181–97.

Samuelson, P.A. (1963), 'Comment on Ernest Nagel's "Assumptions in economic theory"', *The American Economic Review*, May; reprinted in J.E. Stiglitz (ed.) (1966), *The Collected Scientific Papers of Paul A. Samuelson*, vol. 2, Cambridge, MA: MIT Press, pp. 1772–8.

Schenk, H. (1999), 'Industrial policy implications of competition policy: failure in mergers', in K. Cowling (ed.), *Industrial Policy in Europe: Theoretical Perspectives and Practical Proposals*, London: Routledge.

Smith, A. (1776), *An Inquiry into the Nature and Causes of the Wealth of Nations: A Selected Edition*, Kathryn Sutherland (ed.), 2008, Oxford: Oxford Paperbacks.

Steindl, J. (1952), *Maturity and Stagnation in American Capitalism*, Oxford: Oxford University Press.

Stigler, G.J. (1947), 'The kinky oligopoly demand curve and rigid prices', *Journal of Political Economy*, **55**, 432–49; reprinted in G.J. Stigler and K.E. Boulding (eds) (1953), *Readings in Price Theory*, London: Allen and Unwin, pp. 410–39.

Stolper, W.F. and Samuelson, P.A. (1941), 'Protection and real wages', *Review of Economic Studies*, **9**, 58–73.

Stopford, J. and Turner, L. (1985), *Britain and the Multinationals*, Chichester: Wiley.

Sugden, R. (1991), 'The importance of distributional considerations', in C.N. Pitelis and R. Sugden (eds) *The Nature of the Transnational Firm*, London: Routledge, pp. 168–93.

Sutcliffe, B. and Glyn, A. (2003), 'Measures of globalisation and their misinterpretation', in J. Michie (ed.), *The Handbook of Globalisation*, Cheltenham, UK and Northampton, MA, USA: Edward Elgar.

Sweezy, P.M. (1939), 'Demand under conditions of oligopoly', *Journal of Political Economy*, **47**, 568–73.

Sweezy, P.M. (1942), *The Theory of Capitalist Development*, London: Dennis Dobson.

Sylos Labini, P. (1964), *Oligopolio e Progresso Tecnico*, Torino: Piccola Biblioteca Einaudi.

Teece, D.J. (1977), 'Technology transfer by multinational firms: the resource cost of transferring technological know-how', *The Economic Journal*, **87**, 242–61.

Teece, D.J. (1983), 'Technological and organizational factors in the theory of the multinational enterprise', in M. Casson (ed.), *The Growth of International Business*, London: G. Allen and Unwin, ch. 3, pp. 51–62.

Teece, D.J. (1988), 'Technological change and the nature of the firm', in G. Dosi, C. Freeman, R. Nelson, G. Silverberg and L. Soete (eds) (1988), *Technical Change and Economic Theory*, London: Pinter, pp. 256–81.

Teece, D.J. and Pisano, G. (1994), 'The dynamic capabilities of firms: an introduction', *Industrial and Corporate Change*, **3** (3), 537–56.

Tether, B.S. (2002), 'Who co-operates for innovation, and why. An empirical analysis', *Research Policy*, **31**, 947–67.

Thomsen, S. and Woolcock, S. (1993), *Direct Investment and European Integration, Competition among Firms and Governments*, London: Royal Institute of International Affairs and Pinter Publishers.

Tiberi, M. (2004), *The Account of the British Empire: Capital Flows from 1799 to 1914*, Aldershot: Ashgate.

Tushman, M.L. and Anderson, P. (1986), 'Technological discontinuities and organizational environments', *Administrative Science Quarterly*, **31** (3), 439–65.

United Nations Conference on Trade and Development (UNCTAD) (1992), *World Investment Report, 1992: Transnational Corporations as Engines of Growth*, Geneva: United Nations.

United Nations Conference on Trade and Development/Division on Transnational Corporations and Investment (UNCTAD/DTCI) (1994), *World Investment Report 1994: Transnational Corporations, Employment and the Workplace*, Geneva: United Nations.

United Nations Conference on Trade and Development (UNCTAD) (1995), *World Investment Report 1995: Transnational Corporations and Competitiveness*, Geneva: United Nations.

United Nations Conference on Trade and Development (UNCTAD) (1996), *World Investment Report 1996: Investment, Trade and International Policy Arrangements*, Geneva: United Nations.

United Nations Conference on Trade and Development (UNCTAD) (1997), *World Investment Report 1997: Transnational Corporations, Market Structure and Competition Policy*, Geneva: United Nations.

United Nations Conference on Trade and Development (UNCTAD) (2001), *World Investment Report 2001: Promoting Linkages*, Geneva: United Nations.

United Nations Conference on Trade and Development (UNCTAD) (2002), *World Investment Report 2002: Transnational Corporations and Export Competitiveness*, Geneva: United Nations.

United Nations Conference on Trade and Development (UNCTAD) (2004), *World Investment Report 2004: The Shift Towards Services*, Geneva: United Nations.

United Nations Conference on Trade and Development (UNCTAD) (2009a), *World Investment Report 2009: Transnational Corporations, Agricultural Production and Development*, Geneva: United Nations.

United Nations Conference on Trade and Development (UNCTAD) (2009b), *UNCTAD Training Manual on Statistics for FDI and the Operations of TNCs, Vol. I Flows and Stocks,* Geneva: United Nations. http://www.unctad.org/en/docs/diaeia20091_en.pdf.

United Nations Conference on Trade and Development (UNCTAD) (2011), *World Investment Report 2011: Non-Equity Modes of International Production and Development*, Geneva: United Nations.

Van den Berghe, D.A.F. (2003), *Working Across Borders: Multinational Enterprises and the Internationalization of Employment*, Rotterdam: Erasmus University.

Vaupel, J.W. and Curhan, J.P. (1974), *The World's Multinational Enterprises: A Sourcebook of Tables Based on a Study of the Largest US and Non-US Manufacturing Corporations*, Geneva: Centre des Etudes Industrielles.

Verbeke, A. (2003), 'The evolutionary view of the MNE and the future of internalization theory', *Journal of International Business Studies*, **34,** 498–504.

Venables, A.J. (1998), 'The assessment: trade and location', *Oxford Review of Economic Policy*, **14** (2), 1–6.

Vernon, R. (1966), 'International investment and international trade in the product cycle', *The Quarterly Journal of Economics*, **80**, 190–207.

Vernon, R. (1974), 'The location of economic activity', in J.H. Dunning (ed.), *Economic Analysis and the Multinational Enterprise*, London: Allen and Unwin, pp. 89–113.

Vernon, R. (1979), 'The product cycle hypothesis in a new international environment', *Oxford Bulletin of Economics and Statistics*, **41**, 255–67.

Westney, D.E. (2005), 'Institutional theory and the multinational corporation', in Sumantra Goshal and D. Eleanor Westney (eds), *Organization Theory and the Multinational Corporation*, New York: Palgrave Macmillan, pp. 47–67.

Westney, D.E. and Zaheer, S. (2001), 'The multinational enterprise as an organization', in A.M. Rugman and T.L. Brewer (eds), *The Oxford Handbook of International Business*, Oxford: Oxford University Press, ch. 13, pp. 349–79.

Wilkins, M. (1988), 'The freestanding company, 1817–1914', *Economic History Review*, **61** (2), 259–82.

Williamson, O. (1975), *Markets and Hierarchies: Analysis and Anti-trust Implications*, New York: Free Press.

Williamson, O.E. (1981), 'The modern corporation: origins, evolution, attributes', *Journal of Economic Literature*, **19**, 1537–68.

Williamson, O.E. (1984), 'Efficient labour organization', in F.H. Stephens (ed.), *Firms, Organization and Labour: Approaches to the Economics of Work Organization*, London: Macmillan, pp. 87–118.

World Trade Organization (WTO) (2005), *World Trade Report 2005. Exploring the Links Between Trade, Standards and the WTO*, Geneva: WTO.

Yamashita, N. (2010), *International Fragmentation of Production. The Impact of Outsourcing on the Japanese Economy*, Cheltenham, UK and Northampton, MA, USA: Edward Elgar.

Yamin, M. (2000), 'A critical re-evaluation of Hymer's contribution to the theory of the transnational corporation', in C.N. Pitelis and R. Sugden (eds), *The Nature of the Transnational Corporation*, London: Routledge, pp. 57–71.

Yamin, M. and Nixson, F.I. (1988), 'Transnational corporations and the control of restrictive business practices: theoretical issues and empirical evidence', *International Review of Applied Economics*, **2** (1), 1–22.

Young, A. (1928), 'Increasing returns and economic progress', *The Economic Journal*, December, 538–9.

Zaheer, S. (1995), 'Overcoming the liability of foreignness', *Academy of Management Journal*, **38** (2), 341–63.

Zanfei, A. (2000), 'Transnational firms and the changing organisation of innovative activities', *Cambridge Journal of Economics*, **24** (5), 515–42.

Zetlin, M. (1974), 'Corporate ownership and control: the large corporation and the capitalist class', *American Journal of Sociology*, **79** (5), 1073–119.

Index

Introductory Note: Because the entire work is about 'transnational corporations' and 'international production' the use of these terms (and certain others which occur constantly throughout the book) as an entry point has been minimized. Information will be found under the corresponding detailed topics.

'Professor Grazia Ietto-Gillies has provided an updated and illuminating analysis of the main forces behind the development of transnational corporations and international production as well as of their effects on innovation, trade and employment. The book has a multi-level architecture and is addressed to both students and researchers.'

    – Nicola Acocella, University of Rome 'La Sapienza', Italy

'In the second edition of her authoritative book, this prominent figure in the study of transnational corporations has achieved an excellent job. The volume is updated and more comprehensive, and also digs deeper into reflection on the growing relevance of transnational corporations in times of a crisis of the world economy. In periods of financial troubles, calling for a new globalizing phase of capitalism in which TNCs' organizational and technological power would overcome the current financialization and liberalization sounds more than sensible.'

    – Wladimir Andreff, University of Paris 1 Panthéon Sorbonne, France

'Do we really need a specific theory to interpret transnational (or multinational) corporations, assessing their impact on the global economy? The answer is yes, and this brilliant and inspiring book by Grazia Ietto-Gillies explains why. She overviews and discusses in a critical way the main theoretical approaches and interpretative frameworks since the seminal thesis of Stephen Hymer, pointing out their key elements, positive contributions, and weaknesses. She argues that transnational corporations are powerful integrators of fragmentation and that differences in terms of resources, institutions, laws and policies determine strength, as in the case of labour markets. Highlighting the specific advantages of transnationality is a key issue in the author's view. Grazia Ietto-Gillies' arguments are sharp and convincing, her style clear. This well-structured book is a welcome, excellent introduction to the theory of the transnational corporation and to the policy issues related to this crucial actor. It will soon become an essential instrument for any student in international business, as well as for any intelligent reader willing to better understand the dynamics of the global economy.'

    – Giovanni Balcet, University of Turin, Italy

'At a time when researchers in international business tend to hide behind increasingly specialized professions, comprehensive overviews of basic perspectives are in high demand. This book fills this need by offering brilliant analyses and comparisons of basic theories within the field. It is an invaluable guide for students, teachers and researchers in international business and the reader will emerge better equipped to understand the realities of today's international production and the role of the modern transnational corporation.'

    – Mats Forsgren, Uppsala University, Sweden

'Grazia Ietto-Gillies successfully gives readers a truly comprehensive perspective of the development on the theory of transnational corporations over one hundred years. It is a marvelous and admirable work, useful and readable not only for scholars and students in this field, but also for government officers and social activists in order to gain a deeper understanding of this complicatedly globalized world. The aphorisms at the beginning of each part clearly illustrate the author's critical standpoint on TNCs.'

    – Masahiko Itaki, Ritsumeikan University, Japan

'The second edition of *Transnational Corporations and International Production* provides not only an appreciable general updating of content, empirics and references reflecting developments, challenges and debates in the real economies – it also offers vibrant insights on the convergence of different theoretical strands on the emergence, role and effects of transnational corporations, as well as on the recent combination/intersection with other disciplines and methods.'

– Lucia Piscitello, Politecnico di Milano, Italy

'Grazia Ietto-Gillies book captures a quite large and complex area of international business from economic and political economy angles. I have been using the previous edition for a number of years and will continue to use this second edition as it keeps pace with the changing area but does it in a very accessible way and on an acceptable number of pages. As it focuses on essentials of theories and on analytical frameworks it does not require yearly updates, but it does help students to read empirical studies. From my experience students like it, as it enables them to capture in a short time the gist of a variety of theories and offers them a useful conceptual perspective how to find their own way in this expanding area. In addition, the book can be used by anybody who wants to get an accessible and quick but thoughtful overview of theories on TNCs and economic effects of TNCs' activities. This book is the reflection of lifetime experience and an indispensable roadmap for anybody who is new to this area.'

– Slavo Radosevic, University College London, UK

'For anyone who wants a teaching resource for the economic theories of multinational firms, this book will be the outstanding choice.'

– Mohammad Yamin, The University of Manchester, UK

'This is an excellent book which dares to accomplish a challenging mission. And it does so very effectively. Grazia Ietto-Gillies explores and acknowledges an extremely large variety of streams of literature that feed into the international business field, without over-simplifying any of the theories, views and insights that are accounted for. The reader thus gets a very useful overview of contributions ranging from those of the noblest and remotest ancestors of the economics discipline to the most promising and recent developments in the analysis of international production, its determinants and effects.'

– Antonello Zanfei, University of Urbino, Italy

Acclaim for the First Edition:

'This book provides a truly excellent span and depth of coverage of alternative theories and perspectives on transnational corporations (TNCs) and their effects on countries. In recent years the international business literature has tended to diverge from the earlier economic-based theories of the TNC, towards on the one hand the management and strategy of the TNC, and on the other the political economy of globalization. This splendid book brings these three strands back together again in a coherent way. It should be a compulsory text for anyone teaching in these fields, and essential reading for any postgraduate student or scholar starting out in this area.'

     – John Cantwell, Rutgers University, USA

'Although globalisation has stimulated competition in the world economy, significant market power remains in the hands of transnational corporations; particularly in software, pharmaceuticals and other high-technology industries. The rapid rise of transnationals in the second half of the twentieth century provoked a wealth of research. This book provides an admirably concise yet comprehensive account of the role of transnationals in the global economy, based on this research. It stands alone as the most authoritative and up-to-date survey of theory, evidence and policy in this field.'

     – Mark Casson, University of Reading, UK

'The overriding purpose of the...work is to provide an accessible introduction to the subject, and the book does this admirably. Ietto-Gillies' vast experience of the subject matter allows her to draw links between the wide array of writers whose work is discussed, and this is made explicit through cross-referencing in each of the chapters to other sections of the book. A further teaching tool is the use of text-boxes which concisely summarise points from each chapter. This simple approach is actually highly effective, and means those readers who are approaching the material for the first time are guided effortlessly through the normally demanding terrain of theoretical argument.'

     – Howard Cox, University of Worcester

'A most imaginative and carefully crafted textbook on the determinants and effects of MNE activity. A really excellent introduction to the subject. It deserves to be widely read by both undergraduates and graduate students taking courses in international economics and business.'

     – John H. Dunning, OBE, University of Reading, UK and Rutgers University, USA

'If one is interested in an introduction into and critical review of theoretical issues, activities and impact of transnational corporations (TNCs), then this is an excellent book to read and have. . . it ought to be read widely by those that are interested in and studying economics, business and management. Both lecturers and students would find useful summaries at the end of each chapter. Practicing economists also need to read it if they want to keep abreast of new developments and findings.'

     – Miroslav N. Jovanovic, *Economia Internazionale*

'Professor Grazia Ietto-Gillies has produced an extremely useful account of the economic and business aspects of multinational production. It is particularly useful to have previous work summarised and reported, with the development of theories and analysis over time described and discussed. This book will be invaluable for courses on international business.'

     – Jonathan Michie, Birmingham Business School, UK

'This book is a welcome addition to the available literature in International Business (IB), responding to the urgent need for more textbooks in this subject. This volume's main aim is to provide a general background/introduction to the IB field. It does so in a clear, well-presented, reader-friendly and didactic way. Its strong focus on economics differentiates it from other recent textbooks in IB that adopt a more managerial, strategy-focused and empirical/case-based perspective. Grazia Ietto-Gillies's book, in contrast, is dedicated to the theories and to the effects of TNCs' activities. . . this book, written by a well-respected and knowledgeable specialist in the field, provided a very pleasant read, and I found it very useful and successful in attaining its aims. Writing a textbook is a complex and challenging endeavour. Ietto-Gillies, with all her experience and knowledge of the field, has achieved this very competently. I believe this volume will be very useful to readers such as students of IB and for related courses at the undergraduate or postgraduate level, especially for students introduced to the subject for the first time, and lecturers and researchers who wish to have an overview of the subject and its development. I will certainly recommend this book to my students and colleagues.'

– Ana Teresa C.P. Tavares, *Transnational Corporations*